FOCUS ON THE MIDDLE EAST

Forthcoming titles in the

focus *series*

of introductory texts

focus *on Southeast Asia*

focus *on South America*

focus *on Sub-Saharan Africa*

focus *on Eastern Europe and the U.S.S.R.*

focus *on East Asia*

focus *on South Asia*

focus on
THE MIDDLE EAST

edited by ALICE TAYLOR

Published in cooperation with
The American Geographical Society

Praeger Publishers
New York • Washington • London

PRAEGER PUBLISHERS
111 Fourth Avenue, New York, N. Y. 10003, U.S.A.
5, Cromwell Place, London SW7 2JL, England

Published in the United States of America in 1971
by Praeger Publishers, Inc.

© 1971 by Praeger Publishers, Inc.

Library of Congress Catalog Card Number: 79-174241

Printed in the United States of America

CONTENTS

Foreword — Alice Taylor   vii

I   AN OVERVIEW

1   The Political Dimension: Colonialism to Nationalism
    — Ian R. Manners   3
2   The Challenge of Change: Petroleum and Planning
    — James A. Bill   9
3   Cities of the Middle East — Robert S. Harrison   17
4   The Desert and the Sown: An Ecological Appraisal
    — Ian R. Manners   27

II   NATIONS OF THE MIDDLE EAST

5   The United Arab Republic — John S. Haupert   43
6   Israel — John S. Haupert   64
7   Jordan — Ian R. Manners   83
8   Saudi Arabia — John S. Haupert   99
9   Yemen and the People's Democratic Republic of
    Yemen — Alexander Melamid   112
10   Eastern Arabia, Kuwait, Bahrain — Alexander Melamid   125
11   Lebanon   139
12   Syria   149

13 The Republic of Turkey — John Kolars   163
14 Iraq — Robert A. Fernea and Elizabeth W. Fernea   179
15 Iran — John S. Haupert, with Gad Soffer   196
    Index   215
    The Contributors   224

MAPS

The Middle East   5
The Middle East: Population   19
The Middle East: Rainfall   29
The Middle East: Relief   30
United Arab Republic   45
The Nile Delta and Suez Canal   53
Sadd Al 'Āli (Aswān High Dam)   59
Israel   67
Jerusalem   79
Jordan   85
The East Ghor Irrigation Project   93
Saudi Arabia   101
People's Democratic Republic of Yemen   117
Eastern Arabia   127
Lebanon   141
Syria   152
Syria: Irrigation Networks   159
Turkey   165
Iraq   181
Iraq: Agricultural Regions and Irrigation   185
Iran: Agricultural Regions   199
Iran: Industries and Minerals   204
Iran: Proposed Industrial Projects   207

FOREWORD

Political and social inequalities, hunger, unemployment, illiteracy, and poor health have been the lot of much of mankind throughout history. Today they are critical problems for millions of people living and working in the less developed nations of Asia, Africa, and South America—the so-called third world—where new ideas, attitudes, and technology have only recently begun to challenge ancient traditions and patterns of living. Seeking solutions, these people are beginning to question political, economic, and social organizations that fail to alleviate poverty and injustice. They are becoming increasingly aware of the consequences of inequitable distribution of land, great disparities in income, rapid and chaotic urbanization, rapidly increasing population, and ecological imbalances. They see the urban rich minority retaining most of the political and economic power while the majority continues to eke out a living barely above the subsistence level. They know that in the highly industrialized affluent nations of the West the average income exceeds theirs greatly—in some cases as much as 10 to 1.

How can such problems be tackled in a nation where a privileged group pursues policies aimed at its own enrichment (the tax system, for instance), while the lowest income and employment group is unorganized and has little means to make itself heard? If there are no broadly based democratic forces that can bring pressure to change the political and economic system, how can it be changed?

Unemployment in the third world has now reached the proportions of the Depression of the 1930's in the West. How can it be reduced when most of the people are undernourished and illiterate, when production and productivity are so low that there is little opportunity to accumulate capital investment in agricultural and industrial development? Moreover, a large portion of the foreign aid received, which might be used as capital investment, now goes to pay foreign debts and the interest on them. Unemployment spells poverty, discouragement, alienation, and unrest.

Frustration is greatest among the members of the new middle class and the young, those most imbued with ideas of equality and material progress. They seek innovations that will give them greater influence in government and society and bring a greater measure of economic well-being. Thanks to education and modern means of communication, they are more aware of injustices than their parents and grandparents, reared in societies where hierarchies in all realms were traditional and unquestioned. The political consequences of economic and social inequalities, unemployment, and increasing population pressures are likely to become more serious in the 1970's. Local governments that ignore such problems may well find it difficult to survive. Nor can any citizen of this small planet afford to ignore them.

In its monthly publication, *focus,* the American Geographical Society has been attempting to disseminate up-to-date and accurate information on problems prevalent in the less developed nations and on the solutions being sought for them. Of particular concern has been the dissemination of such information among young adults in the United States, for they need to learn more about the peoples and cultures of the third world if they are to contribute to the solution of its problems.

New York
July, 1971   ALICE TAYLOR

I AN OVERVIEW

1 THE POLITICAL DIMENSION

Colonialism to Nationalism

Ian R. Manners

As a result of recurrent political crises in the area during the last three decades, the "Middle East" has become a familiar term. Nevertheless, to most people the Middle East remains a rather imprecisely defined region. The prevailing concept of the Middle East, whether as a geographical, cultural, or political entity, would undoubtedly include the United Arab Republic, Israel, and the Arab states of southwest Asia; yet on occasion the Middle East region has been arbitrarily extended to include countries as far apart as Morocco and Afghanistan. Prior to World War II, the Middle East Command of the British Royal Air Force even included Kenya within its sphere of operation. Confusion over the specific geographical or territorial limits that should be used to identify the region appears to stem from a failure to distinguish among the concepts of the Islamic (or Muslim) world, the Arab world, and the Middle East.

Within the Islamic world, schism has resulted in the creation of Shia and Sunni sects; yet there are still strong social and cultural bonds. Islam itself is based on easily understood tenets and principles—"There is no God but the one God, and Muhammad is His Messenger"—and those who conduct their lives according to the laws laid down by the Prophet form a religious community that extends beyond the traditional limits of the Middle East.

3

Stretching from the Atlantic Ocean in the west to the Toros Daglari and Zagros mountains in the east, the Arab world forms part of the larger Islamic world. Like the Islamic world, the Arab world cannot be defined in terms of political groupings, but it includes those areas that were most profoundly affected by the Arab conquests of the seventh and eighth centuries. Not since the Mongol invasions of the mid-thirteenth century has the Arab world had any claim to unity, except in so far as it formed an enclave within the Ottoman Empire, but the impact of a common history and a common culture has been enduring.

It is the inheritance of a common language and a common experience that gives substance to the concept of an Arab nation and to the collective consciousness of the Arabs today. Arabic is spoken by perhaps as many as 90 million persons in Africa and Asia, although numerous local variations exist. With the spread of education and literacy, however, modern literary Arabic increasingly serves as a *lingua franca*. Islam is the religion of the majority of Arabs, but there are religious minorities that also identify themselves as Arabs. It was among the Christian communities in Lebanon and Syria, for example, that the ideas of Arab nationalism were first formulated. As Professor Bernard Lewis has noted, "Arabism as a political movement, as a belief that the speakers of Arabic form a nation with national rights and aspirations . . . dates only from the late nineteenth century, and it was for a long time confined to small and unrepresentative groups, most of them Christian." * Within the Arab world, there are communities, such as the Kurds of Iraq and Berbers of northwest Africa, that have resisted assimilation and have retained their own language or religion or both.

Again, despite the growth of an Arab consciousness during the twentieth century—strengthened by improvements in communication and by the growing hostility of the Arabs to the West and to the state of Israel—certain ambiguities remain in the commitment to Pan-Arabism. In the United Arab Republic, for example, "the term Arab, as used in current speech, is derogatory, denoting a shiftless nomad, someone to be looked upon with contempt by a people who have been settled cultivators from time immemorial." † A similar ambivalence is perhaps evident in Gamal Abdel Nasser's identification of the three circles of Arabism, Islam, and Africa, with each of which he believed Egypt's future to be linked.

---

* B. Lewis, *The Middle East and the West* (New York: Harper and Row, 1966), pp. 86–87.

† S. G. Haim, *Arab Nationalism: An Anthology* (Berkeley: University of California Press, 1964), p. 52.

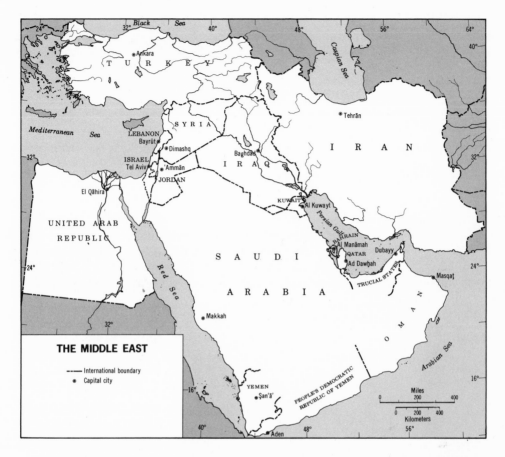

The Middle East is not coterminous with either the Islamic world or the Arab world. It is basically a political concept and represents a projection of European, particularly British, thinking. As originally conceived at the beginning of the twentieth century, the Middle East referred only to Afghanistan, Iran, Iraq, and the Persian Gulf—an area of British-Russian rivalry as distinguished from the Near East, a term essentially identified with the pre-1918 Ottoman Empire. With the collapse of the Ottoman Empire, however, the political groupings that had given validity to the expression the "Near East" disappeared. In particular, the Balkanization of the Arab provinces of the Ottoman Empire into mandated territories after World War I resulted in the establishment of European political dominance throughout southwest Asia.

The region represented essentially a British sphere of influence, French involvement being limited to the administration of the mandate for Syria (including Lebanon). Britain was responsible for the mandated territories of Palestine, Transjordan, and Iraq, while in the Crown Colonies of Cyprus and Aden British rule was direct. In the Persian Gulf, the British position was sustained by treaties with local sheikhs that gave Britain responsibility for defense and the right to establish military bases. In Egypt, despite the opposition of the Egyptian government and despite nominal Egyptian independence, British troops were stationed in the Canal Zone. In the political vocabulary of the period, "Middle East" came to denote the whole area of British involvement. Through frequent references to the British Middle East forces in military communiqués during World War II, the name eventually gained widespread acceptance.

In the postwar period, the expression has been perpetuated through its continued use by various specialized agencies of the United Nations. However, in so far as the name is a reflection of British political thinking, it could perhaps be argued that changed political circumstances have rendered it obsolete. For example, coincident with the decline of British involvement and influence in this part of the world, the North African countries of Tunisia (1958), Algeria (1962), and Morocco (1958) sought and obtained independence from the French. As each of these countries achieved independence, it became a member state of the Arab League. As a result, the distinction that existed through the first half of the twentieth century between the Maghreb, which represented a French preserve, and the Middle East, which represented a British preserve, has in the last decade become less clear-cut.

The Arab League is an attempt to give political expression to the concept of the Arab world. In theory, the league provides a forum for regional cooperation; in practice, the league's effectiveness has been hampered by Arab disunity. In particular, the league proved to be incapable of mobilizing the Arab world either to counter the establishment of Israel or to prevent the enlargement of that state during the Arab-Israeli war of June, 1967. Political cooperation has been hindered both by the differing ideologies of member states—Saudi Arabia and Iraq representing opposite ends of the political spectrum—and by the emergence of a strong sense of nationalism within each state. In this sense, the Balkanization of the Arab world and the European powers' imposition of arbitrary boundaries on the region created major obstacles to the realization of Arab unity.

Such differences have been reinforced by unequal advances in education and economic development and by long-standing local rivalries and animosities. These find expression in such inter-Arab conflicts as the military involvement of Saudi Arabia and the United Arab Republic in the recent civil war in Yemen; the border dispute between Iraq and Kuwait; and, more recently, the increasingly outspoken demands by West Bank leaders in Jordan for an autonomous state. Since June, 1967, further disagreements have developed as a result of the emergence of a Palestinian consciousness and the divergent attitudes of states such as Jordan and Syria toward the activities of the Palestinian *fedayheen* (guerrillas).

Nor has the Arab League been outstandingly successful in promoting economic cooperation among member states. Again, this is at least partly understandable in view of the political evolution of the region in the twentieth century. As Professor Charles Issawi has pointed out,

> Different currencies, linked to those of the Metropolitan Powers, circulated in the various Arab countries and customs barriers impeded trade. . . . As each country gained political independence, it sought to promote its economic well-being through policies designed to develop its own resources as fully as possible. Preoccupied with its own economic problems, no government has modified either its course of action or its plans in the light of developments in other parts of the region.*

The last few years, however, have seen increasing economic cooperation within the Arab world. The Kuwait fund for Arab Economic Development, for example, makes loans available to member states of the league. The Mukheiba Dam, an integral part of Jordan's Yarmuk Project, and the Suez Canal improvement scheme are both financed by the fund, although work on these projects has of necessity been suspended since the June war. In 1969, further loans were made to Lebanon and Yemen for agricultural development programs. Furthermore, since the June war, both Jordan and the United Arab Republic have received large-scale aid from Saudi Arabia, Kuwait, and Libya. Finally, the currently emerging federation among Libya, the United Arab Republic, Syria, and possibly the Sudan includes a provision to coordinate economic development and to reduce tariff barriers between member states of the federation.

Increased Arab political and economic cooperation has tended to emphasize the political division between the Arab countries of the Middle East and the northern tier states of Turkey and Iran. In part, this is a reflection of divergent historical experiences since the end of World War I. In the first place, under Reza Shah and Mustafa Kemal (later to be called Ataturk), both Iran and Turkey were able to retain their national sovereignty. Also, both rulers embarked upon a policy of modernizing and

---

* C. Issawi, "The Bases of Arab Unity," *International Affairs* XXXI (1955), p. 44.

westernizing many aspects of traditional life. Women, for example, were emancipated (at least by law), and European dress was encouraged. At the same time, in view of their common boundary with the Soviet Union and in the light of past history, Iran and Turkey have consistently been more sensitive to Soviet policies than have the Arab states. Both countries have consequently followed a more pro-Western policy since World War II. With Britain and Pakistan, for example, they were founder members of the Baghdad Pact, later known as the Central Treaty Organization (CENTO). Finally, both states have pursued a less hostile policy toward Israel. Iran, for example, supplies the bulk of Israel's crude-oil requirements. The continuing dispute between Iran and Iraq over navigation rights on the Shatt al Arab further reflects the political division between the Arab world and the northern tier states.

2 THE CHALLENGE OF CHANGE
Petroleum and Planning

James A. Bill

Tradition and Change • The Professional Middle Class •
The Petroleum Catalyst • Planning for Development •
The Fight for the Future

The Middle East is one of the most tumultuous areas in a world convulsed by the forces of revolutionary change. International war between the Arabs and Israel, internal war in the Yemen, tribal conflict in Iraq and Iran, and repeated coups in Syria and Iraq are among the more dramatic indications of this situation. Since 1918, there have been literally hundreds of cases of political assassination or attempted assassination in the Middle East.

Violence, however, is only one symptom of a situation in which conflict and tension are on the increase in all systems and at all levels. Great-power rivalry and ideological confrontation take place in a setting where communist cadres are outlawed, capitalist ideas are berated, Islamic tenets are ignored, and socialist movements are deeply divided. Gaps widen and divisions deepen as new groups and classes make profoundly new demands upon a traditional system. The Nassers exist alongside the shahs and sheikhs, while airplanes and computers challenge the camels and abacuses. It is within this general context that one must discuss the process of development.

Tradition and Change

The traditional Islamic social system was characterized by great elasticity. The Prophet's message stressed the brotherhood of all Muslims; as a result, rigid class lines were uncommon in the Muslim Middle East. Social mobility was a key pattern in the system, and Middle Eastern history abounds with dramatic instances of this phenomenon. The Ottoman, Safavid, Fatimid, and Mamluk dynasties were founded and built by men who rose from the lowest orders of society. Grocers and cobblers have become Prime Ministers, and slaves and soldiers sultans and shahs.

Despite this mobility mechanism and the professed ideals of brotherhood, traditional Middle Eastern society also witnessed great division and inequality. Dramatic rises usually were due not to equality of opportunity, professional skill, or individual merit but, rather, to personal connections, persistent intrigue, and chance. Power flowed informally and personally, and goals were achieved by twisting and bending one's way through the maze of individual relationships. Long-term planning and institutional efficiency made little sense in such an environment, where insecurity and uncertainty prevailed.

Yet the traditional Islamic system represents one of the most resilient and enduring systems in world history. New challenges and forces were absorbed and digested whenever and wherever they appeared. The fundamental sociopolitical relationships consistently weathered the changes involving dynasties, monarchs, and invaders. New rulers and elites were easily enmeshed in the traditional web of personalism and institutionalized tension. The Crusaders from the West and the Mongols from the East burned themselves out in the Middle East as the Islamic patterns of survival by submission and advancement by maneuver continued and prevailed.

The traditional patterns of the Islamic Middle East have also possessed the capacity to absorb economic growth and accelerating wealth. The expansion of cities and the construction of gigantic and complex edifices have represented little difficulty for the system. Physical development and material advancement, indeed, have helped to buttress and reinforce persisting social relationships.

Now, however, profoundly new forces, which challenge these patterns, have appeared. These forces demand transformation, and their drive to uproot rests at the heart of the conflict and change that characterize the Middle East today.

The Professional Middle Class

The major challenge to tradition in the Middle East is a new social class whose members derive their power from the skills and talents that they have gained from their modern education. This nonbourgeois middle class is composed of teachers, writers, students, bureaucrats, technocrats, journalists, engineers, and middle-ranking army officers. The coups and revolutionary take-overs in the Middle East are often led by individuals drawn from this class. These professionals demand fundamental changes in education, health, administration, government, and justice. Many of them criticize the personalism and uncertainty of the traditional system and call for rationality, efficiency, and security. Primarily because of their modern education, they entertain entirely new values and attitudes, which they are in an excellent position to transmit to the masses of their fellow countrymen.

The professional middle class is a burgeoning force, and in many Middle Eastern countries it is now doubling in size every ten years. In such countries as the United Arab Republic, Turkey, Iran, and Lebanon, it already accounts for nearly 10 per cent of the population. In other societies, such as Saudi Arabia, it is only now beginning to appear in noticeable numbers, and less than 2 per cent of the population can be classified in this category.

The professional middle class is the most dynamic social force now present in the Middle East. The sons of Syrian merchants, Egyptian peasants, Iranian mullahs, and Iraqi soldiers are obtaining higher education, and many are moving into salaried and professional positions, where they can play a key role in the formation and transmission of new ideas.

In Turkey and the United Arab Republic, this class has come to power and is now occupied with implementing reforms. In Iraq and Syria, it has taken political power but has failed to heal debilitating intraclass dissensions. In Iran, Saudi Arabia, and Jordan, the new class remains locked out of the political arena. In all these countries, however, members of the professional middle class are playing a crucial role in shaping attitudes and life styles at every level of society.

The Petroleum Catalyst

The Middle East is the world's largest oil-producing area, and Iran, Saudi Arabia, and Kuwait are among the top half dozen or so oil-producing countries in the world. In 1967, Middle Eastern wells produced 496 million tons of crude oil; 1970 production reached more than 689 million tons. In terms of future production, it is important to point out that Middle Eastern countries contain 62 per cent of the world's published proven oil reserves. And these figures, if anything, underestimate the situation. More dynamic analysis reveals the tremendous momentum being built up in Middle Eastern oil production. Important recent discoveries have been made in Iran, the United Arab Republic, and Syria. Petroleum experts estimate that, by 1975, Iran will pass Venezuela, which now stands as the top noncommunist oil-producer after the United States. In 1969, the United Arab Republic achieved oil self-sufficiency.

Increased oil production means increased oil revenues, which are crucial for national development. Oil revenues continue to skyrocket, and the governments of Middle Eastern countries can now expect to receive more than $5 billion a year from this source in the near future. Iran, Saudi Arabia, and Kuwait will soon be receiving more than $1 billion each in oil revenue per year. Such increases are due not only to increased efficiency and production but also to increasing organization among the oil-producing countries. The key development in this regard was the establishment of the Organization of the Petroleum Exporting Countries (OPEC) in 1960. Even at the time of its creation, the five members (Iran, Iraq, Kuwait, Saudi Arabia, Venezuela) of OPEC produced over 90 per cent of all crude oil crossing international boundaries. The now united producing countries have been receiving higher and higher percentages of the revenues as the once revolutionary 50-50 division between country and company has shifted to 75-25 and even 80-20. As a result of an agreement signed in February, 1971, by six Persian Gulf oil-producing nations—Iran, Iraq, Saudi Arabia, Kuwait, Abu Zaby, and Qatar—and twenty-three international oil companies—mostly American and a few British and Dutch firms—oil-company payments to the six nations will rise by more than $10 billion over the next five years.

High production and huge revenues, however, do not necessarily indicate development and modernization. Such resources can be used to prop up decadent and unpopular political regimes as well as to reinforce crumbling traditional institutions. However, there is no doubt that petroleum is an important catalyst of change. The oil industry stimulates development in that it (1) helps to raise the Gross National Product and contributes to foreign-exchange receipts; (2) stimulates the growth of other industry, especially in related areas such as petrochemicals and natural gas; (3) provides opportunities for local employment and technical training; (4) gener-

Courtesy Arab Information Center

The juxtaposition of traditional and modern is striking in the Middle East, especially where income from petroleum is swelling the national coffers. Vast sums are now available to speed the modernizing process. Here, Bedouins bring their camels to drink water from a well dug along the Trans-Arabian Pipeline Company's 1,068-mile petroleum pipeline. Such wells, bringing water to formerly dry places, have induced many traditionally nomadic groups to settle in tent villages nearby.

ates revenue that can be used for national development programs; (5) introduces new personal and business relationships into the culture; and (6) heightens aspirations and expectations among the citizenry.

The last two points are especially significant, for they strike directly at traditional sociopolitical relationships. The members of the professional middle class, represented in this case by the oil technocrats, engineers, economists, and administrators, are continually exposed to new methods, which they pass on to others in their societies. They are also the ones whose aspirations are whetted and who in turn sharpen the expectations of their countrymen. There is little doubt that many of the changes evident in everyday patterns of life have been stimulated by the oil industry.

Planning for Development

Planning organizations and five-year plans abound in the societies of the Middle East. In countries such as Iran and Iraq, between 60 and 70 per cent of the money used for development projects is derived from oil revenues. An examination of the investments of various Middle Eastern planning organizations reveals that most emphasis has been placed upon agriculture, communication and transportation, industry, education, and social-welfare projects. Changes in all realms of life are now being effected by planning organizations and agencies.

Change is evident in everyday occupational and recreational life. Stenographers and typewriters are replacing calligraphers and scribes; tractors are taking the place of oxen; motels and restaurants increasingly stand in place of caravansaries and teahouses. The carpet and metal industries have been transformed by the machine. Throughout the Middle East, herdsmen and mule-drivers listen to transistor radios while television sets now adorn village teahouses. The urban young, at least the males, flock to the movie houses, which are increasing in number. Dance halls, gambling clubs, ski resorts, and bowling alleys are becoming popular among the urban middle and upper classes. The patterns of dress are constantly changing, as veiled women do their shopping in tennis shoes and street cleaners go about their business in sport coats.

The nearly 3-per-cent rate of population growth in the Middle East means that the population of every country in the area, except Israel, Lebanon, Saudi Arabia, and the Yemen, will double in the next twenty-five years. This trend has occurred alongside intensive rural-urban intrasocietal migration. There is a flooding movement from the villages and countryside to the provincial cities and national capitals. In many Middle Eastern countries, therefore, the society has come to be dominated by a gigantic, sprawling capital city. Kuwait, where nearly 75 per cent of the population resides in Kuwait City (Al Kuwayt), is the extreme case. But Beirut (Bayrut) accounts for 19 per cent of Lebanon's population, Amman for 16 per cent of Jordan's, Cairo (El Qahira) for 14 per cent of Egypt's, and Tehran for 10 per cent of Iran's. With this migration have come unemployment, shantytowns, slum areas, and urban congestion.

Government agencies have tried to confront the problems inherent in this urbanization process by designing programs and plans in housing, health, and education. Housing projects are being developed and expanded throughout the Middle East. Public and private investment is constructing 10,000–12,000 new homes a year in Syria and 40,000 new dwellings annually in Iraq. But the effort is minimal when measured against the 1965 statistics, which revealed three million substandard housing units in Iraq and 250,000 in Syria.

Important strides have been taken in health care, and the number of physicians and hospitals has increased sharply in many places. Control over such diseases as malaria has been dramatic (though recent setbacks indicate that this ailment will continue to be a problem in some areas). Despite some encouraging trends, however, the medical situation continues to be deeply inadequate. In Iran, for example, half of the country's 6,000 doctors are located in Tehran. Of the 3,000 doctors practicing in the provinces, 2,500 are situated in the provincial capitals. This results in a ratio of 1 doctor per 300,000 people in the Iranian countryside. Many of the best Iranian doctors are practicing abroad: some 900 Iranian physicians work in New York and another 700 in Munich.

In the field of education, the rates of enrollment expansion are running much higher than the rate of population growth. Between 1963 and 1967, primary-, secondary-, and higher-education enrollment in six Middle Eastern countries rose from 12 million to 16.4 million students—a 35-per-cent increase in only four years. During this short period, secondary-school enrollment more than doubled in Saudi Arabia and nearly tripled in Syria and the United Arab Republic; university enrollment doubled in Iran and Iraq.

Progress in quality must also be considered. The traditional preoccupation with rote memory is still prevalent in the area, and qualified teachers are in severely short supply. There is a particularly serious gap in technical education: fewer than 3 per cent of Middle Eastern students are enrolled in vocational or technical schools. The problem is aggravated by the "brain drain," as thousands of students being educated in Europe and America decide not to return to their homelands. The spread of education is the prime stimulant in the growth of new classes whose commitment is crucial to the processes of development.

The Fight for the Future

The key to national and local change in the Middle East is not petroleum or planning organizations or education. All these are, of course, intimately involved and important: petroleum provides capital, plans and projects represent goals and guidelines, and education develops intellectual talent and technical skills. But the capital must still be rationed and allotted, plans must be integrated and implemented, and education must be made creative and relevant. Only the political system can relate and consolidate these variables; only the political system can sponsor national integration and human commitment.

The traditional patterns of personalism, fragmented planning, administrative rivalry, incoherent violence, and inadequate health and educational reform continue to thwart the forces of social transformation. These patterns remain prevalent in planning organizations, as ministers, deputy ministers, public groups, private groups, committees, councils, and institutes constantly compete with one another. A 1967 United Nations study of development planning in six Middle Eastern societies concludes that the "social chapters of development plans lack depth, breadth, and interrelation with the other parts of the plans."

Yet the accumulating changes in petroleum production, population, urbanization, health, housing, and education promise to influence the social patterns in a way that will require more effective and deep-seated action. These changes continually alert Middle Easterners to new opportunities and possibilities. It is the people, therefore, who will demand the kind of planners and politicians who will implement and accelerate fundamental changes in all aspects of life. It is in this sense that the changes now flashing through the Middle East acquire their most profound significance.

3 CITIES OF THE MIDDLE EAST

Robert S. Harrison

*The Urban Expansion • The Form and Structure of Cities •
Urban Functions • The Widening Gap*

Cities are not new to the Middle East. By 3000 B.C., the urban centers of
Memphis, Thebes, Babylon, and Nineveh had emerged, based on the
fertility of the Nile Valley and Mesopotamia. Although these ancient
civilizations collapsed in time, the idea of the city spread in the eastern
Mediterranean and also North Africa through the Phoenicians, Greeks, and
Romans. After the seventh-century Arab conquests, urban life flourished
in such Muslim centers as Baghdad, Damascus (Dimashq), and Cairo (El
Qahira).

Again and again political vicissitudes have changed the fortunes of
cities. Damascus was overshadowed by Baghdad after the latter's rulers
took over the Arab Empire; in the eighteenth century, the capital of
Persia (now Iran) was shifted from Esfahan in the southwest to Tehran
in response to the rise of Russian power to the north. When the Turkish
Empire collapsed and Syria was established, centrally located Damascus was
chosen over Aleppo (Halab) as its new capital, and the capital of Turkey
was transferred from Istanbul to Ankara in 1923.

Although individual cities may decline, certain locations appear to have
permanent advantages. Babylon was succeeded in turn by Ctesiphon and
Baghdad; Cairo lies across the Nile (Bahr el Nil) and twelve miles north
of the site of ancient Memphis. Perhaps more than elsewhere, urban growth

in the Middle East has been a reflection of the development of commerce and trade routes, because of the position of the area in the crossroads of Asia, Africa, and Europe. Towns grew along and at the termini of the great caravan routes linking the lower Tigris-Euphrates with the Levant, at the northern ends of trans-Saharan routes, and along the northern highway connecting central Asia with the eastern Mediterranean via the Black Sea. Cities developed as ports—Beirut (Bayrut), Haifa, Basra, Alexandria (El Iskandariya), Trabzon—at important land-route and water-route crossings (Baghdad, Istanbul), and at the nodes of caravan routes in places that controlled important natural routes (Damascus, Aleppo).

Certain towns grew because of their religious significance. Mecca (Makkah) remained a small rest stop for caravans until it became the Holy City of Islam. Now it attracts 500,000 pilgrims a year—a major source of income. Similarly, the growth of Jidda (Juddah), the port for Mecca, and Medina (Al Madinah) has been connected with pilgrimage, as has that of Jerusalem, Holy City for three faiths: Christianity, Islam, and Judaism.

In this predominantly dry area, a major factor influencing the choice of town sites has been the availability of water supplies. For example, Damascus developed where the Barada River permits extensive irrigation farming. Defensive sites were also chosen, as in Istanbul and Cairo. The only natural advantage of Jerusalem, in view of its inaccessibility, inadequate water supplies, and distance from main caravan routes, was its rocky hilltop site. Good harbors were utilized wherever possible, as at Beirut's Bay of Saint George and Alexandria's narrow isthmus, which was free of silting and protected by the peninsula of Faros.

In the nineteenth century, Europeanization further stimulated town growth: Many old cities expanded, and new towns were built. The Turkish coal-mining towns and the oil port of Abadan owe their origin to such modern economic activities.

The Urban Expansion

The population of the Middle East is mainly rural, but urbanization is increasing rapidly, and in Muslim states urban populations now represent 25 to 40 per cent of the total. In Turkey, the urban population increased from one-quarter in 1935 to one-third in 1960, and in the United Arab Republic, the growth was proportionately even greater. In addition, the rate of urban increase is itself increasing, and urban populations are expanding faster than rural populations: in the U.A.R., 3 per cent per year compared with 1 per cent; in Iraq, 3.8 per cent compared with 1.4 per cent. Consequently, there are now some 18 million people inhabiting fifty-seven cities of more than 100,000 population, and there are five cities with more than a million inhabitants: Cairo, 4.5 million; Tehran, 2.7 million; and Alexandria, Istanbul, and Baghdad, with 1.8 million each. These five account for 66 per cent of the population of centers with over 100,000 inhabitants. Although Israel has no "million" city, it is the most highly urbanized nation in the Middle East; more than 80 per cent of its inhabitants live in cities.

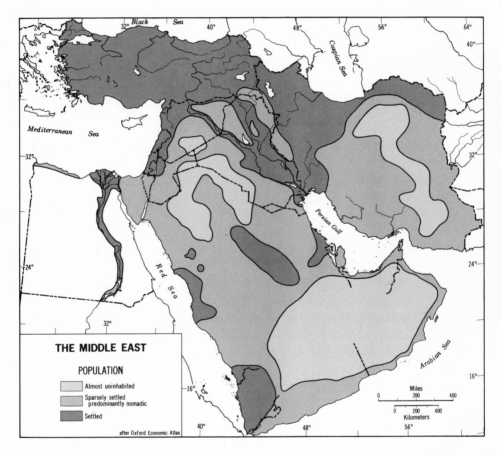

THE MIDDLE EAST

POPULATION

Almost uninhabited

Sparsely settled
predominantly nomadic

Settled

after Oxford Economic Atlas

Urban population growth has not been due primarily to natural increase. Although death rates are lower in cities than in the more primitive countryside (for example, 12 per 1,000 in Damascus compared with 27 per 1,000 in poor rural areas), birth rates are also lower (29.3 per 1,000 in Damascus compared with over 45 per 1,000 in rural localities). Instead, the

CITIES OF THE MIDDLE EAST   19

increase has been a result of massive migrations to the cities, stimulated by overcrowding on the arable land and the attractions of urban employment. In just one year, 1947, Cairo, for example, gained 600,428 by in-migration, 28 per cent of the total population of the city. Migrants have been attracted by employment possibilities in building and construction, especially when modern urban sectors and ports are being developed. They go to cities where a building boom is paralleling an oil boom. They seek jobs in industrial and service occupations, although the capacity of industry to absorb labor is limited in most places. They join the police or the armed forces. And, in the case of the relatively few migrants with special talents, they may find private employment as traders and shopkeepers. Further, the cities are magnets because they offer educational, social, and cultural attractions. All this has created tremendous housing and employment problems and has led to the growth of overcrowded *bidonvilles* (shantytowns) around many large cities, often lacking such elementary facilities as sewage disposal.

The rate of urban population increase varies with the extent of economic development. Modern commercial and industrial cities have had the greatest increase: Cairo, with a population of 790,939 in 1917, now has 4.5 million; Abadan, established in 1910 as an oil port, had grown to 280,000 by 1969. Old cities untouched by modern development have grown far less rapidly.

The Form and Structure of Cities

Although the morphology of towns has undergone changes as a result of Western influences, modern economic development, and urban in-migration, many distinctive features of the traditional Muslim city remain. The great mosques in the heart of the *medinas,* or old cities, are striking features, their minarets dominating the skyline, as in Cairo and Istanbul. Equally impressive are the ramparts surrounding the old cities, which recall the political instability of these areas in the past and their need for military protection. The citadel—the fortified administrative center—was often built within an angle of the walls or alongside them. Well known are the Citadel of Saladin, which dominates Cairo from an escarpment on the east side of the city, and that of Istanbul, located in the center of a steep-sided peninsula overlooking the strategic Sea of Marmara and the Golden Horn.

Other important structures of the *medinas* were the *khans,* centers of wholesale trading with lodgings for merchants, and the *hammam,* public baths whose function as centers of social life has been largely taken over by cafés. Houses face inward to courtyards, turning blank walls to the street, reflecting traditional social attitudes and the desire for privacy. Within their walls, the *medinas* developed a network of narrow, winding alleys—often confusing to the modern tourist. Streets in the commercial quarters are broader than residential "streets," many of which are only three feet wide. But there are more important thoroughfares running through the old cities, and some of these are wide enough for a motor vehicle.

Many *medinas* are now being modified in the interests of development. Streets are being widened and straightened, and old structures are being torn down to make way for new public buildings and offices. Unfortunately, in some towns renewal projects in the *medinas* are destroying historical and aesthetic landmarks, which, ironically, are a source of considerable tourist income. In Tripoli (Tarabulus), for example, the city government has constructed motorable streets across the *medina* with little respect for old buildings or attention to external appearance.

The variety of minority groups in the Middle East has produced the most characteristic feature of traditional towns: division into quarters based on cultural differences. The inhabitants are areally differentiated by religious sect, linguistic group, or place of origin, rather than by social class. Members of a sect often concentrated in the interests of group solidarity, but a more important influence was the Ottoman *millet* system, whereby minority groups were recognized as semi-autonomous communities, each occupying a distinct quarter (*hara*). The *hara* was a self-contained unit with its own officials, headed by the *seyh,* who performed administrative, legal, and police functions. With their own public buildings and defensive gates, the *harat* were quasi-independent, and even today they may be distinct in their associations with particular politicial parties. There are or were Jewish, Greek Orthodox, Armenian, Maronite, Coptic, and Shia *harat* in all the large cities, such as Istanbul, Cairo, Damascus, Baghdad, and Jerusalem. Where cultural grouping is more significant than differentiation by social or economic class, it is not uncommon to find imposing residences immediately adjacent to humble dwellings.

Characteristic of the Middle East are the *suqs,* craft and trading quarters in which each street concentrates on one activity and artisans and shopkeepers are traditionally connected with strong corporative organizations similar to medieval guilds. In some cases, a particular trade is monopolized by a certain cultural group, as with the Christian goldsmiths of Tripoli. The *suqs* are arranged around the center of the *medina;* the high-value goods are usually sold near the chief mosque, where goldsmiths, jewelers, incense

Courtesy Saudi Arabian Public Relations Bureau

An old man in Hofuf, Saudi Arabia, displays his wares in a tiny narrow stall typical of traditional markets in the Middle East. With his scale he measures out grains and nuts—but he also sells boxes of imported detergent and cans of tomato paste.

and perfume sellers, and booksellers are located. Farther away are quarters dealing with leatherwork, textiles, and carpets, while the outermost quarters house the dirtier or noisier trades of metalworking, tanning, dyeing, and pottery-making. Near the city gates are the food markets, selling vegetables, fruit, eggs, and meat.

In the past, the areas immediately outside the *medina* walls were occupied only by cemeteries and, frequently, by piles of urban refuse; beyond them were irrigated gardens or cultivated fields. It is in this zone that modern sections of the cities have tended to develop, first in Egypt under the progressive regime of Muhammad Ali but especially during the period of the European mandates after World War I. Here, wide, straight streets, regular street plans, gridlike or radial, and building styles directly reflect European influences. Cathedrals, museums, theaters, large shops, and government buildings were erected. As the modern sectors expanded rapidly, new residential areas came into existence, and the process of suburbanization began. Cairo expanded spectacularly: From the base of the Citadel, it spread west across the Nile and north to include the residential suburb of Heliopolis. European influences also brought the development of port and warehouse areas and industrial districts.

In spite of all this expansion, overcrowding is characteristic of all large centers from Baghdad to Cairo. Thousands of migrants live in squalor in the outer rings of *bidonvilles*. Prosperous or upper-class families are moving out of the *medinas*, being replaced by poor migrants who live in conditions as deplorable as those in the shantytowns. Today, many cities display their prosperity in newly constructed offices, public buildings, luxury apartments, and suburban villas, but the greatest need is for low-cost housing projects to eradicate the blight of the *bidonvilles*.

Urban Functions

One of the chief functions of Middle Eastern cities is commercial: The *suqs* have been the center of this activity and remain active even though traditional crafts are declining and wares now include cheap imported textiles and shoddy plastics. International trade is concentrated in a relatively few major ports, such as Alexandria, which handles two-thirds of the United Arab Republic's maritime foreign trade, and Haifa, which handles over 80 per cent of Israel's trade.

Towns also have long been centers of craft industries. Although competition from foreign and local manufacturers has caused a decline of small-scale industry, various centers have maintained their traditional reputation for quality. Well-known goods, much sought after by tourists, include the silk, brocade, and wrought copper products of Damascus and the carpets of Esfahan.

Modern manufacturing, apart from the steel industry, petroleum-refining, and chemicals, consists mainly of consumer industries based on agricultural products or on conversion of imported materials. It is heavily concentrated in the towns: Alexandria and environs has the United Arab Republic's largest concentration of manufacturing establishments; Tel Aviv–Jaffa (Tel Aviv–Yafo) has 67 per cent of Israel's industry. Urban concentration of industry is related to the presence of large markets and, in the case of port cities, to imports of fuels, raw materials, and machinery.

Towns have traditionally been political centers. Some are both administrative and economic capitals: Baghdad, for example. Where cities have been chosen as new capitals, economic development has often followed, as in Ankara after 1923 and Tel Aviv–Jaffa after it became the transitional seat of the Israeli government in 1948. And cities have always played an important cultural role. With their trading interests, commercial contacts, and diverse ethnic and cultural minorities, they have been more receptive to new ideas and much less conservative than the countryside. It was from the towns that the cultural influence of Greece, Rome, and Byzantium spread through the Middle East, and cities such as Baghdad, Damascus, and Cairo, where literature and the arts flourished, were the great centers for the diffusion of Islamic civilization. Other centers of learning include Beirut and Alexandria.

The cities have also been points of entry for Western influences and ways of life, as indicated by their modern schools and social services, movie theaters, night clubs, hotels, and restaurants. The cities were the first to accept European-style dress and the first to develop more liberal attitudes toward the position of women in Muslim society. Through the press, radio, and television, it is the cities that have become the most powerful propagators of modern social and political ideas.

The Widening Gap

In a largely desert zone, cities stand out as islands of activity, and the contrast between rural poverty and urban wealth is very great. In the Middle East this contrast has been accentuated by urban interest in long-distance trade rather than local development, so that urban dwellers have

These modern homes in Riyadh, Saudi Arabia, incorporate traditional Arab decorative motifs in an adaptation of modern-style architecture. Note the bicycle, now a favorite mode of transportation, and the cyclists in traditional robes.

often had more in common with distant cities than with local rural populations. Towns were sometimes able to provide food from their own oases, but they commonly depended on alliances with nomadic tribes for the protection of their caravans. Political insecurity further heightened the contrast; while commerce and industry prospered within the protection of city walls, the countryside was frequently ravaged by nomadic invasions. Political control needed the security of the cities, which were often centers of alien rule—Greek, Roman, Arab, Turkish, European—thus further divorcing the town from the countryside.

Culturally, the contrasts are striking. Religious attitudes and practices in the cities are far more flexible than in the countryside. Another powerful divisive force has been the emergence of a new middle class. The liberal, educated, and adaptable city-dweller rarely sees eye-to-eye with the poor, illiterate, and conservative farmer. Differences in faith sometimes play a part in the urban-rural division, as in Tripoli, a predominantly Muslim city surrounded by Christian rural areas. Urban wages are higher than rural wages, and the economic disparity between towns and countryside is widening as the urban concentration of industry and commerce develops. Modern health facilities are to be found largely in the cities, and, in rural areas, therefore, the incidence of disease is greater, death rates are higher, and life expectancy is lower. Educational facilities are similarly concentrated, particularly at the secondary and higher levels. The mass media—newspapers, movie theatres, radio and television stations—are centered in the cities. Beirut and Tripoli have over 70 per cent of Lebanon's cinema capacity, and Cairo has half of all radio receivers in the United Arab Republic. As a result, social evolution is occurring far more rapidly in the cities than in the rural areas. Because of education, birth control, and higher living costs, birth rates in the city are declining and smaller families are becoming more common. Jobs in the cities make it possible for young people to live more independent lives and to break away from the patriarchal and extended family. Uprooted migrants, detached from traditional tribal or family authority, often drift into crime in the cities if they cannot obtain employment. Education, modern attitudes, and the decline of the patriarchal family have also brought a questioning of old religious values. Education for girls is much more common in cities than in rural areas. Urban women are entering universities and professional careers, and polygamy has all but disappeared, although the traditional veil is still quite common in the towns. Accumulation of wealth in the cities has often led to the concentration of political power among a relatively few individuals, but on the other hand the urban middle class has been the principal instigator of reforms. And, while the cities today undoubtedly have tremendous problems, it is here that the greatest hopes for the future lie.

4 THE DESERT AND THE SOWN

An Ecological Appraisal

Ian R. Manners

The Environmental Complex · *Nomadic Pastoralists* · *Irrigation Farmers* · *The Potentialities of Arid Lands*

Despite a diversity of culture and society, ranging from nomadic pastoral to sophisticated urbanite, and a diversity of environment, ranging from torrid desert to semiarid steppe, the peoples of the Middle East are united by their common concern with water, its sources, and its availability. "We made from water every living thing," says the Koran (Quran), and water is indeed the most valuable of resources. In a difficult environment, life is everywhere dominated by the need to discover, conserve, and divert water from wells, streams, and the larger perennial rivers that flood briefly each winter. The major irrigation projects on the Nile (Bahr el Nil), the Jordan, and the Euphrates (called variously Firat and Al Furat) and the hand-dug wells of the Bedouin thus have a common purpose.

The unity of the region in terms of the general risk of moisture deficiency is immediately apparent, but the specific conditions affecting the availability of moisture for plant growth vary both spatially and temporally. As a result, a variety of strategies have been developed by the peoples of the Middle East, which, by overcoming the problems of water shortage, have enabled their cultures to survive and flourish under arid conditions.

The Environmental Complex

As far as human occupancy is concerned, the lands of the Middle East are uniformly hazardous. But the nature of the risk varies from one part of the region to another; different parts of the Middle East present different problems and opportunities for human occupation. In particular, there is a basic contrast between the arid zone, where climatic conditions throughout the year are too dry to permit any form of cultivation without supplementary irrigation, and the areas of seasonal aridity, where rainfall during the winter months is usually adequate to permit crop cultivation using dry farming techniques.

The arid zone, where extensive grazing is the only practical form of land use, has traditionally been the preserve of the nomadic pastoralist, while the seasonally arid zone has been the preserve of settled cultivators. However, the border between the fields of sedentary farmers and the grazing grounds of the pastoral nomads is rarely sharply defined, and there exists a broad transitional zone where the variability of rainfall conditions and the uncertainty of its time of occurrence impose severe restraints on farming activities.

A study by Wallen and Perrin de Brichambaut, for example, concluded that the minimum annual rainfall necessary for dry-land farming in the Middle East was seven inches. But the report also concluded that, because of the variability of rainfall conditions, agriculture might be marginal in areas with a mean annual rainfall of as much as eleven inches.* If these figures are taken as an indication of the range of values within which annual rainfall and variability may restrict the regular practice of dry land farming, it will be evident from the map of mean annual rainfall that large parts of the Middle East are highly marginal for rainfed agriculture. In areas receiving less than seven inches per year, the average rainfall is insufficient to permit agriculture even during the winter months without some form of irrigation supply. Where average rainfall is between the critical annual values of seven and eleven inches, the variability of rainfall conditions is likely to result in crop failure in a number of years. The probability of experiencing drought conditions can be calculated, but, while a farmer may have a rough idea of the risks over a decade, in any particular year he must make his decision with no guarantee as to

---

* C. C. Wallen and G. Perrin de Brichambaut, *A Study of Agroclimatology in Semi-Arid and Arid Zones of the Near East,* Food and Agricultural Organization, UNESCO, and World Meteorological Office Interagency Project (Rome, 1961), pp. 95–96. Rainfall in the Middle East is totaled for the period from October to September; thus all the rainfall falling during the winter cropping season is included in the total for a single year.

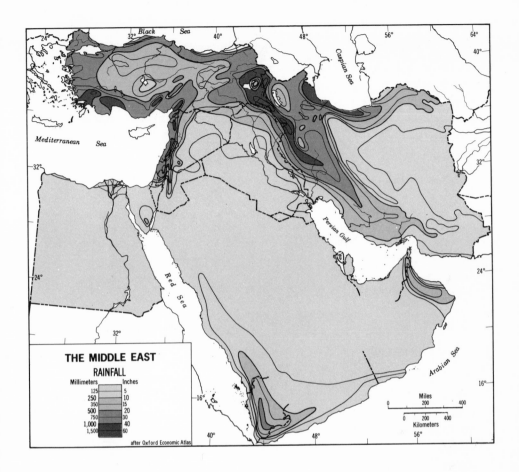

THE MIDDLE EAST
RAINFALL
Millimeters Inches
125   5
250   10
350   15
500   20
750   30
1,000 40
1,500 60
after Oxford Economic Atlas

whether that year's rainfall will be adequate. Only in areas with a mean rainfall of more than eleven inches per annum is there a minimal risk of crop failure due to drought.

These theoretical limits must not, of course, be considered as clear-cut boundaries, since factors other than the amount and variability of rainfall influence the feasibility of rain-fed agriculture. In marginal areas, for example, soil characteristics—in particular, the ability of the soil to retain moisture—take on added significance for farming operations. Reasonable distribution of rainfall throughout the crop-growing season is as vital as the total amount.

Again, any critical threshold values that are suggested may be modified by such technological advances as the development and introduction of drought-resistant seeds or moisture-conserving practices. Moreover, economic pressures may force agriculture into the marginal areas. In Jordan,

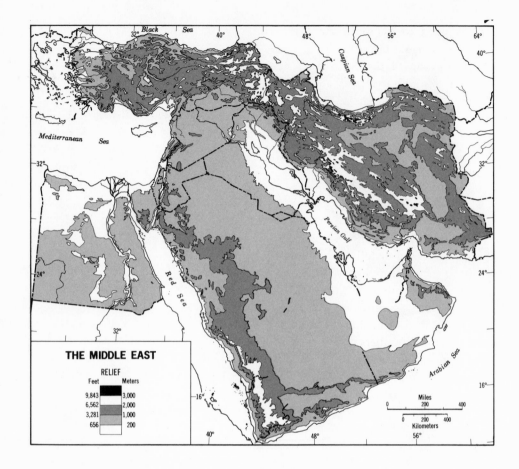

THE MIDDLE EAST

RELIEF

Feet	Meters
9,843	3,000
6,562	2,000
3,281	1,000
656	200

Miles
0   200   400

0   200   400
Kilometers

for example, attempts are frequently made to grow a winter cereal crop by rain-fed methods at places such as Al Mafraq, located on the fringe of the desert, where there is only a 20-per-cent probability of receiving more than eight inches of rainfall during the crop-growing season; but this is a reflection of population pressure on the land rather than its suitability for rain-fed agriculture. A succession of more favorable years—perhaps coinciding with the humid stages of minor climatic fluctuations—may also result in an expansion of agriculture into the marginal areas. But, with the return to median or more arid conditions, the contraction of the sown area and the abandonment of particularly rash frontier settlements are inevitable.

As a result of such processes and forces, however, the transition zone separating the desert from the sown has experienced marked changes in occupancy. Moreover, on occasions, even those areas that are traditionally considered to lie well within the cultivated zone have become involved in the struggle between the desert and the sown. The centuries following the breakup of the Arab Empire, for example, were a time of political instability and accelerating agricultural decline. During the fourteenth and fifteenth centuries, the movement of nomadic peoples in increasing numbers into the settled areas further interrupted and interfered with the orderly cycle of activities that characterize sedentary agricultural systems. Ultimately, in the absence of a strong authority to protect the cultivators, the traditional life of the nomads prevailed. In place of the settled agriculture of antiquity, therefore, there appeared a seminomadic type of farming, characterized by sporadic cropping, heavy dependence upon livestock, and frequent movements of population from place to place. Irrigation works constructed during the Roman, Byzantine, and early Arab periods either were destroyed or fell into disrepair.

The transformation of the cultural landscape during these centuries intensified the deterioration of the total land resource, which had begun during the last millennia B.C. The drastic destruction of the true climax vegetation cover for lumber and for fuel; the grazing and browsing activities of excessive numbers of livestock, particularly goats; soil erosion as a result of poor agricultural techniques; and the absence of a protective vegetation cover—all combined to alter the ecological balance over large parts of the Middle East and contributed to the present, highly degraded landscape.

It was the evidence of this transformation, in particular the existence of abandoned settlements and irrigation works in regions that are virtually desert today, that led to the suggestion that the climate of the Middle East had undergone a marked change since Roman times, involving progressive dessication. This hypothesis, however, has not been supported by recent archaeological and stratigraphical research, which suggests that the climate has remained essentially stable in the historic period and that the advance of the desert must be ascribed to man's own activities in altering the ecological balance.

To suggest that there has been no pronounced change in climatic conditions within historical times does not, of course, imply that there has not been minor short-term fluctuation. Rainfall records, for example, indicate a gradual increase in aridity in the Middle East during the first half of the twentieth century. At Jerusalem, mean annual rainfall for the period 1921–50 was only 19.5 inches compared to 25 inches for the period 1881–1910; the intervening averages show a progressive decline. Evidence from other areas confirms this trend: The level of the Dead Sea, for instance, has dropped 9.8 feet since 1910. However, this appears to represent a minor, short-term trend rather than a secular trend toward increasing aridity. It is of interest to note, for example, that during the most recent thirty-year period (1931–60) Jerusalem had an average annual rainfall of 19.2 inches.

Nomadic Pastoralists

Among the array of strategies developed by man in the Middle East to counter the difficulties and uncertainties of the environment, nomadic pastoralism was long considered one of the earliest forms of adaptation. However, it is now generally agreed that the nomadic way of life followed rather than preceded the domestication of plants and animals, the cultivator having far greater opportunities to domesticate wild animals than the hunter or gatherer.

The ecologic basis for nomadism in southwest Asia is the availability of seasonally productive natural pastures. In Iran, for example, nomadism is adjusted to altitudinal variations in the seasonal occurrence of pasture. In spring, nomadic groups among the Lur, the Bakhtiari, and the Kurds move from their winter grazing grounds in the foothills of the Zagros Mountains and follow the retreating snow line into areas of higher altitude, where snowmelt and cooler temperatures facilitate the growth of summer vegetation. On the return journey in the fall and before winter rains revive the pasture lands at lower altitudes, the herds survive on the stubble of harvested fields. In this instance, the complementary nature of summer and winter pastures is the basis of nomadism. In Arabia, nomadism is characterized by movements of peoples and animals from the oases, which are occupied in the dry season, to winter and spring pastures in the desert. In both instances, the nomads have no permanent place of residence and follow essentially fixed routes between grazing areas.

It is worth noting that the livestock herded by nomadic groups have different rates of movement, different environmental tolerances, and different pasture preferences. In some areas these differences are exploited by the nomads, thereby ensuring the fullest possible use of pasture resources. Barth has noted, for example, that in southern Kurdistan the foothills of the Zagros are utilized by sheep-raising Kurdish nomads during the winter. As they vacate the area in spring and move to higher altitudes, camel-herding Bedouin move in from the desert to escape the summer drought. Their camels thrive under conditions too severe for sheep and utilize the summer pasture that is available in the foothills. At the onset of the rainy season, the camel herders return to the desert and the sheep herders to the foothills.*

The mobility and independence of nomadic tribes present the central state authorities with numerous administrative problems. In many instances, the solution favored by the state has been enforced sedentarization of nomads. This policy was vigorously pursued in Iran during the 1930's, for example, when entire groups were resettled as agriculturalists in specially built villages far from their tribal territories. Although such policies may be politically expedient, they tend to overlook the fact that some form of livestock husbandry is the only viable form of economic activity under the ecological conditions existing in the arid zone.

Integration of the nomadic tribes into the economic and political functioning of the state could perhaps be achieved more effectively by improving the economic efficiency of pastoralism. Improved grazing control, for example, including a reduction in the numbers of livestock, would contribute to the improvement of both livestock and vegetation. Also, the establishment of artificial pastures in the cultivated zone might encourage free-range graziers and their livestock to become less dependent on arid and semiarid pastures and facilitate the integration of village and nomadic societies.

Irrigation Farmers

The seasonality of climatic conditions in general has a marked impact on farming operations in the semiarid zone. For example, climate imposes a distinct seasonal rhythm upon agricultural activities, involving a period of rest during the summer months in those areas without a perennial irrigation supply. As already noted, however, the semiarid zone is not completely lacking in water resources; rather, it is characterized by marked seasonal fluctuations in the potential water supply. Rainfall is, of course, the ultimate source of water for irrigation purposes, but the surplus of moisture remaining after evapotranspiration has occurred will be differently distributed in time and space according to local conditions. Many perennial wadis (intermittent streams) in the Middle East, for example, have regimes highly unsuited to the needs of irrigation farmers, maximum flow occurring in the winter months of least irrigation need. If storage facilities are not available, most stream flow, including both flood flow and winter ground-

* F. Barth, *Principles of Social Organization in Southern Kurdistan* (Oslo: Oslo University Press, 1953), p. 13.

water flow, will be lost. Other wadis have an ephemeral flow, which dries up completely during the summer.

In general, it is only in those areas that have exogenous water supplies—that is, where the water supply is drawn from rivers originating in more humid areas, as in the case of the Nile and the Euphrates—or that have groundwater supplies that a reliable water supply is available for irrigation development. As a result of variations in water-supply conditions, both the opportunities for irrigation development and the technology used to obtain and apply water differ greatly from one part of the region to another.

The *qanat,* for example, represents an extremely sophisticated technique for the development of groundwater resources. *Qanats* are believed to be a Persian invention dating back to the first millenium B.C., but knowledge of the technique was disseminated throughout the Middle East, North Africa, Spain, and the New World by the Romans, the Arabs, and the Spaniards. The physical basis for these irrigation systems is a combination of mountainous terrain and sedimentary basins, such as occurs in central Iran, where rainfall on the mountain ranges actively recharges the aquifers in the alluvial fans bordering the highlands. In the fans, groundwater moves underground toward the centers of the sedimentary basins. In excavating a *qanat,* vertical shafts are dug at intervals to the groundwater table and a gently sloping tunnel is excavated to abstract the groundwater, which eventually emerges at the surface, giving rise to a small "oasis" of irrigated fields. Many such tunnels are several miles in length, tapping groundwater lying several hundred feet below ground level. The graded nature of the tunnel also permits the flow of water by gravity, obviating the need for pumping and, at the same time, minimizing evaporation losses.

In Egypt, the traditional basin method of irrigation, which permitted effective utilization of the floodwaters of the Nile, represents a very different strategy. Each year, mud embankments were constructed in the flood-plain area dividing the irrigable land into a series of shallow basins. Floodwaters were then diverted into the basins to depths of several feet and retained for several weeks. Crops were planted in the fall as the floodwaters subsided, utilizing moisture stored in the soil. Such a system allowed the cultivation of only a single crop each year. In the twentieth century, the construction of barrages and dams to conserve floodwater for distribution during the season of low discharge has resulted in perennial irrigation techniques, replacing the traditional basin method. In the Orontes and Euphrates valleys, where the present flood plain of the rivers is incised to considerable depths below the main irrigable terraces, large water wheels (*norias*) are still used to lift water to the upper terraces. The wheels are turned by the flow of the river, and buckets lift the water into the distribution channels.

In the Middle East, as elsewhere, demands upon the water supply are presently increasing. In many areas, further intensification of land use, whether by extending the area under cultivation or by multiple cropping in those areas already cultivated, is dependent upon more effective management and use of the available water supply. Although the twentieth century has also seen major advances in technology, providing opportunities for more productive use of the resource base, in many parts of the region political, social, and economic factors have thus far hindered efforts to apply such technology.

An exception is perhaps the speed with which modern well technology has been adopted. Local farmers have long been accustomed to sinking hand wells to tap groundwater for agricultural and domestic purposes, but

Courtesy National Council of Tourism in Lebanon

Because rainfall in much of the Middle East occurs infrequently throughout the year or only in the winter months, farming is hazardous except where a reliable supply of water is available from rivers or wells. In the barren area shown here, the traditional wooden plow, which is attached to the mule's yoke, is still widely used, and harvests are likely to be both meager and uncertain.

modern techniques of well-drilling have permitted intensive development of this resource. In the southern Jordan Valley, for example, the successful boring of a well on land belonging to the Arab Development Society near Jericho in 1950 set off a wave of well-drilling activity. Between 1950 and 1961, when restrictions were finally imposed, a total of 588 wells were drilled in this part of the Jordan Valley.

Groundwater resources, however, frequently represent the accumulation of many centuries' infiltration of rainfall and are consequently susceptible to exhaustion if the rate of withdrawal exceeds the present rate of recharge. In the instance of the Jordan Valley, a serious overdraft situation had been created as early as 1960, and the recent history of most wells shows continuous lowering of the water table. There are similar signs of falling water tables in Saudi Arbian oases, where the water on which many cultivators and pastoralists depend may represent "fossil" groundwater— that is, moisture that infiltrated the aquifers underlying the area during the pluvial periods of the Pleistocene. In the coastal plain of Israel, with-drawal of groundwater has resulted in the intrusion of saline waters into the aquifers, endangering the quality of the water supply.

Such examples of resource degradation serve as an effective reminder of the problems and hazards of development in a marginal environment. Even more deleterious changes may be observed in other irrigation projects, where waterlogging, due to a lack of adequate drainage facilities and over-application of irrigation water, and salinization, due to improper applica-tion, combine to reduce crop yields and to remove large areas of land from productive use. In Iraq, an estimated 30 per cent of the irrigated land requires salinity control.

The Potentialities of Arid Lands *

The implications of the world's accelerating rate of population growth have led some experts to consider the vast, sparsely peopled arid lands as major food-producing regions. A common line of thought appears to be that increasing the amount of water available for irrigation would make it possible to dramatically increase the productivity of the arid zone.

As already indicated, however, the arid lands of such regions as the Middle East pose serious problems for man. Considering the effort and investment required, the opportunities for economic development are

---

* This section is based mainly on material contributed by David H. K. Amiran, of the Hebrew University, Jerusalem.

limited. Also, the people of the region frequently do not command the advanced technological and managerial competence required for the intensive utilization of such a difficult and uncertain environment. In particular, regional development projects introduce new elements and factors into the landscape, which must upset the existing ecological balance. As a result of man's intervention, the productivity of certain areas has been markedly increased, as in those irrigated areas where salinization and water-logging have been avoided. But in other areas, man's activities have brought about a serious deterioration of water, soil, and vegetation resources, and, with increasing pressure of population on these resources, the rate of deterioration is likely to accelerate. Attempts to restore and improve the resource base must take note of the fact that any environmental system constitutes a complex of interdependent components and interacting processes. Any projected change by man, therefore, must involve consideration of all the processes that interact to shape that particular environment. Unfortunately, examples of ecologically unsound planning—such as irrigation projects without adequate drainage—are all too common.

In view of the difficult environmental conditions in arid zones, no development project should be initiated without the most careful and comprehensive planning. Planning teams should include geographers trained to study natural environments and the modifications that will occur as a result of the projected development. Economists should evaluate the economic feasibility of the projects, the cost of the necessary infrastructure, and the economic potential and feasibility of marketing. Sociologists should evaluate the human aspects of the people involved—the social attitudes, habits, and adaptability of populations already in the area and of those to join them from elsewhere. Finally, and definitely last in order, engineers should plan and implement the technical installations within the framework of the project. In view of the practice in many parts of the Middle East, it should be stated explicitly that one cannot commit a greater error than to try to *engineer* arid-zone development projects. The restricted choices of an arid climate leave little margin for inefficiency.

Suggested Readings for Part One

Aramco Handbook. *Oil and the Middle East,* rev. ed. Dhahran, Saudi Arabia: Arabian American Oil Company, 1968. A comprehensive, up-to-date study of the Middle East, particularly of the impact of the oil industry on all phases of life. Excellent maps and illustrations in color. Carefully indexed with extensive bibliography.

BAER, G. *Population and Society in the Arab East.* New York: Praeger, 1964. A demographic and social study of the Middle East, which describes the expansion of urbanization, the structure and institutions of towns, and features of urban society.

BERGER, MORROE. *The Arab World Today.* Garden City, N.Y.: Doubleday, 1962. An analysis of changing everyday life in the Arab world.

BRICE, WILLIAM C. *South-West Asia.* London: University of London Press, 1966. A general survey of outstanding historical, social, and economic events.

CANTOR, LEONARD M. *A World Geography of Irrigation.* London: Oliver and Boyd, 1967. Ch. 9, South-West Asia, pp. 135–38. An up-to-date summary of irrigation projects.

CLAWSON, MARION; HANS H. LANDSBERG; and LYLE T. ALEXANDER. *The Agricultural Potential of the Middle East.* New York: American Elsevier Publishing Company, 1971. This study, sponsored by the Rand Corporation–Resources for the Future, concludes that the Middle East possesses the physical capacity to triple its agricultural output within a generation.

CRESSEY, GEORGE B. *Crossroads: Land and Life in Southwest Asia.* Philadelphia: Lippincott, 1960. An excellent text on the Middle East, with a good bibliography.

DICKSON, R. H. P. *The Arab of the Desert.* London: Allen and Unwin, 1949. An excellent description of traditional Bedouin life.

DOUGHTY, CHARLES M. *Travels in Arabian Deserts.* New York: Random House, 1937. A classic of travel in Arabia in the nineteenth century providing much insight into Bedouin attitudes.

FISHER, W. B. *The Middle East.* New York: Dutton, 1963. A general outline of the growth of towns and the urban way of life in the Middle East. Regional chapters provide information on each of the large towns.

———. *The Middle East: A Physical, Social, and Regional Geography.* London: Methuen, 1971. An up-to-date analysis of factors contributing to the emergence of new systems and new patterns in Middle Eastern society.

Gibb, Sir H., and H. Bowen. *Islamic Society and the West,* vol. I, part I. London: Oxford University Press, 1957. A valuable picture of life in the traditional Muslim city in the eighteenth century; describes the structure of the city, the organization of quarters and craft corporations, industry and commerce.

Halpern, Manfred. *The Politics of Social Change in the Middle East and North Africa.* Princeton, N.J.: Princeton University Press, 1963. A study emphasizing the social and political dimensions of change.

Lawrence, Thomas Edward. *The Seven Pillars of Wisdom.* New York: Doubleday, 1935. Lawrence of Arabia's story. Contains excellent descriptions of Bedouin life and attitudes and historical accounts of some of the tribes and their distribution.

The Middle East and North Africa, 1968–69. London: Europa Publications, 1968. A compendium of statistics and information relating to the various countries of the Middle East and North Africa.

Thesiger, W. *Arabian Sands.* New York: Dutton, 1959. Travel with Bedouins in the Ar Rab al Khali. Well told.

Warriner, Doreen. *Land Reform and Development in the Middle East: A Study of Egypt, Syria, and Iraq.* New York: Oxford University Press, 1962, esp. Chs. 1 and 2, pp. 1–70. Revision of a classic study on land-reform innovations in the Middle East. Provides excellent critique and comparison of land-reform processes in these three Arab states.

———. *Land Reform in Principle and Practice.* New York: Oxford University Press, 1969. A study of the aims, problems, and implementation of land-reform laws.

II NATIONS OF THE MIDDLE EAST

5 THE UNITED ARAB REPUBLIC

John S. Haupert

The Desert and the River • *An Arid Climate* • *The Land and the Small Farmer* • *Land Reform and Agricultural Development* • *The Chief Crops* • *Industry and Natural Resources* • *Urbanization and Transportation* • *The Current Economic Crisis* • focus *on the Aswan High Dam* • focus *on the Suez Canal*

Proud of its rich and ancient civilization, and conscious of its location on the African and Asian continents, and its affinity with the Mediterranean world and the other Arab states, the United Arab Republic (formerly Egypt) in recent years has based its foreign policy on the principle that it is an African, Mediterranean, Arab, and Asian nation, and it has emerged as the dominant power in the Middle East. Paradoxical situations have arisen, however, in practical politics, as witness the country's continued hostility to Israel and its Western supporters, yet defiance of traditional Arab monarchies; its championship of non-alignment, yet acceptance of direct economic and military support from the Soviet Union and communist-bloc nations.

Internally, an intensely nationalistic revolutionary elite that seized power from the monarchy in 1952 introduced substantial changes in the political and socio-economic system. The regime of President Gamal Abdel Nasser, supported by a small technically educated middle class, a growing urban proletariat, and the great mass of small farmers, was able to effect some basic reforms designed to increase agricultural production, extend arable land, and generate the skills and capital necessary for further industrialization. Upon the death of President Nasser on September 28, 1970, Anwar

Sadat, who succeeded him, announced his intention to continue Nasser's policies in these respects.

The Desert and the River

Virtually all of Egypt is included in the huge desert belt that stretches from the Atlantic Ocean through the Arabian Peninsula eastward into central Asia. Rectangular in shape, the nation has a total area of about 386,000 square miles, approximately the size of Texas and New Mexico combined. Four major physical regions can be distinguished: the Sinai Peninsula, the Red Sea Highlands, the Western or Libyan Desert, and the Nile Valley and Delta.

The Sinai Peninsula, linking Africa and Asia, consists of a dissected limestone plateau rising southward in a confusion of granite and metamorphic rocks dominated by Gebel Katherina (8,644 feet). To the east, the highlands plunge abruptly to the Gulf of Aqaba. There are no perennial streams, and rainfall ranges from five inches in the north (higher in the mountains) to practically zero at the southern tip; agriculture is limited to a few oases along the Mediterranean coast.

The Red Sea Highlands were formed by the uptilting of crystalline basement rocks associated with the Rift Valley. Like the Sinai, the highlands are deeply dissected by ephemeral rivers running to the Nile River (Bahr el Nil) and the Red Sea. The desert escarpments in many areas are close to the river, and it is only between Asyut and Luxor that cultivation on the east bank covers any extensive area. Rainfall is less than four inches per year, and settlements occur only in a few places where underground water has been tapped along the Red Sea coast.

The Western Desert is an uninterrupted expanse of basement rocks covered by horizontal sediments with gentle gradients; its elevation is less than 1,000 feet. There are large oases a few hundred miles west of the Nile in artesian depressions (*kavirs*) of internal drainage where water is found close to the surface and is available for agriculture if free from salts. The largest and deepest of these basins is the Munkhafad el Qattara, with its badlands and salt marshes. In the big oases of the "New Valley," fresh water and sandy but arable soils support considerable agricultural colonies; recently drilled deep wells will irrigate 43,000 acres of arable land. The settlements of El Siwa, El Wahat el Bahariya, El Wahat el Dakhla, and El Wahat el Kharga form a huge S-shaped curve from the latitude of Aswan northward to the Munkhafad al Qattara depression. About forty miles south

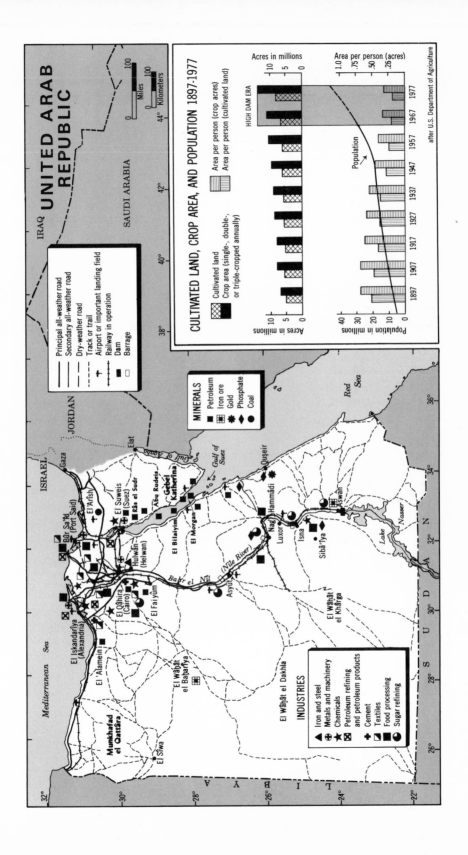

UNITED ARAB REPUBLIC

Principal all-weather road
Secondary all-weather road
Dry-weather road
Track or trail
Airport or important landing field
Railway in operation
Dam
Barrage

MINERALS

Petroleum
Iron ore
Gold
Phosphate
Coal

INDUSTRIES

Iron and steel
Metals and machinery
Chemicals
Petroleum refining and petroleum products
Cement
Textiles
Food processing
Sugar refining

CULTIVATED LAND, CROP AREA, AND POPULATION 1897-1977

Cultivated land
Crop area (single-, double-, or triple-cropped annually)
Area per person (crop acres)
Area per person (cultivated land)
Population

Acres in millions
Area per person (acres)

HIGH DAM ERA

1897 1907 1917 1927 1937 1947 1957 1967 1977

Acres in millions

Population in millions

after U.S. Department of Agriculture

IRAQ

SAUDI ARABIA

JORDAN

ISRAEL

Gaza

Mediterranean Sea

Red Sea

Gulf of Suez

Nile River

LIBYA

SUDAN

Munkhafad el Qattâra

El Sîwa

El 'Alamein

El Iskandarîya (Alexandria)

Bûr Sa'îd (Port Said)

El 'Arîsh

El Suweis (Suez)

Râs el Sudr

Abu Rudeis

Gebel Katherina

El Bilaiyim

El Morgan

El Qâhira (Cairo)

Hulwân (Helwan)

El Faiyûm

El Wâhât el Bahariya

El Wâhât el Dakhla

El Wâhât el Khârga

Asyût

Nag' Hammâdi

Luxor

Isna

Sibâ'îya

Aswân

Lake Nasser

Quseir

Elat

Bahr el Nîl

Miles
Kilometers

of Cairo (El Qahira) is the Al Faiyum depression, which receives fresh water by canal from the Nile River.

The Nile is the lifeline of Egypt, determining the patterns of life and occupation of the vast majority of its people. The contrast between the lush, fertile, green Valley and Delta regions and the adjacent barren brown deserts is absolute.

Where the Nile enters the United Arab Republic, it becomes part of Lake Nasser, the immense reservoir that is rising behind the Aswan High Dam (Sadd el Ali) (see pp. 57–63). In the entire stretch between Aswan and the Delta, the Valley is only about twelve miles wide. This is where most Egyptians live, outside of the Delta, and this is the main area of basin irrigation, which will be replaced by perennial irrigation now that the Aswan High Dam has been completed. The latter type of irrigation allows the sowing of two or three crops on the same plot of land each year. Already, four-fifths of the cultivated area of Egypt is under perennial or gravity-flow irrigation, with the proportion increasing toward the Delta.

An Arid Climate

The main feature of the Egyptian climate is its almost uniform aridity. Alexandria (El Iskandariya), on the extreme western edge of the 135-mile-wide Delta, receives eight inches of rain annually, and the early morning fog that appears here and elsewhere over the Delta during spring and early summer brings a little additional moisture beneficial for plant growth. But Cairo, 155 miles south of the Mediterranean, averages only 1.5 inches; Asyut, farther south, gets 0.2. Rainfall is also capricious; in many places it may come in measurable quantities only once in two or three years. Owing to the large extent of desert, hot dry sand winds (*khamsin*) are fairly frequent, particularly in spring, and cause discomfort to men and damage to crops.

In the northern coastal areas, temperatures range between a mean summer maximum of 99° F. and a mean winter minimum of 57°. In inland areas the range is greater: stifling 114° maximums and chilly 42° minimums.

The Land and the Small Farmer

Unlike many African states, the United Arab Republic has few problems stemming from ethnic or religious diversity. Most Egyptians are identified as

Hamitic, although Levantine characteristics are evident in the north, particularly in the major cities, and Nubian peoples predominate south of Aswan. Wealth and position being equal, the person with lighter skin enjoys social advantages although overt discrimination is not condoned. Apart from 2 million Coptic Christians and 100,000 Greeks, Lebanese, Armenians, and Jews, the population is made up of Muslims who speak a local dialect of Arabic. Since the Arab-Israeli war in 1967, an exodus of foreigners has occurred because of discriminatory measures taken by the government. These include Greeks, Armenians, Italians, and Jews. The Jews, once numbering 65,000, have been reduced to 2,500 or less.

More important than the composition of the population is its phenomenal growth. From 10 million in 1900, it increased to 27 million in 1961 and was estimated in July, 1970, to be about 34 million. The abrupt increase has been a result primarily of improved health care, which has sharply reduced the death rate among infants. In 1940, for example, the death rate was 26.3 per 1000 population; by 1967, it had dropped to 14.2 Today 42 per cent of the population is under fifteen years of age, which creates heavy demands for jobs and housing. At the present rate of growth of 2.88 per cent per year—high by world standards—a demographic projection might indicate a doubling in half a century.

Despite the extremely fertile soils in the productive areas, the great efficiency of labor per agricultural unit, and the current expansion of acreage and increased yields, output cannot keep up with the population growth, and the cultivated land per person has been declining. Furthermore, since 96 per cent of the nation is desert, all but 1 per cent of the people live in the Valley and Delta of the Nile and in the Suez Canal (Qana el Suweis) Zone; overcrowding and pressures on the land have pushed densities up to as much as 6,000 persons per square mile in some areas of the Delta. Under these circumstances, the *fellahin* (small farmers), who comprise 70 per cent of the population, are likely to continue to suffer from low standards of living, inadequate diet, and such enervating diseases as bilharzia (caused by a snail-borne liver fluke), which is increasing as a result of the extension of perennial irrigation.

Land Reform and Agricultural Development

One of the main causes of poverty in Egypt has been the unequal distribution of land. Prior to the first Agrarian Reform Law, instituted in 1952, two

Courtesy United Nations

Irrigation by traditional methods involves continual and arduous labor. The two farmers pictured here are using a system of buckets and crude levers to raise water from river level to their fields. In order to do so, they must stand in the water for long periods of time and are almost certain to come in contact with snails carrying the liver fluke that causes bilharzia.

main types of tenure were practiced: private, and *wakf* (held in perpetuity by charitable institutions, public and private); some unreclaimed land was also held by the state. Private land was owned individually without any restrictions on the right of disposal and was operated by owners, tenants, or subtenants. Disparities in land ownership resulted in two distinctive societies: the wealthy landlords, who usually preferred to live in the major cities, and the impoverished *fellahin.*

Two feddans (1 feddan equals 1.038 acres) of land are considered the absolute minimum from which a farm family can derive a mere subsistence living; in 1952, 72 per cent of all landowners owned only 13 per cent of the cultivated land, with holdings averaging about 0.3 feddan. At the other end of the scale, 280 large landowners owned 583,400 feddans (of which 178,000 feddans were the personal property of the monarch). In addition, there were about 1.5 million families (approximately 8 million people) who owned no land at all and lived by sharecropping or casual labor.

Tied to the Muslim law of inheritance that required the equal division of property among male heirs, the small owner subdivided his land into minute holdings. In response, he turned to renting or sharecropping on an additional small area, or leased out his own plot and tried to find employment as a laborer. The tenant, furthermore, paid exorbitant rental rates and was hardly in a better position than a laborer. Primitive technology, wasteful use of capital, and poor seeds and fertilizers kept living conditions at a subsistence level even though productivity per unit was high. The stereotype of the *fellah* as a peasant-owner-cultivator had become invalid. During the period from World War II to 1952, the proportion of land that was rented rose from 17 to 60 per cent, and the prices for land increased fourfold. At the time of land reform, the average rental rate was equivalent to about half of the gross agricultural production.

The 1952 Agrarian Reform Law was designed to attack directly the poverty of the landless farmers by abolishing land feudalism, regulating the land market by fixing a ceiling on private land ownership, and redistributing expropriated land among the tenant cultivators. The main provision of the law was limitation of the size of properties to 200 feddans per landowner plus up to 100 feddans for his children. The second Reform Law (1961) decreed that no person should own more than 100 feddans and restricted the total area that might be held in tenancy to 50 feddans per family. In 1962, foreign-owned agricultural land was expropriated with compensation. Under the new law, compensation was made payable in fifteen-year 4-per-cent negotiable bonds in order to placate landlord resistance.

In 1969, land ownership was further restricted to 50 feddans per person and up to 100 feddans per family. Compensation is now paid equivalent to 70 times the value of the land tax.

To pass such laws is one thing but to apply them is often another. In Egypt, the two were actually the same in the sense that implementation was quick and complete. Redistribution is being done equitably with preference to former tenants who own less than five feddans themselves and to permanent laborers. The size of the holdings granted varies between two and three feddans according to the size of the family. By 1966, agrarian reform had affected 960,000 feddans through redistribution measures and almost 4 million feddans by tenancy regulations, or 17 per cent and 65 per cent, respectively, of all agricultural land. The very large estates have disappeared, but the general pattern of a vast majority of small units has not substantially changed. The installments paid by the new owners of land invariably amount to less than the rent they were charged as tenants.

Critics of land reform have stated that it does not necessarily lead to increased productivity because of the ensuing decrease in the scale of farm operations. However, the incentive of private ownership was expected to be reflected in larger yields. And, in general, a gradual improvement in the *fellah*'s income is an obvious indication of progress after nineteen years of land reform. The Agrarian Reform Authority is presently preoccupied with the supervised cooperatives—membership having been made compulsory. The cooperatives advance loans to members and provide them with seed, fertilizers, livestock, and machinery, together with storage and transport of crops. They also sell all the main crops for the members after deducting installments for the purchase price of the land and interest on agricultural and other loans. Thus far, the cooperatives have been rather successful, and crop yields, especially of cotton, the main cash crop, have risen steadily. Profits accrued by the cooperatives are both saved and invested. Reserves are accumulated as insurance against fluctuating prices, but surpluses are spent on socially useful purposes in the villages, such as clinics, social centers, and public water supplies.

The technical advantage of cooperatives lies in their ability to apply large-scale farming methods to small plots. All the land in the village is divided into fields, each several hundred feddans in size and planted in a single crop. The *fellah* is assigned a holding in three pieces, each in a different field, so that one, for example, might be under cotton, another under corn or rice, and a third under *berseem* (clover). The advantage in being able to plow, irrigate, and spray larger areas is obvious.

The Chief Crops

Despite reforms, however, the United Arab Republic produces only about three-fourths of the foodstuffs it now consumes. Until the Arab-Israeli war in 1967, the remainder had been coming from imports—largely U.S. Food and Peace shipments. Currently, the Soviet Union and Eastern Europe export food to Egypt in the form of grain, meat, and dairy products, but the diet of most Egyptians consists principally of grains such as wheat, rice, corn, and other starchy foods. Most vegetables, fruit, sugar, and oilseeds are produced domestically.

By value, more than 80 per cent of all exports are agricultural, mainly long-staple cotton and textiles, rice, and onions. Since 1956, most of the cotton has gone to the communist states under barter or other trade arrangements. Egypt produces annually 5 per cent of the world's cotton, but, more significantly, it is the major grower of the favored long-staple variety, with 40 to 50 per cent of the world's output. Cotton acreage for 1969–70 was 1.73 million acres, a slight increase over the previous year. Production totaled about 2 million bales and exports amounted to 1.4 million bales, the largest shares being purchased by Japan and India. Rice is the second agricultural export, jumping from 364,000 tons in 1966 to 1.8 million in 1968–69, out of a harvest of 2.48 million tons, thus bringing Egypt closer to self-sufficiency in grain production if the rising trend in rice, wheat, and corn production continues. In 1969, farm production rose 2.9 per cent, equivalent to the prevailing population-growth rate. Meat production, however, continued to lag, creating severe shortages, particularly in the cities.

Industry and Natural Resources

Industrial development has been greatly stimulated in the United Arab Republic since World War II despite shortages of skilled personnel, raw materials, and equipment. The rationale given for industrialization is the alleviation of rural population pressures and the raising of living standards. Most major industrial enterprises are nationalized; however, trade and handicrafts remain in private hands and are actually encouraged by the government with easier credits and hard-currency concessions in order to sustain greater owner confidence in investment and improvements.

At first, expansion efforts concentrated on consumer-goods industries, especially food processing, textiles, and pharmaceuticals, and on building materials. The textile industry is efficiently operated and is diversified, producing cotton, wool, linen, carpets, and clothing. Factories vary in size, with the largest, at El Mahalla el Kubra in the Delta, employing 17,000 persons to work 3,500 looms. Emphasis has now shifted to the development of heavy industry: iron and steel, oil refining, fertilizers, and automobile and agricultural machinery assembly plants.

A considerable array of minerals has been discovered, but only a few deposits have been surveyed, much less exploited. Coal occurs in commercial quantities in the Sinai Peninsula south of El Arish, and significant deposits of iron ore have been mined since 1955 about thirty miles east of Aswan and more recently in the El Wahat el Bahariya. Limestone, manganese, and feldspar, required by an iron and steel industry, are also produced in limited amounts. The fertilizer industry has a promising future. Phosphate reserves estimated at some 200 million tons of rock are found along the Red Sea coast at Quseir and in the upper Nile Valley at Sibaiyah. Half of the production is exported and the rest is converted to super-phosphates for domestic use. Hydroelectric power from the completed Aswan High Dam already supports a fertilizer complex, and the new electric power grid will aid the expansion and dispersal of other heavy and light industries.

The most spectacular project after the Aswan High Dam has been the integrated iron and steel mill at Helwan (Hulwan). Production began in 1958 with two blast furnaces. West Germany and the Soviet Union have supplied coking coal, and the former most of the plant's machinery and equipment. Production reached some 416,700 tons in 1965; fabrication and sintering plants are nearby. There are several disadvantages of the Helwan complex: Costs are high, as iron ore must be moved by rail over 400 miles from Aswan and coking coal must be imported. Nevertheless, it has given the nation domestic supplies of iron and steel and increased its industrial and employment opportunities.

Plans were announced in 1968 for the development of a new Soviet-built complex at Helwan to be completed by 1974. The total cost will be $965 million and the Soviet Union will contribute approximately $160 million in equipment and machinery. Steel production will rise to 1.5 million tons per year, enabling Egypt to be self-sufficient and to export 500,000 tons of steel a year. Repayment to the Soviet Union will consist of rolling-mill products from Helwan and various types of vessels from U.A.R. shipyards.

Egypt's major mineral product is petroleum. The chief oil fields occur on both shores of the Gulf of Suez. The Pan American Company discovered a rich field at El Morgan in 1965 under 100 feet of water, 12 miles from shore and 125 miles south of Suez (El Suweis). Ultimately an agreement was reached between the present two American companies, Phillips Petroleum Corporation and the Amoco-U.A.R. Oil Company, and the Egyptian General Petroleum Corporation, according to which Egypt receives 75 per cent of the revenue (valued at $50 million in 1969) and the investing companies 25 per cent. Twenty-five wells in the El Morgan field are in operation, producing about 15 million tons yearly. Smaller fields were developed by ENI, an Italian firm, at Ras el Sudr in the Sinai. In 1967, the Israelis captured deposits in the Sinai that were yielding 40 per cent of Egypt's oil production, and they damaged the Suez refineries. These were rebuilt, and by 1968 were producing about 6.5 million tons; however, in March, 1969, Israeli shells set fire to storage tanks and again damaged refining facilities. There are two other refineries at Alexandria and nearby El Maks, and production in the latter is expected to be doubled by the addition of a new distillation unit from Czechoslovakia.

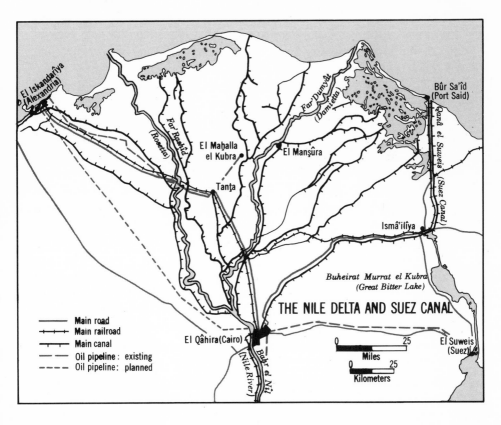

THE NILE DELTA AND SUEZ CANAL

Main road
Main railroad
Main canal
Oil pipeline: existing
Oil pipeline: planned

A production goal of 25 million tons will probably be realized in 1971, thanks not only to additional wells at El Morgan but also to new fields recently discovered west of Cairo, at El Faiyum, and twenty miles south of El Alamein. By 1969, despite the loss of the Sinai fields, the United Arab Republic, as a result of new discoveries, was a net exporter of petroleum, and agreements have been signed to sell petroleum products to Greece, Italy, the German Democratic Republic, the People's Republic of China, the Netherlands, and Bulgaria—the last in exchange for vital wheat shipments.

Following the closure of the Suez Canal in 1967, the United Arab Republic, faced with enormous deficits from the loss of transit tolls, decided to lay a 42-inch-diameter pipeline across the Nile from Suez to Alexandria, a total distance of almost 200 miles. Tankers will deliver crude oil from the Arabian Peninsula to Suez, and others will continue on to Europe from the Alexandria terminal. The pipeline is expected to carry at least 60 million tons of crude oil per year beginning in 1972—almost a fourth of the total amount that was shipped through the canal annually before the 1967 closure. (For additional information on the canal, see pp. 62–63.) Transit fees will bring in foreign exchange that is expected to help recover some of the losses from the canal. A consortium of Western private companies has arranged financing totaling $175 million for the project.

Egypt's domestic requirements for petroleum products continue to expand and constitute over half of all production. Liquefied petroleum gas (butagas) is used widely throughout the country for domestic and commercial purposes, such as cooking and refrigeration; heavy fuel oil (*mazut*) is used by most power stations to produce thermal electricity, by factories to produce their own steam or electricity, and by railroads, which are now dieselized. Increasing output of hydroelectric energy from the Aswan High Dam in the next few years will release additional amounts of petroleum for domestic use or export.

Urbanization and Transportation

At present, 35 per cent of Egypt's people are urban dwellers, and the proportion is rising every year. The large recent influx into the cities has created problems similar to those in many other newly independent nations: Rural migrants are often inadequately assimilated and are subjected to urban slum conditions as bad as, if not worse than, the rural poverty they left behind. Unemployment and underemployment are common. Cairo and Alexandria are the largest cities and the greatest centers of attraction. Cairo, the capital of Egypt and the first city in Africa and in the Arab world, has increased from 3.3 million to 4.5 million people in the short span of eight years. Well-located in regard to rail and road connections with the Delta cities, the city predominates in nearly all political, social, and economic activities except maritime trade.

The Alexandria Governate has the largest single concentration of manufacturing establishments and is Egypt's main port. Imports of machinery, steel, wheat, petroleum, vehicles, and fertilizers, and exports of cotton are handled through this harbor. Eleven other cities have populations exceeding 100,000; Port Said (Bur Said) (283,000) and Suez (264,000) are next in size and serve as centers of the oil-refining, petrochemical, and fertilizer industries as well as refueling stations and staging areas for the Suez Canal.

Egypt's infrastructure is already well developed. Inland water transport is by the Nile and to some extent by irrigation canals. Small sailing craft (feluccas), barges, and some motorized vessels carry most of the trade and passengers. The road and highway system is extensive, and there are more than 6,000 buses and 23,000 trucks in operation. About half of the 40,000 miles of roads are macadamized. Major highways link Egypt with Libya, cross the Suez Canal, and serve some of the oases. An important route, currently being improved, extends south to Aswan. Railroads connect the main centers for a total of 2,700 miles. Cairo is a focal point of international air communications in the Middle East and North Africa; the government-subsidized United Arab Airlines connects the chief cities within the country and with surrounding states. The radio and television system is one of the most modern and powerful in the Middle East.

Illiteracy and a shortage of qualified teachers are still problems, but much progress is being made in building primary and secondary schools and providing greater opportunities for technical and university training. There are several medical schools, and clinics and hospitals are found in all the principal settled areas.

The Current Economic Crisis

There is little doubt that the pace of industrialization and agricultural development accelerated after 1960. Official accounts show that the average annual rate of growth of national income between 1952 and 1959 was a little over 4 per cent (with about 1.5-per-cent annual per-capita growth), and that between 1960 and 1965 the yearly growth rate rose to 7 per cent. But, on the other hand, it has been obvious that the Egyptian economy has been severely strained. The deficit in the balance of trade grew from $96 million in 1960 to $465 million in 1966. Cotton, the main source of foreign exchange, earned more than $325 million in 1965 but dropped to $292 million in 1966 and registered an additional 11-per-cent decrease in 1967. The Suez Canal brought in no income at all. The tourist industry, the third largest earner of foreign exchange, provided almost $100 million in 1966, but the expected $138 million revenue in 1967 did not materialize because of the war with Israel. Since then, most tourists have avoided the United Arab Republic and other Arab states involved in the war.

Rapid industrialization has forced heavy imports of industrial raw materials, but exporting finished goods has been difficult. The quality of exports is at times unsatisfactory, and prices are high owing to low productivity. Steel from the Helwan plant, for example, costs more than twice as much as imported steel. The Nasser automobile plant has had to shut down periodically for lack of foreign exchange to pay for imported components, and other state-owned industries were unable to operate at full capacity because of a lack of imported parts and raw materials.

By 1968, Egypt owed about $3 billion to various foreign countries, and foreign-exchange reserves had narrowed to a mere $48 million. Beginning in 1969, however, industrial production turned upward in response to an austerity program and increased about 12 per cent by the end of 1970. The Gross National Product is now well over $4 billion, and, for the first time in years, a small surplus was realized in the balance of payments. The national budget for 1969–70 was $4 billion, but military expenditures required $1.1 billion, or about 25 per cent of the total. The financial burden of rebuilding the shattered armed forces after the 1967 war is aided by gifts of aircraft, tanks, and missiles from the Soviet Union. A crucial factor in the current budget surplus is the yearly subsidies of $266 million from the oil-rich Arab states of Libya, Saudi Arabia, and Kuwait that just offset the losses from the Suez Canal and nothing more.

The government has also altered its economic plans, which now call for a three-year "achievement stage" entailing further expansion of industries that can provide relatively quick returns, especially the processing of foodstuffs and the manufacture of cotton textiles. National income has risen by 3 to 5 per cent since 1968, partly because of higher taxes. It is hoped that employment will increase by 3 per cent to partly offset the severe unemployment created by several hundred thousand refugees relocated inland from badly damaged cities in the Suez Canal battle zone.

The commonly held view is that the root of the United Arab Republic's problems is the high growth rate of the population and the accompanying low growth in annual per-capita income, which now stands at only $100. However, in this respect the U.A.R. is similar to other developing nations, most of which do not have Egypt's expanding irrigated agriculture and petroleum resources.

focus *on the Aswan High Dam*

Southern Egypt's Aswan High Dam, completed in 1970, is one of the most impressive and significant irrigation and hydroelectric projects in the world. To the list of stupendous monuments erected by the pharaohs of old, history may well add President Nasser's great dun-colored colossus on the Nile River.

The dam is of such importance to the economic future of the United Arab Republic that special government agencies—the High Dam Authority and the Aswan Regional Planning Project—were established to supervise all activities related to it and to ensure that the country's great dream became a reality. It is spectacular from an engineering viewpoint: Designed to impound 100 million acre-feet of water, it will eventually reach 360 feet above the river bed and have three times the capacity of Hoover Dam. The installation is expected to produce over 10 billion kilowatt-hours of hydroelectric power, which is more than Grand Coulee Dam and second only to the Bratsk Power Station in Siberia.

The dam is also creating Lake Nasser, the second largest artificial lake in the world; it will extend some 310 miles southward, across the Sudanese border, and will average 14 miles in width. The lake is now about 200 feet deep at the sluice gates and will reach 300 feet by 1972, when the reservoir will be almost filled and the great complex fully operational. However, the construction of the dam is only one step toward the ultimate objective of using the available waters of the Nile River more completely for the benefit of Egypt's millions.

The revolutionary government that came to power in 1952 was committed to a policy of social and economic reform. Faced with the specter of a population explosion and diminishing food supplies, the new regime quickly concluded that construction of a single massive integrated irrigation-hydroelectric project on the Nile would be *the* panacea. The perennial irrigation to be realized by a high dam project, coupled with land reform and the greater use of fertilizers, would assure the United Arab Republic

Courtesy United Arab Republic Tourist Office

The Aswan High Dam, finished in 1970, utilized the latest techniques in engineering and construction. Besides generating large amounts of electric power, the dam will regulate the flow of the Nile so as to provide irrigation water all year round to many hundreds of thousands of acres, thus making it possible to grow two and even three crops a year in the same field. A portion of this cropland will be used to increase cotton production, one of the mainstays of the United Arab Republic's economy.

of reliable food supplies. The additional hydroelectric power would create the basis for industry and free much of the country's oil for the export market.

In 1956, the United Arab Republic turned to the Soviet Union for aid in financing and constructing the high dam after the United States and Britain had canceled their offer in protest against Nasser's political policies. A site was selected 450 miles south of Cairo, just five miles from the Aswan Dam built by the British in 1902. Of primary importance in site selection was technical feasibility—that is, the width and depth of the valley and the

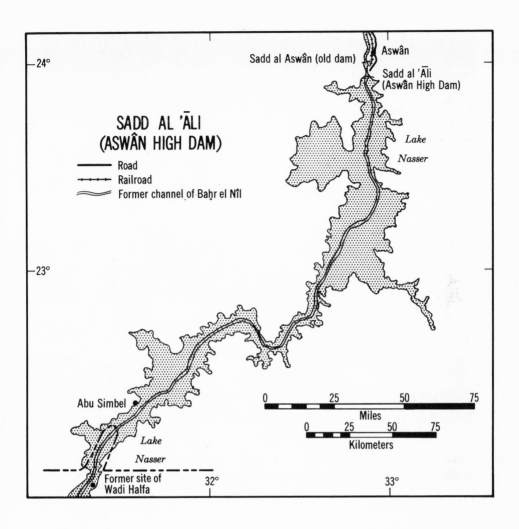

**SADD AL ʾĀLI
(ASWÂN HIGH DAM)**

——— Road
+–+–+ Railroad
≈≈≈ Former channel of Baḥr el Nîl

Sadd al Aswân (old dam)

Aswân

Sadd al ʾĀli
(Aswân High Dam)

*Lake
Nasser*

Abu Simbel

*Lake
Nasser*

Former site of
Wadi Halfa

24°

23°

32°

33°

0   25   50   75
Miles

0   25   50   75
Kilometers

porosity of the bedrock. A secondary consideration was the flooding of villages and fields in southern Egypt. Some 70,000 Nubians in Egypt and northern Sudan, threatened with inundation in 1965, had to be relocated on the higher riverine terraces and adjacent desert plateaus. Archaeological teams, aided by UNESCO, drew up plans to rescue historical sites from the rising waters. The most famous monument, the sandstone statuary and columns carved 3,000 years ago at the order of Pharaoh Ramses II at Abu Simbel, was cut into huge blocks and reassembled 200 feet higher. Certain other problems had to be taken into account regarding the aftermath of construction: for example, the tremendous amount of water that would be lost through evaporation in an arid region and the fertilizer deficiency that might result in northern Egypt when the silt that had enriched the soil for centuries was retained in the reservoir. There is also some indication that soil salinity may become a problem if adequate drainage systems are not installed, and that the reduced sediment in the Nile waters may reduce plankton and organic carbons and hence the fish catch in the eastern Mediterranean.

Storage of water behind the high dam will enable the nation to irrigate 1.3 million acres of unreclaimed farm land and to put another 700,000 of the present 6 million acres of cropland under perennial irrigation so that two or three crops a year can be grown. The main commercial crops affected will be rice, wheat, corn, and millet. Water available from the Aswan High Dam will make possible substantially increased acreages of rice, which presents an economic opportunity regardless of whether the objective is direct internal consumption or the export of rice in exchange for wheat. The output of corn will also increase because for the first time it can be planted and irrigated in both summer and winter, thanks to a year-round supply of water. Lake Nasser is also being rapidly developed as a giant fishery to supply a valuable protein supplement to the meager diet. The catch in 1969 amounted to 6,500 tons.

By 1970, the Aswan High Dam Project had cost $782 million. Of this cost, the Soviet Union supplied $325 million through two long-term loans for equipment and technical assistance; a small repayment has been made. In the earlier stages of construction, Soviet technicians numbered about 2,000, and Russians operated most of the power shovels and drills and placed most of the blasting charges. But, as Egyptian enthusiasm for the project developed, particularly after the coffer-dam was completed in 1964, Soviet technicians gradually relinquished their positions to Egyptians. Most of the actual work has been carried out by the government-owned Arab Construction Company at Cairo, one of the largest in the Middle East, which has employed as many as 40,000 Egyptian engineers and laborers.

The project was completed in mid-1970, and already "Egypt's Siberia," the Aswan region, is being transformed into an industrial complex of more than 100,000 people. International agencies are involved in providing counterpart funds to augment massive Soviet assistance. The United Nations has established a special fund of $1.6 million to found a research center to explore nearby mineral deposits. The Ford Foundation has supplied foreign experts to help chart the orderly development of industry, agriculture, mining, recreation, tourism, and transport and communication.

Laborers released upon completion of the dam are to be absorbed into a chemicals-metals industrial complex based on local deposits of iron ore, phosphates, copper, and possibly other minerals. When the related projects are finally completed, it is hoped that the national income will be in excess of a half billion dollars a year, thus repaying the cost of the dam in only two years.

By 1967, the dam had effectively eliminated the seasonal rise and fall in the level of the Nile. More than 100,000 acres of previously uncultivated desert lands have been irrigated in the United Arab Republic and the Sudan from Lake Nasser. The Aswan Dam will provide a stable and guaranteed discharge of 74 billion cubic yards of water a year, with 55.5 billion cubic yards allocated to Egypt and 18.5 to the Sudan. This additional water will assure an increase in agricultural production of 25 per cent and 15 per cent, respectively.

By August, 1968, seven of the twelve big Soviet-built generators had been activated—the others will have been so by 1971. Each generator is capable of producing 175 megawatts of power. A quarter of the total power will be used to drive irrigation pumps in southern Egypt. Another 20 per cent will provide power for an aluminum plant with an annual output of 100,000 tons. Two transmission lines now carry about 1,000 megawatts to Cairo, or half of the projected annual output when the dam is fully operational. However, considerable power will be lost in long-distance transmission over expensive power lines: The core areas of the United Arab Republic still remain Cairo, Alexandria, and the Delta, far north of the energy-producing site.

Offsetting problems related to distance and accessibility are the growth potential of Aswan industries and the stimulation of Nile traffic to unite southern and northern Egypt more effectively. The installation of three locks between Cairo and Aswan will permit heavy barges to ply the waterway, thus raising river cargo traffic to about 10 million tons a year. The lake will also be developed as a major recreational area for Egyptians. Foreign tourism will be encouraged by the construction of new hotels and the establishment of easy water transportation via hydrofoil to the salvaged antiquities.

Yet the Aswan High Dam, while making the river a more potent weapon in the war against hunger and for supplying power for industrial development, is not the complete solution to all the nation's economic and population problems. Raising the standard of living will require consistent and efficient effort in all areas of the infrastructure. The United Arab Republic is importing close to one-fourth of its food supplies, and under current agricultural practices it would appear that the planned 25-per-cent increase in agricultural output will at best only equal present food imports.

focus *on the Suez Canal*

Opened in 1869, the Suez Canal extends from Port Said in the north for a distance of 101 miles via the Great Bitter Lake (Buheirat Murrat el Kubra) to Suez on the southern end.

In 1956, the United Arab Republic nationalized the international Suez Canal Company, which had been run by the British under a concession that was to terminate in 1968. The Egyptian operation and modernization of the canal between 1956 and 1967, when it was closed as a result of the Arab-Israeli war, were among the nation's greatest technical achievements. Egyptians not only ran the canal efficiently but improved it and increased the transit fees so that the canal became the nation's second source of foreign funds, In 1955, the last year of foreign administration, the canal earned $74 million from 14,466 ship transits; in 1965, a record number of 20,289 ships paid almost $200 million. This remarkable performance was repeated in 1966, with revenues amounting to $266 million at the prevailing sterling exchange rate.

Much of this increase resulted from the growing dependence of European nations on Persian Gulf oil, which amounted to 250 million tons in 1965 and brought in 73 per cent of all canal revenues. In that year, an additional 40 million tons of dry cargo were transshipped: Ores, raw materials, and bulk foodstuffs moved northward; machinery, manufactured goods, and fertilizers moved southward. Another factor influencing the increased traffic and revenues was the modernization program made possible by a World Bank loan of $56.5 million in 1959. The entire length of the canal was dredged to permit the passage of fully loaded tankers with a draft of 38 feet and a capacity of 60,000 tons. (Ships with capacities of up to 106,000 tons have passed through the canal, but only when they are empty.)

In 1966, the United Arab Republic revealed plans designed to retain the lucrative transit trade, which is threatened by the trend toward employing supertankers. A ten-year plan, to cost $126.5 million, financed by the nation's central budget and the canal authority, would deepen the canal to accommodate tankers with a 57-foot draft and a 205,000-ton capacity.

The loss of revenue while the canal is closed is an overwhelming blow to the development plans of the country. Losses in canal fees have been calcuated at $300 million per year. At this writing, there is some prospect that the canal will be reopened in the not-too-distant future because of its importance to the economy and national pride of Egypt and to world shipping. (It has been estimated that the canal carried 15 per cent of the world's ocean trade.) Western European nations are pressing for a reopening to ease rising shipping costs. International oil companies say that the canal has a place in their economic thinking despite their earlier claims that the supertanker had outmoded the canal. The Soviet Union would like to see the canal in operation for defense and political reasons. The United Arab Republic would welcome the $300 million revenue per year. Israel hopes that the reopening of the canal might be the first step toward permanent peace. However, the problems remain formidable, for the canal is only one element in the long-drawn-out Arab-Israeli conflict. Nevertheless, diplomatic and economic planning is underway.

Suggested Readings

GRAY, ALBERT I. "The Egyptian Economy—Prospects for Economic Development." *Journal of Geography,* LXVI, no. 1 (Dec., 1967), pp. 510–18. Considers some of the major advantages for and hindrances to economic development of the U.A.R. in relation to the nation's physical and social resources.

KANOVSKY, E. "The Economic Aftermath of the Six Day War." *Middle East Journal,* XXII, nos. 2 and 3 (1968), pp. 131–43, 278–96. A brief summary of economic conditions in the U.A.R. from 1960 through 1967.

NOUR EL DIN, NABIL. "The High Dam and Land Reclamation in Egypt." *Mediterranea,* XX (April, 1968), pp. 262–69. Background information on factors necessitating land reclamation followed by a description of how the Aswan High Dam will benefit the nation through projects to be undertaken upon its completion.

SAAB, GABRIEL S. *The Egyptian Agrarian Reform, 1952–1962.* New York: Oxford University Press, 1967. Tables. A history of agrarian reform movements as they affected distribution of land and social changes. Appendixes study various reclamation projects in depth.

STEVENS, GEORGIANA G. *Egypt—Yesterday and Today.* New York: Holt, Rinehart, and Winston, 1963. Maps, photographs, bibliography. A concise history of Egypt skillfully blended with a consideration of modern trends.

6 ISRAEL

John S. Haupert

Varied Climate and Landscape • *The Negev* • *Refugees and Immigrants* • *Modern Farming* • *Transportation and Communications* • *Minerals, Industry, and Foreign Trade* • focus *on Jerusalem*

One has only to arrive in the bustling industrial and urban complex of Haifa or visit a new settlement in the Negev Desert to realize that the people of Israel have accomplished a near miracle in the twenty-two years since nationhood was achieved. Despite such serious obstacles as small size, a polyglot population, a land damaged by centuries of abuse, a paucity of natural resources, acute shortage of water, and hostile neighbors, Israel has forged a growing economy and a viable society. Among the many nations that have become independent since World War II, it is a prodigy to be watched and studied, an example of what can be accomplished in a land with limited resources by the application of modern techniques.

Varied Climate and Landscape

Israel's borders—as defined by the 1949 armistice agreements signed with Egypt, Jordan, Lebanon, and Syria—are disproportionately long and odd in shape. The country's greatest length from north to south is 262 miles and its width varies from only 9.5 miles on the Sharon Plain to 70 miles along a line from the Gaza Strip to the Dead Sea.

Within its small pre-1967 area of 7,993 square miles, approximately that of New Jersey, Israel has a variety of climates. In general the summers are exceedingly dry; rain comes in winter from cyclonic westerlies, usually in the form of a few heavy downpours that create excessive runoff and severe soil erosion on unprotected slopes. The total amount of rainfall varies critically from year to year; it also varies considerably from north to south and from east to west. In the north, 3,000-foot mountains in Galilee may intercept up to 40 inches of precipitation a year from Mediterranean storms, whereas Elat in the far south receives only 1.2 inches annually. Haifa, on the coast, averages 25 inches a year; Jerusalem, only 19.2. Snow generally falls in winter in northern Galilee and in Jerusalem (elevation, 2,650 feet).

Temperatures are determined primarily by altitude and distance from the Mediterranean Sea. In the interior valleys and highlands, especially in the Negev, they are higher in summer and lower in winter than on the coastal plains. In August the temperature may rise to 100° F in Jerusalem and even higher in the Jordan Valley or at Sedom on the Dead Sea, where there is little air circulation. Winter and summer temperatures at Tel Aviv–Jaffa (Tel Aviv–Yafo), on the other hand, rarely go below 50° or above 90°.

Israel also has greatly varied landscapes, with four main regions: Galilee in the north, a series of mountains dissected by numerous valleys; the coastal plains of Zevulun, Sharon, and Shefelah; the hills of Samaria and Judea, to the north and south of Jerusalem, respectively; and the Negev Desert in the south, which occupies more than half of Israel's total area.

In the limestone uplands of Galilee, Samaria, and Judea, a southern extension of the Lebanon Mountains (Jabal Lubnan), thousands of acres of barren hillsides have been planted with coniferous forests to replace the original Mediterranean vegetation, which had long been cut away or overgrazed. The trees, which anchor the soil and help to reduce erosion, are already beginning to yield much needed timber. Separating the Galilean uplands from the Samarian block is the Yizreel, a tectonic trough with a floor of rich, deep, black soil weathered from limestone and basalt. In the past half century, this valley has been transformed from an uninhabited malarial swamp into one of the most fertile and densely populated agricultural regions in the land, where farmers apply modern technology to produce a great variety of crops with surpluses for urban areas and export. From the Hula Valley in the northeast, which contains 60 per cent of Israel's water resources, the Jordan River plunges southward into Lake Kinneret (called variously the Sea of Galilee and Lake Tiberias), 665 feet below sea level, and flows sixty-five miles farther into the Dead Sea, its ultimate destination.

The deeply dissected Galilean uplands with a few fertile valleys support small Jewish cooperative settlements and Arab villages. The Judean Hills, which are more arid and have little soil cover, include the Jerusalem "corridor." Before June, 1967, it tapered from a width of about twenty miles at its western base to a tip about five miles wide at the site of the then divided city. After the brief Arab-Israeli war of that year, Israel unilaterally annexed eastern Jerusalem and incorporated it into a single municipality, which now has a population of 270,000.

The 120-mile-long coastal plain is actually the core area of Israel, for it contains the major cities and agricultural lands and the great majority of the people. Narrow and discontinuous in the north, where the Galilean Hills reach the sea, the plain widens out between Acre (Akko) and Haifa.

Since independence, spectacular industrial advances have occurred in the few miles between these two cities, in addition to the development there of entrepôt ports and market centers for western Galilee. Heavy industry on Haifa Bay now includes a steel-rolling mill, an oil refinery, a cement plant, a chemical and fertilizer factory, and a pharmaceutical plant. Haifa, with a population of over 200,000, is Israel's largest port and the focus of maritime commerce.

Where the Carmel Range approaches the sea, the coastal corridor is only 200 yards wide, barely sufficient for road and railroad lines. Farther south is the Sharon Plain, 10 to 20 miles wide. It is formed by alluvium originating in the hills of Samaria and Judea, but it is dune-fringed along the coast, where sand has tended to encroach on agricultural lands unless held in place by grasses and trees. The fertile sandy loam soils support the country's main citrus belt, in addition to other fruits, olives, vegetables, cereals, and fodder.

Tel Aviv–Jaffa, which lies in the heart of the coastal plain, is Israel's largest city (nearly 400,000) and its commercial and cultural center. It was founded only in 1909, as a Jewish counterpart of Jaffa, and absorbed the latter when the Arab population moved out in 1948. If the peripheral suburbs are included, the greater metropolitan area has well over 700,000 residents.

The lowlands of Shefelah, south of Tel Aviv–Jaffa, are less productive than the Sharon Plain and the Yizreel, primarily because of meager rainfall, consequent heavy irrigation requirements, and the prevalence of wind-blown sand. Arising among the coastal dunes are two new cities: Ashdod

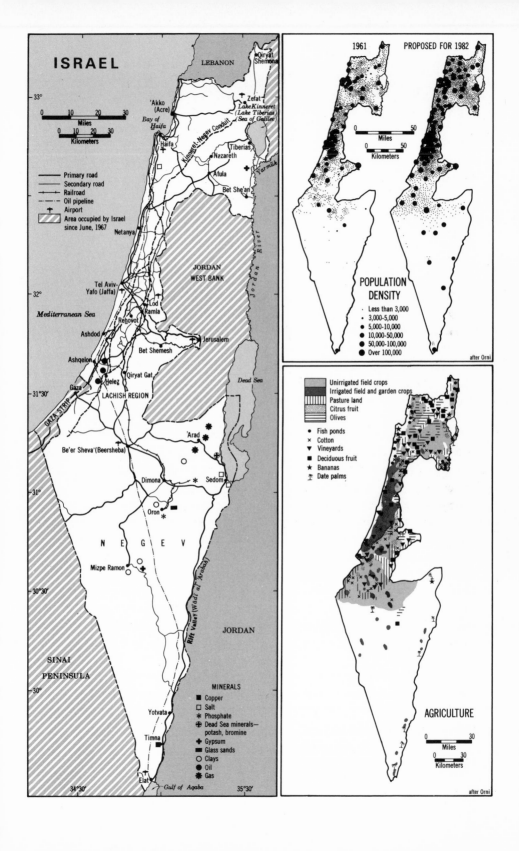

ISRAEL

-33°

0 10 20 30
Miles
0 10 20 30
Kilometers

LEBANON

— Primary road
— Secondary road
+ Railroad
—·— Oil pipeline
+ Airport
▨ Area occupied by Israel
since June, 1967

'Akko
(Acre)

Zefat
Lake Kinneret
(Lake Tiberias
Sea of Galilee)

Qiryat
Shemona

Bay of
Haifa

Haifa

Kinneret-Negev Conduit

Tiberias
Nazareth

Afula

Yarmūk

Bet She'an

Netanya

-32°

Mediterranean Sea

Tel Aviv-
Yafo (Jaffa)

Lod
Ramla

Rehovot

Ashdod

Ashqelon

Helez

Gaza

Qiryat Gat

LACHISH REGION

GAZA STRIP

-31°30'

JORDAN
WEST BANK

Jordan River

Jerusalem

Bet Shemesh

Dead Sea

'Arad

Be'er Sheva' (Beersheba)

Dimona

Sedom

Oron

-31°

N E G E V

Mizpe Ramon

-30°30'

Rift Valley (Wadi al 'Arabah)

JORDAN

SINAI
PENINSULA

-30°

Yotvata

Timna

Elat

Gulf of Aqaba

34°30'

35°30'

MINERALS
■ Copper
□ Salt
✳ Phosphate
⊕ Dead Sea minerals—
potash, bromine
✚ Gypsum
▬ Glass sands
○ Clays
● Oil
✻ Gas

1961   PROPOSED FOR 1982

0   50
Miles
0   50
Kilometers

POPULATION
DENSITY

· Less than 3,000
· 3,000-5,000
• 5,000-10,000
● 10,000-50,000
● 50,000-100,000
● Over 100,000

after Orni

▨ Unirrigated field crops
▨ Irrigated field and garden crops
▥ Pasture land
▨ Citrus fruit
▨ Olives

• Fish ponds
× Cotton
▼ Vineyards
■ Deciduous fruit
★ Bananas
⚘ Date palms

AGRICULTURE

0   30
Miles
0   30
Kilometers

after Orni

(27,000) and Ashqelon (38,000). The former, only twenty miles from Tel Aviv, is the center of a modern industrial development area. A deep-water artificial harbor has been completed, and the port is now second only to Haifa since the closure of Jaffa port a few years ago. The government planning authority envisages a population of 250,000 for Ashdod in twenty-five years; the port will handle the exporting of agricultural products from the Negev and minerals from the Dead Sea. The prime industry in Ashqelon, besides plywood and textiles, is tourism.

The Negev

The southern half of Israel is occupied by the Negev Desert, a region shaped like the tip of an arrow with its base in the north extending from the Mediterranean Sea south of Gaza eastward along the southern slope of the Judean Hills to the Dead Sea depression. It is confined on the east by the great Rift Valley (Wadi al Arabah), on the west by the 1949 military armistice line, and on its southern tip by the Gulf of Aqaba. Most of the Negev consists of a low plateau from 1,000 to 2,000 feet in elevation covered by thin sedimentary rocks folded upward in the center; in the south, the granitic basement complex is revealed near Elat. At the edge of the Rift Valley, the slopes fall steeply hundreds of feet amid a tangle of dry stream beds to the lowest point on the earth's surface, the Dead Sea, whose surface is 1,286 feet below mean sea level. Except for the northern Negev, upland soils are of the generally sterile red and gray desert varieties.

In 1966, a master plan was launched to regulate the development of the Negev as far south as Mizpe Ramon in coordination with national and regional considerations. The northern Negev represents Israel's principal future land reserve since a quarter of the area is considered arable and it is very sparsely populated. Among the fundamental goals of the plan are the achievement of maximum population density; expansion of the cultivable area within the limits of fertile soils and efficient use of water resources; promotion of industries using local crops and minerals; development of the urban aspects of newly founded cities and towns; and careful evaluation of prospective sites for new urban centers. Airlines and new roads will connect all inhabited parts of the Negev with the rest of the country. Permanent settlements will be established for the presently nomadic people of the area.

Courtesy Israel Office of Information

Giant pressure pipes of prestressed concrete, 108 inches in diameter, convey water from Lake Kinneret (Sea of Galilee) in northern Israel southward to the Negev Desert west of Beersheba. These pipes, now buried underground, are part of the integrated national system of water management that has made it possible to cultivate many thousands of formerly dry acres and vastly increase yields per acre in the past two decades.

The region around Beersheba (Beer Sheva) particularly is undergoing an amazing transformation from nomadism and dry farming to irrigated intensive farming of both subsistence and industrial crops. The city itself has experienced a phenomenal growth in only two decades, from 1,400 people in 1950 to almost 70,000 at present, most of whom are recent immigrants from abroad. It has become the major focus for urban and agricultural activities, the principal highway and railroad junction, and the administrative center for the Negev.

In the central and southern Negev, agriculture is limited to a few settlements dependent upon local springs or wells that contain considerable amounts of salts and chlorides. The largest is the Yotvata Kibbutz, where drip irrigation and hydroponics make possible the export of winter vegetables. With the exception of Elat and the copper-mining town of Timna, the very arid southern part of the Negev is almost empty. However, the new port city of Elat, on the 6.3-mile coastal littoral on the Gulf of Aqaba, has achieved a population of 10,500 in the last fifteen years. Several factors have contributed to its rapid growth. The closure of the Suez Canal to Israeli shipping brought trade that would normally use the ports of Ashdod and Haifa. Elat is also a convenient outlet for Negev minerals: phosphates from Oron, potash from the Dead Sea, and copper cement from Timna. The most important shipments that move through the port are petroleum imports, largely from Iran, totaling 4 million tons per year.

One of the factors limiting the growth of Elat has been the lack of potable water for residential and industrial purposes. In 1966, a dual-purpose plant was erected, combining a multistage flash-type evaporation plant with a steam power station that now supplies the town with electricity and 80 per cent of its drinking water.

Refugees and Immigrants

Only about one out of six Arabs remained in the new state of Israel after the 1949 armistice; the rest formed the basis of the present Palestinian refugee population perched on the frontiers in several Arab countries. A total of 1.39 million are registered with the United Nations Relief and Works Agency. Israel contends, however, that the total number of actual refugees emanating from the wars of 1948 and 1967 is much smaller.

Since the time of statehood, the original Jewish population of 655,000 has been augmented by more than a million immigrants, including a half million Jewish refugees from Arab countries. Approximately 65 per cent of the present population was born elsewhere. Very few of the new residents had any agricultural experience, and less than half had any vocational or professional training. The task of settling, educating, and integrating these people into the social and economic fabric of the nation is comparable in magnitude to the absorption by the United States of some 5 to 10 million new citizens every year for fifteen years, and it has been achieved for the most part without endangering a relatively high standard of living (annual per-capita income is about $1,600).

The Jewish population is now about 2.45 million; the non-Jewish population living within the 1949–1967 boundaries stands at 335,000, mostly Arabs, of whom 70 per cent are Muslims, 20 per cent Christians, and 10 per cent Druze, an Islamic sect. At present, the Jewish population is increasing at a rate of only 2.1 per cent per year; the Arab population is increasing at a rate of 3.9 per cent. Israeli Arabs enjoy full citizenship, but, with the exception of the Druze, do not serve in the armed forces. The population of the administered areas (Jordan's West Bank, Syria's Golan Heights, the Gaza Strip, and the Sinai Peninsula) totals about one million Arabs, including 236,000 in refugee camps and in East Jerusalem. Thus, the combined population of Israel and the occupied Arab lands is about 3.8 million, with a ratio of two Jews to one Arab.

Two basic types of settlement exist in the agricultural sector: the more flexible *moshav*, the cooperative small holders' settlement, and the classical *kibbutz*, a collective settlement popular in the pre-independence era. Economic decisions in the *moshav* are basically the responsibility of the individual farm family within the framework of national and regional planning; however, purchasing, selling, and other services are handled cooperatively under the supervision of the Settlement Department of the Jewish Agency. This organization is responsible for establishing 375 settlements with a population of 130,000 on the land owned by the state and the Jewish National Fund. The institutional structure of the *moshav* is adjusted to meet the needs of new settlers, who are often from a traditional society composed of merchants and craftsmen and who must be transformed into commercial farmers. Holdings in this type of settlement are about twelve acres per family and are capable of realizing high incomes from intensive agriculture.

The *kibbutzim*, the unique collective villages that introduced modern farming into the Middle East, have found it necessary to become more adaptable as the movement has slowed perceptibly. The 85,000 members of the 235 *kibbutzim* comprise only 3.5 per cent of the total population, but in the years 1960–66, their agricultural output rose by 70 per cent without a significant increase in numbers. Many of these settlements have been turning away from orthodox *kibbutz* philosophy to launch collective industries with hired labor and to promote cooperation between blocks of villages; these new activities, it is hoped, will provide additional income as a cushion against fluctuations in market prices for agricultural products. The *kibbutzim* in 1969–70 had a total of 160 industrial enterprises, employing 15,000 workers and producing goods valued at $125 million. Agriculture now provides only 50 per cent of the total income of the *kibbutzim*, while industry provides 35 per cent; the remaining 15 per cent is derived from outside work of the membership.

Modern Farming

In the last two decades, Israel has developed a primitive agricultural system into one of the world's most modern and sophisticated operations. Through national planning, large areas that centuries of neglect had left unfit for cultivation have been rehabilitated. Swamps have been drained, erosion controlled, dunes anchored, and irrigation extended. In coordination with these reclamation programs, new crops and cropping patterns were introduced.

The cutivated area in 1948 was about 400,000 acres; it now totals 1.1 million acres, of which about one-third are irrigated. Afforestation of 85,000 acres includes avenues of trees along 550 miles of roadside. Nearly 900,000 additional acres, mostly in the northern Negev, could be irrigated if sufficient water were at hand, but Israel utilizes 90 per cent of all water now available from runoff and groundwater sources. Agricultural policy, therefore, strives for maximum crop yields with the minimum use of water and establishes priorities for crops that will increase self-sufficiency and those that can replace imports and become valuable earners of foreign exchange.

Although self-sufficiency in food grains has been a long-term goal, Israel has concentrated its principal efforts on the production of high-protein, low-calorie foods such as milk, eggs, poultry, fish, fruit, and vegetables and is now nearly self-sufficient in these products. Hybrid varieties of wheat, expanded cultivated areas, and ample rainfall resulted in a record 200,000 tons produced in 1967 (compared to a previous average of 40,000), but only 58 per cent of the country's wheat requirements were met; self-sufficiency is still a long way off. Feed grains, beef, animal fats, and oils are other major food products that must be imported. At present, the United States, Israel's primary source of agricultural imports, supplies many of these.

Citrus fruits are the most valuable crop by far, and production has increased from 868,000 tons in 1965 to over 1 million. This phenomenal rise is largely due to increased plantings in the Negev. Some 700,000 tons, comprising 80 per cent of the value of all agricultural exports, are sold abroad, mostly to Western Europe.

Industrial crops, introduced ten years ago, are a feature of the five new regional-development bloc schemes, in which every town and village is linked in a regional system and the entire area is planned as one economic unit. A number of farm villages (usually four or five) are grouped around a rural center, which generally contains an elementary school, a cultural center, a dispensary, and farm services. The rural centers are then linked to an urban center with industries, a secondary school, and central administrative, social, health, and agricultural services. The Lachish Region, inaugurated in 1955, is the most advanced of these projects. Fifty-. six nucleated villages with a total population of 17,500 are organized around the urban center, Qiryat Gat (18,000). Some 65,000 newly cultivated acres produce sugar beets, cotton, ground nuts, tobacco, and vegetables. Farmers are also engaged in beef-cattle raising and dairy farming. To process these products, industrial plants have been established in Qiryat Gat, including textile mills, a sugar mill, and slaughterhouses. Enough cotton is currently being raised in Israel to export as well as to meet local demands.

Agriculture is the main consumer of water in Israel, using from 80 to 85 per cent of the total (industrial and urban consumption currently comprises about 17 per cent of it). Most significant to national development has been an integrated water-distribution plan, which includes drilling wells, maintaining storage reservoirs, establishing sewage-reclamation projects for the reuse of municipal and industrial waste waters, developing careful pumping techniques, controlling intermittent floods, improving brackish waters, preventing seawater incursions, and finding economically feasible methods of seawater conversion. The largest project is the Kinneret-Negev water-transfer system, completed in 1964; its purpose is to move water from Lake Kinneret into the northern Negev and to integrate all the existing regional waterworks into one grid. At present the annual capacity of the project is 320 million cubic yards. According to the latest studies, the annual quantity of water available when all proven resources are developed will be about 1.6 billion cubic yards. Yet this will provide only enough water to irrigate 40 per cent of the irrigable land.

At present, the desalination of seawater is extremely expensive, and so far it has been used only to supply drinking water and to improve existing brackish water in southern Israel. It is hoped, however, that recent technological progress will ultimately make desalinized water cheap enough to be used more generally. A significant step is the proposed dual-purpose atomic reactor to be built on the Mediterranean coast south of Tel Aviv–Jaffa. The reactor is to supply power and heat for a desalination plant to service both the Negev and the populated areas around Gaza. Plans for the project at the moment are at a standstill, but if and when the plant goes into operation the cost of water should be about 25 cents per 1,000 gallons. This is still more than twice the price Israeli farmers normally pay, so water costs will have to be minimized through government subsidy.

Transportation and Communications

Even prior to Israeli statehood, communications and transport enjoyed a paramount position in the economy for political and social, as well as economic, reasons, and they still do. An efficient infrastructure of roads and railroads and telephone services has been established. Low-cost public transportation by buses has been encouraged, while the purchase of passenger autos has been restricted in order to curb rising foreign-currency expenditures. Nevertheless, problems of traffic density in urban areas have increased in severity, and in recent years attempts have been made to eliminate bottlenecks and build multilane highways between Haifa, Tel Aviv–Jaffa, Jerusalem, and Elat. The roads connecting Elat to Haifa provide for the first time a "dry-land Suez Canal" between the Red Sea and the Mediterranean.

Politically, the maintenance of a state-owned system of air and sea transport is of crucial importance because these are the nation's sole outlets to the rest of the world. In times of crisis, foreign companies tend to refrain from operating to and from Israel. Government activity has concentrated on developing the national airline, El Al, and on developing harbors with associated axes of roads and railroads. Thirteen international airlines maintain regular flights to Lod Airport, the main facility; Jerusalem Airport (Kalandia) serves the capital; and Arkia, the internal airline, services Haifa, the Hula Valley, Beersheba, and Elat. El Al carries tourists primarily, about half the persons who visit Israel annually. It is also an important carrier of freight, especially fresh vegetables and flowers.

Israel has 112 ships, with a total capacity of 1.5 million tons (1968), and three ports. Haifa, the largest, handles 56 per cent of total cargoes (excluding fuel); the second deepwater port at Ashdod, opened in 1965, handles 38 per cent; and Elat, with its modern facilities for bulk loading, 6 per cent. The three ports totaled 6.2 million tons in 1968–69.

The dieselized state-owned railroads, despite the obsolescence of much of the track and rolling stock, have continually extended their lines (454 miles) southward into the Negev, reaching Dimona in 1965, and on to the Oron phosphate works. Another link is being built to the Arad region.

Minerals, Industry, and Foreign Trade

A variety of mineral resources for industry have been discovered in recent years by extensive geological surveys and by testing. The Dead Sea, which has a higher salt concentration than any other body of water in the world, is Israel's prime source of mineral resources: Its reserves of chlorides of magnesium, sodium, calcium, and potassium are estimated at some 40 to 50 billion tons. Production of potash reached 710,000 tons in 1967, and government aid and loans from the World Bank are financing further expansion. About 460,000 tons were exported in 1967 for a return of $13.6 million. The Dead Sea also has made Israel one of the world's top producers of bromides, most of which are sold to Europe.

The sedimentary rocks of the central Negev are the second most important source of minerals. Phosphate rock with a phosphorous content of 23–25 per cent is mined at Oron, and the ore is calcinated to raise the phosphorous content to 33–35 per cent. Production reached 483,000 tons in 1966–67. The Oron mines are operated in conjunction with processing plants in Haifa, which produce superphosphate fertilizers, phosphoric acid, and dicalcium phosphate for export. From the Ramon "Crater" twenty-five miles southwest of Oron, glass sands and ball and fire clays are trucked to Beersheba, where glass, ceramics, tiles, and porcelains are manufactured. High-quality gypsum is also found here and sent by rail from Beersheba to cement factories at Ramla and Bet Shemesh.

A third mineral complex lies in the crystalline rocks and the Nubian sandstone series of the Elat Hills. Granites are quarried near Elat and cut for ornamental building stones. Of the great variety of lesser ores in the southern Negev, only copper is exploitable. The mine is at Timna at the edge of the Rift Valley, fifteen miles from an adequate labor supply at Elat and convenient to the north-south highway. The ore is low-quality copper carbonate, and there are proven reserves of about 20 million tons. Copper cement is one of the principal exports from the port of Elat.

Small amounts of poor-grade iron have been found in Galilee but must be combined with local scrap and imported ores (from Spain and West Germany) to meet the 450,000-ton annual demand of Acre's steel mill. Israel has no coal and little hydroelectric power. The harnessing of solar energy is in its initial stages, and a 24,000-kilowatt atomic thermal reactor near Dimona has been operating since 1964. The chief source of energy has been oil imported from Iran, plus small amounts from Helez and methane gas from near Arad. At present, oil fields near Abu Rudeis on the Israeli-occupied eastern coast of the Gulf of Suez are supplying 2 million tons a year; because of its high sulphur content and the expense involved in any major alterations of the Haifa refinery, however, the oil is marketed abroad in crude form.

The petroleum is pumped through a 16-inch, 250-mile-long pipeline to Haifa, but a 42-inch oil pipeline has just been completed between Elat and Ashqelon. This line, of enormous potential value, both politically and economically, will ultimately reach a capacity of 60 million tons a year (most of which will be refined and sold abroad), or approximately one-fourth of the oil tonnage that passed through the Suez Canal each year before its closure during the Arab-Israeli war in 1967. Supertankers will have easy access to the Elat and Ashqelon oil terminals.

Israel turns out a wide variety of industrial products: processed food and beverages, textiles, machinery and metal products, steel, chemicals and petroleum products, wood products, transport equipment, electrical equipment, rubber and plastics, books and magazines, leather goods, and paper and cardboard. One of the most lucrative industries is diamond cutting and polishing; exports provided 38 per cent of the foreign revenue in 1969.

Industrial production is increasing rapidly: It was valued at $2.3 billion in 1966 and is expected to reach $3.5 billion annually within the next few years. Between 1955 and 1966, industrial exports rose from $63 million to $407 million, and the total was $527 million in 1968.

The government provides loans for industrial undertakings and encourages the investment of foreign capital, especially in enterprises that will save foreign currency by producing goods and services that would otherwise have to be imported. During the next few years, the emphasis will be mainly on industries based on local raw materials and those that have low transport requirements. Another trend is the growing self-sufficiency of the national defense industries.

Israel is still confronted by an adverse balance of trade because of capital imports and investments. The deficit stood at $437 million in 1967 and $585 million in 1968. Nevertheless, the country is enjoying an economic boom, and in 1968 the Gross National Product increased by 13.2 per cent, an unprecedented rate. The value of exports totaled $680 million in 1968–69, an increase of 15 per cent over the previous year, with the major expansion in industrial goods. The largest single earner of foreign revenues is the diamond industry. Tourism is a close second, and citrus fruits and products take third place. Imports include metals, machinery, vehicles, and wood products.

Unlike many of the other newly emerging nation-states, Israel has not suffered from a shortage of trained personnel for modern agricultural, industrial, and managerial enterprises, but difficult years lie ahead. As long as the political situation in the Middle East remains unstable, Israel is likely to have a serious deficit in its balance of payments. It may continue to have access to large amounts of foreign capital, but will this be sufficient to strengthen the economy and provide a place for its immigrants and security for its citizens?

focus *on Jerusalem*

Jerusalem is an ancient city, possibly 5,000 years old. It was a Bronze Age Jebusite stronghold until its capture by King David in about 1000 B.C. and the seat of the Jewish monarchy until its destruction by the Babylonians in 586 B.C. The persistence of Jewish settlement, however, resulted in a renaissance under Persian, Hellenic, and then Roman rule, culminating in the destruction of the ancient city and the second temple by the Emperor Titus in A.D. 70. The Muslim period, which commenced in A.D. 638, continued for many centuries under a succession of Arab, Mamluk, and Turkish leaders (except for a Christian interregnum from 1099 to 1187). The "Old City" walls, following the approximate limits of the Roman city in the second century, exist today; they were restored by Sultan Suleiman I, the Magnificent, in 1541. After 400 years of Ottoman Turkish rule, the city was liberated by the British in 1917, after having changed hands more than twenty-five times.

The natural setting of the Old City was a favorable one, but the modern city lacks most of the assets that normally assure the growth and development of an urban center. It has one rail and one highway link with the coastal plain and one first-class highway eastward to the Jordan Valley, but only second-class roads to the north and south. The agricultural hinterland is limited; therefore, food and industrial products as well as electricity and even water must be conveyed to the city. The deeply dissected limestone topography limits effective planning as well as hindering and increasing the costs of actual construction. Jerusalem's long existence can be attributed primarily to its importance as a religious center for the three great monotheistic faiths: Judaism, Christianity, and Islam. An added significance of the city is that the "new city" of Israeli Jerusalem became the *de facto* capital of the new nation-state in 1949.

Traditionally, the old walled city was divided into sectors or "quarters," Muslim, Christian, Armenian, and Jewish. The remainder of the city consisted of the Haram esh Sharif, or Temple Mount, where the famed Dome of the Rock and Aksa Mosque were built on the foundation of Herod's Temple, of which only the Western (Wailing) Wall remains.

Although there were separate Arab and Jewish sections within and beyond the Old City walls, there was considerable intermingling of the populace. At the time of the first Arab-Israeli war, in 1948, only 1,700 Jews lived within the Old City walls with about 25,000 Arabs. When the British Palestine Mandate was terminated in 1948, fighting had already begun for the possession of Jerusalem by Jewish armies within Palestine and Arab armies within and without the city. The signal for hostilities to begin was the United Nations General Assembly Resolution of November 29, 1947, providing for the partition of Palestine and the establishment of Jerusalem as an international city, a *corpus separatum*. At no time did the international community acting through the United Nations recommend that the city be assigned to either Israel or Jordan. Israel's claims of sovereignty have been recognized by some states but not by the United States, the United Kingdom, France, the Soviet Union, and many others. When a truce was arranged between Israel and the Arabs on July 15, 1948, the United Nations Truce Supervision Organization was entrusted with the maintenance of peace along the cease fire lines and in the no man's lands and demilitarized areas, such as the Mount Scopus enclave one mile inside Jordan, containing the old Hebrew University and Hadassah Hospital, which Israel retained.

Cut off from each other, the two Jerusalems developed distinctive characteristics, separate economies and laws, and national points of view. Jerusalem-Jordan became the center of the Hashemite Kingdom's lucrative tourist industry. The Israeli sector grew quickly under the impact of immigration and planning; government offices and the new Hebrew University and Medical Center were built, and commercial and light industries were established. The Mandelbaum Gate was the only official crossing point for tourists entering Israel from Jordan or for Israeli-Arab Christians who wished to visit the holy places during religious holidays. Normal communications, such as mail, cables, or telephone calls, were not possible. As in West and East Berlin, separate municipal services developed.

During the June, 1967, six-day war, the Old City was captured by

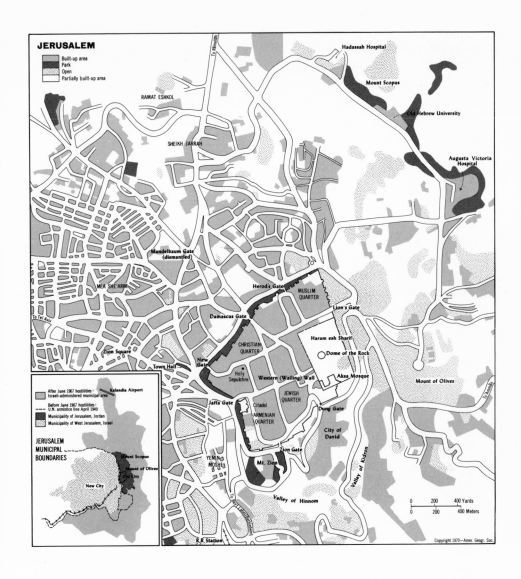

Israeli troops, and the two cities were fused by a unilateral decision of the Knesset (the Israeli Parliament). Although Israel has not yet referred to the act of unification as "annexation," the nation's leadership and a majority of its citizens apparently consider the fusion an irrevocable act. Census figures released shortly after the war, of which the battle for Jerusalem was a part, revealed a population of 65,857 in eastern Jerusalem, including 24,000 in the congested Old City. Muslims numbered 55,000 and Christians 10,000 in the entire urban area. When added to the 200,000 people of western Jerusalem, the total figure made Jerusalem the second largest city in Israel.

At first the problems of incorporation seemed insurmountable, given the disparity between the feudalistic economy and rigid class structure of Arab Jerusalem and the Western-oriented, egalitarian Israeli society. The government's basic desire was to achieve normalization of daily life and, wherever possible, improvement, particularly in the areas of employment, commerce, and municipal administration. The first act of Mayor Teddy Kollek was to remove all physical barriers, such as security walls and barbed wire. The Mandelbaum Gate was dismantled, and severed roads were connected and repaved to allow free movement of the population throughout the city and, indeed, to other portions of Israel as well as the occupied West Bank of Jordan. Dilapidated buildings in the former no man's land were demolished, repairs were carried out on the Old City walls, and compensation was paid to religious groups for minor damages incurred to holy sites during the fighting. The water systems were connected, ensuring eastern Jerusalem a reliable supply. School facilities were somewhat improved, and the Ministry of Education now provides a free high school education to residents of eastern Jerusalem.

Arab functionaries still run their own quarter and serve in the all-city administration. Arab laborers have been provided work in projects throughout the city at higher wages than before. About 4,000 are employed in the western part of the city, mainly in building and industrial work. Some unemployment exists, however, mainly among clerical workers, the unskilled, and those involved in the tourist industry.

Reunification has not been achieved without some difficulties and hostilities, though Kollek has contended that the city has thus far been comparatively free of violence, with a minimum of strife during the four years of Israeli occupation. The obliteration of homes of suspected terrorists and the requisitioning of about twenty-nine acres of slums near the Western Wall to restore the ancient Jewish Quarter forced the removal of 600 Arab families to new homes provided by the municipality. Arab businessmen at first suffered from the loss of tourist business and paid high prices to Israeli wholesalers when their cheaper goods from Jordanian sources were depleted. However, new laws have given Arabs equal economic rights with other Israeli citizens, and they do enjoy some tax relief. Arab banks remained closed, their accounts in Amman (Jordan) still blocked, thus limiting new investments. The Israeli pound is the only legal currency in the city. However, Israel has granted loans to Arab businessmen and is investing huge sums in the Arab sector. Meanwhile, tourism is beginning to revive the hotel and restaurant business of eastern Jerusalem. Yet, many Arab professional people are earning much less than they did before because efforts are being made to lessen the gap between the privileged few and the underprivileged many.

In 1968, under the expropriation laws of Israel, which authorize the government to confiscate privately owned unused lands with compensation to the owners, 838 acres in the Sheikh Jarrah sector were transferred to the municipality for construction of low-cost housing for Israelis. Housing units are now under construction in the new suburb, Ramat Eshkol, that will accommodate 1,400 families by the end of 1971. This scheme is in accordance with the government policy of settling Israelis on controversial lands as the surest means of ultimately retaining them. By 1971, there are to be 10,000 Jews living in this area: about half in Ramat Eshkol and the remainder in two other settlements, French Hill and Givat Hamivtar, on either side of the Jerusalem–Ram Allah Highway.

A master plan for Jerusalem has been announced setting goals to the year 2010. A population of 850,000 is assumed, of whom 450,000 are to be Jews. One of the premises is that, by 2010, peace will prevail between Israel and Jordan and relations between the city's two sectors will, therefore, be completely normal. The Old City itself is planned primarily as a center of religious institutions and tourism. It will also continue to be a residential area, but a less congested one. Already western Jerusalem's congested commercial "triangle," pressing on Zion Square, is extending itself, under the impetus of mutual trading, toward the Damascus and Jaffa Gates in the Old City.

As long as the size of a city's hinterland is unknown, no regional planning and only a limited amount of city planning can be done. The final boundaries of Israel, much more than the urban boundaries of Jerusalem, will determine the city's occupational structure, rate of development, demographic distribution, traffic requirements, and economic dynamism.

Outwardly, Jerusalem appears to be a single city. It has become a link between Israel and the Arab world; its citizens may travel and exchange their views freely. Yet, social integration may take years to accomplish, even after settlement of the Arab-Israeli dispute. One of the major sources of encouragement to the Jerusalem Arabs is the fact that the great powers continue to regard Jerusalem as an international city. Israeli "annexation" has been condemned by the United Nations and the international community in general. Most Arabs would prefer a settlement arranged by the great powers that would end Israeli control. Whatever the outcome, the reunification of Jerusalem is a unique experiment in the history of. the Middle East.

Suggested Readings

BEN-DAVID, JOSEPH, ed. *Agricultural Planning and Village Community in Israel.* Paris: UNESCO Arid Zone Research Series, XXIII, 1964. Describes the planning and social processes that went into settlement of the arid regions of Israel, with special emphasis on the problems of creating new communities.

DASH, J., and E. EFRAT. *The Israel Physical Master Plan.* Jerusalem: Ministry of the Interior, Planning Department, 1964. A comprehensive report on the objectives and present status of physical planning from the point of view of the engineer and architect.

DOHERTY, KATHRYN B. *Jordan Waters Conflict.* New York: Carnegie Endowment for International Peace, International Conciliation Series No. 553, May, 1965. A review of the various plans to harness the waters of the Jordan.

ORNI, E. and E. EFRAT. *Geography of Israel.* Jerusalem: Israel Programs for Scientific Translations, 1964. The first comprehensive study of the geography of Israel to appear in English. Considerable material on the physical and historical geography, supplemented by a briefer treatment of economic conditions.

7 JORDAN

Ian R. Manners

Landscape and Climate • *The People* • *Agriculture* • *Nonmetallic Minerals* • *Manufacturing and Handicrafts* • *Tourism* • *The Future* • focus *on the East Ghor Irrigation Project*

The Hashemite Kingdom of Jordan, a country about the same size as the state of Indiana, has existed in its present form only since 1950. It incorporates the former Amirate of Transjordan, a largely desert kingdom created from the Arab provinces of the Ottoman Empire after World War I, and that part of Palestine remaining in Arab hands when the 1948 Arab-Israeli war ended. Under the Israel-Transjordan Armistice Agreement, Transjordan retained control over the annexed territory, which included most of the hill country of Samaria and Judea, as well as the Old City of Jerusalem. In 1950, this West Bank district was formally merged with Transjordan, and the enlarged state was renamed the Hashemite Kingdom of Jordan. More recently, as a result of the Arab-Israeli war of June, 1967, the West Bank and the Old City of Jerusalem were occupied by Israel, depriving Jordan of much of its most productive agricultural land and of an area that contained the country's major tourist attractions.

Landscape and Climate

The Jordanian landscape is bewildering in its variety, but the basic contrast is between the desert and the sown, between light brown and green. During the long summer drought, only an occasional irrigated field interrupts the over-all aridity, and barren hillsides and bare valley slopes dominate the landscape. The rainy season usually begins in late October and continues until March or April, with the heaviest rains occurring in January and February. In the spring months following the winter rains, even the desert blooms with a profusion of iris and other wildflowers.

Even during the winter months, however, scarcely a sixth of the country is sufficiently humid for rain-fed cultivation. The better-watered region, which receives between ten and twenty-five inches of rain a year, essentially comprises the western slopes of the Judean and Samarian hills on the West Bank and the western edge of the Transjordan Plateau from Irbid in the north to Madaba in the south on the East Bank. In this area, villages are crowded closely together, and during the winter months every acre of cultivable land is intensively cropped. But, within this comparatively well-watered area, local variations in relief may influence the areal distribution of the rainfall. Thus, the leeward slopes of the Judean and Samarian hills, together with the southern portion of the Jordan Rift Valley (Wadi Araba) depression, lie in a marked rain shadow. Here, even during the rainy season, cultivation is possible only where there is some form of supplementary irrigation water.

The Rift Valley itself, which runs from Lake Tiberias (Sea of Galilee) in the north along the length of the Jordan Valley and the Wadi Araba to the Gulf of Aqaba in the south, is perhaps the most dramatic feature of the landscape. The relatively flat valley floor is three to fourteen miles wide and is bordered along its western and eastern margins by extremely steep escarpments. In its northern section, the valley is traversed by the Jordan River, which empties into the landlocked Dead Sea, 1,286 feet below sea level. The Wadi Araba section of the Rift Valley, to the south of the Dead Sea, is dessicated and barren.

Jordan's East Bank consists of an arid plateau sloping gradually eastward from the uplands overlooking the Jordan Rift Valley toward the desert interior. East of the line of the Hejaz (Al Hijaz) Railway and south of Madaba, climatic conditions gradually deteriorate until the viable limit for dry land farming is finally reached. This is the frontier zone between the desert and the sown, between the grazing grounds of the desert nomads and the fields of the settled cultivators. Farther east, the plateau consists of rock outcrops and vast expanses of *hamada,* a forbidding desert of stone, gravel and flint chips, and sand. In the southern part of the country, going toward the Saudi Arabian border, the same sequence occurs, and the land becomes progressively more arid, with only occasional patches of stunted scrub and thorn vegetation. This region is far too remote from surface water sources to be irrigated.

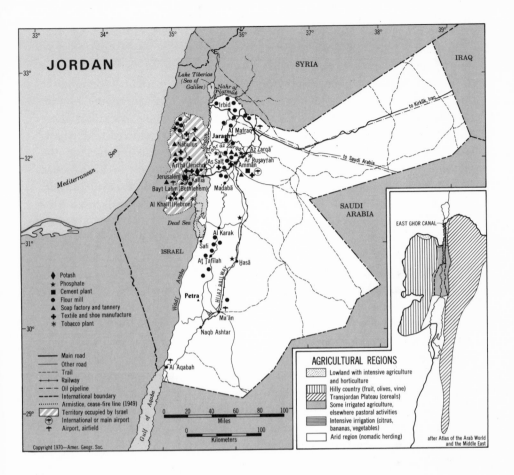

Clearly, agricultural activities in Jordan are much influenced by rainfall conditions. The greater part of the country is desert or semidesert, but even in the more humid areas rainfall often varies considerably from one year to another and drought conditions are not uncommon. In this difficult environment, life is dominated by the need to discover, conserve, and divert water from wells, streams, and the larger perennial rivers that flood briefly each winter.

Climatic conditions not only limit the cultivable area but also impose a distinct seasonal rhythm upon agricultural activities, necessitating a period of rest during the summer months in places that lack a perennial irrigation supply. Traditionally, a cereal crop is grown during the winter season, but the country is potentially capable of producing a far wider range of crops. Temperatures in the depression of the Jordan Valley, for instance, are tropical rather than temperate, and the high temperatures, together with the freedom from frost during the winter months, permit the cultivation of such crops as citrus, bananas, sugar beets, cotton, and rice. Again, in theory at least, the favorable winter climate in the Jordan Valley should allow the local farmers to compete advantageously throughout the Middle East in the early market for fresh fruit and vegetables. To exploit these conditions fully, either the farmers must have a better agricultural education and more commercial awareness than they do at present, or the planning authorities must have a greater degree of control. In the absence of these factors, long-standing traditions and practices continue to prevail, and even on the newest irrigation projects many farmers still persist in cultivating a single winter cereal crop.

The People

Although annexation of the West Bank in 1948–49 only slightly increased the size of the country, as a result of the influx of some 350,000 refugees from the area of Palestine that became Israel, the population of the new state of Jordan was nearly three times as large as that of former Transjordan. Since 1950, both the resident and the refugee populations have increased rapidly, at a rate in excess of 3 per cent a year, placing further strain on the country's limited resources. In 1967, immediately prior to the June war, the estimated population of Jordan was 2.1 million, of whom 722,687 persons were registered as refugees with the United Nations Relief and Works Agency (UNRWA).

The geographical distribution of the population reflects the agricultural potential of the nation; the population is concentrated in the northwest, where rainfall is usually adequate for some form of cultivation. Thus, the average density over the whole country is only approximately 58 persons per square mile, but the density per square mile of cultivated land is more than 500 persons—a much more meaningful indicator of the pressure of population.

Since 1950 there has been a steady migration of people from the West to the East Bank, and, by 1961, approximately 53 per cent of the population lived on the East Bank. This movement is a part of the general drift from rural areas to the towns. Industrial development in Jordan has been largely concentrated in the major towns of the East Bank, and the movement of people to these urban areas has been at least in part a response to the attraction of better employment opportunities. Other causes of the migration have been such negative factors as scarcity of arable land and the resulting underemployment and intense population pressure in rural areas. Thus, although the unemployment rate is high in the major towns, the drift from the countryside is likely to continue. As a result of this migration and the influx of refugees from the June, 1967, war, Amman, which in 1952 had a population of only 108,000, had grown to a city of 450,000 by 1968.

The vast area to the east of the Hejaz Railway is almost uninhabited except for nomadic and seminomadic herders of camels, sheep, and goats. In 1961, according to the census, the nomads numbered less than 53,000 persons. The camel herders live in the true desert, and their life is a constant struggle for food, pasture, water, and protection from winds and sun. They are at present experiencing economic difficulties because of the gradual replacement of the camel by the truck, and many of them are reluctantly becoming sedentarized.

Prior to the 1967 war, approximately one-third of the population was designated as refugees. The presence in Jordan of this economically depressed and politically unstable group created formidable social and economic problems. A number of refugees, who brought with them capital, technical skills, and a progressive outlook that was largely lacking in the country before 1948, have made valuable contributions to Jordan's economic growth. Most Palestinian refugees, however, still live in UNRWA camps and have not become integrated into the economic life of the country. Projects to provide them with employment through public works have had little success thus far, and permanent resettlement has been slow because of the reluctance of many refugees to surrender their claims to compensation or their hopes of returning to their former homeland, and because of a severe shortage of arable land in Jordan.

During and after the war of 1967, there was a further migration of some 200,000 persons from the occupied area of the West Bank to the East Bank. This new group of refugees included Palestinians from the camps near Jericho (Ariha) as well as West Bank residents.

Agriculture

Jordan is primarily an agricultural country: About one-third of the economically active population is engaged in agricultural activities, which on the average contribute one-fifth of the country's Gross Domestic Product.

The prospects for arable agriculture are best in the upland regions to the east and west of the Jordan Valley, and within this area every possible acre of land, however small and unpromising, is intensively cultivated. In addition, to meet the needs of the large and growing population, Jordanian farmers have also plowed up marginal land toward the desert interior, where the risk of drought is too great to justify arable agriculture. Throughout the sown area, yields vary markedly with rainfall conditions; where a farmer has to depend on rainfall alone, the fluctuations in yield may cause severe hardship. The major crops on unirrigated land include wheat, barley, sesame, olives, grapes, and figs. Essentially the same type of farming is practiced on both East and West Banks, although on the wetter, western slopes of the Judean and Samarian hills there is a greater concentration on olive and vine cultivation together with the production of some vegetables. In the drier areas of the East Bank, cereal cultivation and livestock-rearing predominate.

A requisite for increasing agricultural output in Jordan is more water to irrigate more land, and future agricultural development is closely dependent on better use of the country's water resources. Full utilization of these resources not only will enable more land to be brought under the plow but, by improving yields and permitting double cropping, will also bring a significant increase in agricultural production on land already under cultivation. The prospects for extension of the irrigated area are best in the Jordan Valley, where large areas of fertile land remain undeveloped or are used only for limited rain-fed cultivation or grazing. With the completion of the East Ghor Irrigation Project, the northeastern portion of the valley between the Yarmuk River (Nahr al Yarmuk) and the Wadi Zarqa is now intensively irrigated, although recent raids by Israel have severly damaged the main canal. Elsewhere, irrigation is restricted to the area watered from small side wadis, wells, and occasional springs.

Unfortunately, further extension of the irrigated area in the Jordan Valley is hindered by the highly erratic and seasonal flow of the rivers. At present, the surface stream flow reaching the valley during the summer months is fully appropriated for irrigation. Stream flow is greatest, however, during the rainy season, when irrigation requirements are at a minimum, and as a result a large volume of surplus winter flood flow runs to waste into the Dead Sea. To help solve the problem, small storage dams have recently been completed on the wadis Ziqlab, Shuayb, and Kafrein, but plans to conserve the surplus flow of the Yarmuk River, by far the largest of the rivers flowing into the Jordan depression, have been hampered by political considerations. Lake Tiberias would be an ideal natural reservoir, but, because its use is prevented by the continued Arab-Israeli confrontation, Jordan began the construction of a storage dam on the Yarmuk at Mukheiba in 1965 and planned to build a second dam farther upstream at Maqarin. Work on the Mukheiba Dam has been virtually at a standstill since June, 1967, when Israeli military forces occupied Syrian territory along the northern bank of the Yarmuk. It had been envisioned that completion of these projects would have made available a water supply adequate for the entire Ghor.

In areas too dry for rain-fed cultivation or too remote from sources of water for irrigated agriculture, the raising of livestock, primarily sheep and goats, is the main economic activity. Although the goat has been called the "desert maker," it is a good producer of milk in areas inhospitable to sheep or cattle. Currently there are about 680,000 goats and 1 million sheep in Jordan. The number of livestock exceeds the carrying capacity of the natural pastures, so efforts are being made to thin out the herds and to improve their quality.

Nonmetallic Minerals

Jordan possesses few mineral resources of economic significance. The known deposits of metallic minerals—manganese, iron, barites—are all too small to be worth mining. The most valuable resources are of such nonmetallic minerals as potash (potassium chloride), which can be recovered from the Dead Sea brines, and phosphate, but at present only phosphate is being commercially exploited. The potash and other salts present in the waters of the Dead Sea have not been recovered in significant quantities since the destruction of the works at Kallia in 1948. This extraction plant, located at the northern end of the Dead Sea, was one of two formerly operated by the Palestine Potash Company, using the solar-evaporation method of recovery. (The other plant is situated at Sedom, on the southern shore of the Dead Sea, within Israel, and was reconstructed and modernized in 1955.) Jordan's present development plans include the construction of a new plant at Safi, on the shore of the Dead Sea, with an annual capacity of 500,000 tons. To facilitate the transportation and export of the potash, a new road was to be constructed to link Safi with the port of Al Aqabah. Because of the 1967 war, these projects have not yet been undertaken.

High-grade phosphate deposits are now mined in considerable quantities, and production rose from 25,000 tons in 1952 to 1.1 million tons in 1967. With further development of the Hasa deposits, production is expected to exceed 2 million tons by 1975. Most of the phosphates are exported to markets in India, Yugoslavia, Czechoslovakia, and Poland, and provide Jordan's largest source of foreign exchange. The phosphate rock occurs in a broad band extending from Ar Rusayfah, about twelve miles northeast of Amman on the Zarqa Road, through Amman and Hasa as far south as Naqb Ashtar, but workable deposits are found only at As Salt and Hasa.

The Ar Rusayfah mine, operated by a partly government-controlled firm, has been worked for many years; the deposits at Hasa, estimated to be in excess of 30 million tons, have only recently been exploited. The Hasa deposits are suitable for mining by open-cast methods, and production costs are therefore considerably lower than at Ar Rusayfah. This fact, together with the more favorable location of Hasa in relation to the port of Al Aqabah, should give the Hasa mines a growing share of the total output. Additional storage and loading facilities are under construction at Al Aqabah to enable the port to accommodate the anticipated increase in phosphate exports. At present, the phosphate is transported by road to Al Aqabah from Hasa and Ar Rusayfah.

Manufacturing and Handicrafts

Industrial development in Jordan has only recently begun to advance beyond the handicraft stage. Factories were almost nonexistent before 1948, for all manufactured goods were imported from Palestine under a free-trading agreement. The formation of Israel and the closing of the frontier, by cutting Jordan off from the main trading and industrial centers in the coastal plain of Palestine, helped to establish a small domestic market for such essentials as building materials, basic household goods, and foodstuffs. All of these are now at least partially supplied by local industry.

In spite of the growth that has occurred, opportunities for large-scale industrial development are restricted because of the limited range of locally available raw materials and the small size and low purchasing power of the domestic market. The most important industrial enterprises are a cement plant, which raised its total production to 374,400 tons in 1966, and a petroleum refinery, with a capacity of 350,000 tons, which draws its crude oil from the Trans-Arabian Pipeline that crosses Jordan. Other industries are concerned primarily with processing agricultural and pastoral products.

Although much of the recent industrial growth has taken place in and around the capital of Amman, the Jordanian Government has especially encouraged the development of Al Aqabah's shipping and commercial facilities and is planning to build a new resort adjacent to the old town to promote tourism. In 1950, Al Aqabah was only a small fishing village; its importance as Jordan's only maritime outlet was enhanced by the effective partitioning of former Palestine, which totally disrupted the existing transportation and marketing patterns. The country's overseas trade previously passed westward through Haifa on the Mediterranean coast of Palestine. Transport facilities to Al Aqabah have been greatly improved by the completion of the "Desert Highway" linking it with Amman; at the port, better loading facilities and deepwater berths are now capable of accommodating ships of up to 20,000 tons.

The production of handicrafts—mother-of-pearl, embroideries, jewelry, and olive-wood products—has been concentrated in Jerusalem and Bethlehem (Bayt Lahm). Most of the work is done in small shops, only a few of which are mechanized. The tourist souvenir industry is aided by the government, since it is an important earner of foreign exchange.

Tourism

The sector of the economy that suffered most from the war of 1967 was tourism, for Jordan's places of religious, historical, and archaeological significance were on the West Bank: the Church of the Holy Nativity, the Church of the Holy Sepulchre, the Via Dolorosa, the Mount of Olives, the Garden of Gethsemane, Jericho, Solomon's Pools, and the seventh-century mosque of Haram esh Sharif. Nearly a half million tourists used to visit Jordan annually, and the revenue derived from tourism made a significant contribution toward improving the country's balance-of-payments position. Jordan is at present making an effort to revive tourism on the East Bank, where the major attractions are the Roman ruins at Jarash, the rock city of Petra, and the Crusader castles, but the results have so far been disappointing.

The Future

Prior to 1967, Jordan had made some progress in solving its formidable social and economic problems. The trade imbalance, which was covered by foreign aid, was still very large (the amount spent annually on imports—chiefly foods, manufactured goods, and mineral fuels—was more than seven times that received from exports), but the rapid growth of the tourist industry and the increase in phosphate exports were encouraging trends. In addition, the East Ghor Irrigation Project (see below) and the attendant land-reform program were significant steps toward improved agricultural output and greater social progress.

The 1967 war and continued hostilities in the Jordan Valley, however, have brought the loss of the productive West Bank, the collapse of tourism, and the disruption of agricultural activities in the East Ghor project—major setbacks to Jordanian hopes of reducing the balance-of-trade deficit and the level of overseas aid. The war of September, 1970, between Palestinian commando forces and the Jordanian Army, which ended with a shaky cease-fire agreement, further complicated the situation, for it is now clear that the Palestinians seek not only greater economic opportunities but also the creation of an independent Arab state of Palestine. Again, recent demands by West Bank leaders for an autonomous state pose further political problems for the Jordanian government.

focus *on the East Ghor Irrigation Project*

The Jordan Rift Valley, or El Ghor, as it is referred to locally, lies entirely below sea level and extends for a distance of nearly seventy miles from Lake Tiberias in the north to the Dead Sea in the south. Throughout its length, the Ghor is bordered by steep escarpments, so that, from within, the impression is of an almost continuous mountain range. The River Jordan follows a meandering course along the central axis of the depression, although the present flood plain (El Zor) is incised to depths of up to 165 feet below the main surface of the Ghor. The wide, flat terrace surface of fertile marls and clays between the margin of the depression and the Zor is the most characteristic landscape of the Ghor. Through the long, dry summer months, it has an extremely barren appearance, broken only by the lush greenery of "oases" of irrigated farm land.

Although soils in the Ghor are potentially very productive, agricultural development is severely hampered by aridity. Rainfall is generally sparse and unreliable, and, even in the moister northern section of the valley, it is barely sufficient to permit farming by rain-fed methods. Farming is therefore heavily dependent on some form of supplementary water from springs, wells, or rivers. Outside irrigated areas, the primary form of economic activity is the grazing of large flocks of sheep and goats.

The River Jordan and its main tributary, the Yarmuk, account for the

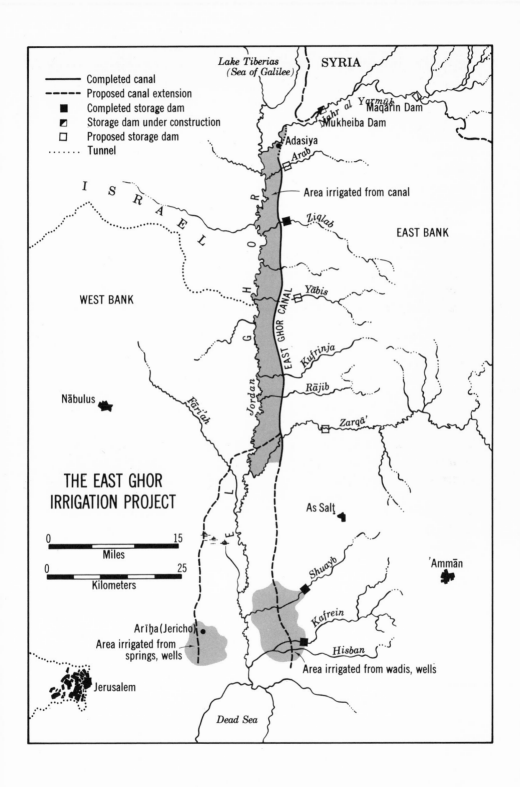

THE EAST GHOR
IRRIGATION PROJECT

Legend:

── Completed canal
─ ─ ─ Proposed canal extension
■ Completed storage dam
▨ Storage dam under construction
▢ Proposed storage dam
⋯⋯ Tunnel

Lake Tiberias
(Sea of Galilee)

SYRIA

Nahr al Yarmūk
Maqārin Dam
Mukheiba Dam

Adasiya
Arab

Area irrigated from canal

EAST BANK

Ziqlab

I S R A E L

G H O R

WEST BANK

Yābis

EAST GHOR CANAL

Kufrinja

Jordan

Rājib

Fāri'ah

Nābulus

Zarqā'

As Salṭ

0   15
Miles

'Ammān

0   25
Kilometers

Shuayb

Arīḥa (Jericho)
Area irrigated from
springs, wells

Kafrein

Hisban

Area irrigated from wadis, wells

Jerusalem

Dead Sea

greater part of the water resources available for irrigation in the Ghor. The watershed of the Jordan drainage basin, however, crosses a number of political frontiers: Parts of Israel, Jordan, Syria, and Lebanon lie within the catchment area. The intense competition between these states for a share in the available water has inevitably caused problems. A number of plans have been put forward for the unified development of the water resources of the Jordan Basin, irrespective of political boundaries, but the failure of Israel and the Arab states to reach any form of political agreement has prevented implementation of these plans. In the circumstances, the riparian states mainly concerned, Israel and Jordan, have proceeded with the construction of rival irrigation schemes that are not only costly but mutually harmful.

Jordan's East Ghor Irrigation Project involves the diversion of the Yarmuk River to provide an irrigation supply for approximately 30,000 acres of arable land in the northeastern part of the Ghor. Only a small proportion of this area represents land brought under cultivation for the first time. In the past, the land was partially irrigated, receiving an irregular supply of water from the side wadis that flow into the Ghor between the Yarmuk and the Dead Sea. Stream flow in these smaller wadis is limited in amount, subject to considerable seasonal and annual variations, and smallest in volume during the hot, dry summer months, when the need for irrigation water is greatest. Farmers were consequently able to grow only a single winter cereal crop and left the land lying parched and fallow through the summer months. The main impact of the project, which has made available a reliable and adequate water supply, has been to enable farmers to cultivate their land throughout the year and to raise two or more crops annually.

Construction of the project was begun in August, 1958. By the summer of 1966, water was being delivered through the irrigation system to most of the land commanded from the main East Ghor Canal. The canal offtakes from the Yarmuk approximately five miles above the Jordan-Yarmuk confluence, close to the village of Adasiya, where the flow of the river is diverted through a side channel excavated below the natural bed of the river. From the diversion point, a horseshoe-shaped tunnel a mile in length carries the water through a rocky spur to the head of the main canal. The canal, which is lined with cement to reduce the loss of water by percolation, runs parallel to the River Jordan for a distance of forty-five miles, terminating to the south of the Wadi Zarqa. An extension of five miles was under consideration in 1966, but construction was indefinitely postponed following the Arab-Israeli war of June, 1967. Lateral canals, also lined, distribute the water to the farmers' fields, which lie between the main canal and the Jordan. The favorable topography of the Ghor, sloping gently westward toward the Jordan and southward toward the Dead Sea, enables the entire area to be irrigated by gravity flow.

The East Ghor Project has had a tremendous impact on farming practices. In particular, the pattern of land use within the project area has shifted away from the traditional cultivation of cereal crops to a more commercially oriented form of agriculture. In 1965–66, for example, over half the cultivated area was planted with vegetable crops, especially tomatoes, eggplant, melons, cucumbers, peppers, and potatoes. The acreage devoted to such perennial crops as citrus fruits and bananas has also increased significantly since the completion of the project. Such crops not only provide the farmer with a high financial return per acre but also have an export potential. Fresh fruit and vegetables are now shipped in considerable quantities to Kuwait and other Persian Gulf states.

Wheat, however, remains the most important individual crop. In part this is because some farmers are reluctant to abandon their traditional ways of farming to concentrate on crops that are in general more labor-demanding; in part because they lack capital to invest in such things as fertilizers, pesticides, and fruit trees; and in part because the Ghor lacks adequate storage facilities for perishable crops, which must therefore be sold immediately and often disadvantageously. The construction of a new marketing center on Wadi Yabis will help to overcome the last of these problems.

In an attempt to improve agricultural practices in the project area, in particular to encourage farmers to experiment with new crops, improved seeds, fertilizers, and pesticides, the Agricultural Extension Service provides a technical-assistance-and-advice program. Cash loans and incentive grants are made available to farmers through the recently established cooperative societies, but, more important, farmers are encouraged to adopt better methods of irrigation. At present, farmers are often wasteful and extravagant in their use of water. The traditional method of applying water, for example, is simply to open the gate leading from the distribution channel and allow the water to flow freely across the field. Unless the field has been carefully prepared and leveled in advance, many parts will remain untouched, while other parts will receive too much. At the same time, the uncontrolled flow of water in the direction of greatest slope means that the water has little chance to infiltrate the soil. The net result is that most water simply runs off the field. Not only is precious water wasted, but also there is a serious danger of soil erosion while the crops tend to remain underwatered. As part of the extension program, agents assist the farmer in preparing and leveling his field for irrigation to ensure more efficient application of the water.

The program of land reform that accompanied the construction of the East Ghor Irrigation Project was the first of its kind in Jordan. Before its enactment, the outstanding features of the agrarian system in the project areas were those common to most unreformed land systems in the Middle East. There was, for example, a very unequal distribution of property, the greater part of the area being owned by large, absentee landowners living in Amman or Nablus (Nabulus). There were smaller landowners, too, but a large portion of the agricultural population owned no land at all and lived either as tenant farmers on the large estates or as casual farm laborers.

The large number of small, uneconomic holdings, incapable of providing a farmer and his family with even a subsistence living, were another unhappy feature of the system. Even more alarming was the downward trend in the size of farms as a result of increasing population pressure. As elsewhere, the "land hunger" enabled landlords to subdivide their property into ever smaller farms for leasing and at the same time charge higher and higher rents. Some sharecropping tenants handed over as much as two thirds of their crop in rent to the landlord. Such features of the land system, together with the fragmentation of even the smallest holdings and the insecurity of tenure, were obvious obstacles to any form of agricultural development.

Under the East Ghor Canal Law, all land in the project area was appropriated, and compensation was paid to landowners on the basis of preproject land values. New holdings were then designed and demarcated by the East Ghor Canal Authority, since an efficient layout of distribution canals could not have been effected within the previous chaotic pattern of small, fragmented holdings. In most instances, the new irrigation units were rectangular, the best shape for good farm management and the application of irrigation water. The new units were then reallocated to landowners and farmers, priority being given to those who had previously owned land in the project area.

This reorganization and consolidation of farm holdings provided an opportunity for reform of the landownership pattern by actual redistribution of property. Under the Canal Law, no single landowner in the project area is now allowed to own more than 50 acres or less than 7.5 acres, and there is a direct prohibition on the subdivision of farms, either through sale or inheritance, into units smaller than the minimum. The lower limit of 7.5 acres, if intensively cultivated, is considered to be the minimum needed to attain a decent standard of living and at the same time help repay the costs of the project's construction.

During the reallocation of land, landowners who had previously owned more than 7.5 acres were allowed to acquire land in proportion to their previous holdings on a sliding scale up to a maximum of 50 acres. Land owned in excess of this amount was retained by the East Ghor Canal Authority for allocation to other farmers. Where the landowner had originally owned less than 7.5 acres, the Canal Authority allocated him additional land to increase the area to the minimum required by law. Thus a considerable redistribution of property has taken place. Both the very large estates and the numerous small properties have disappeared, and a medium-sized landowning proprietary class has been created. In the process, however, there has been a 20-per-cent reduction in the number of landowners in the project area. As a result, not all the previous landowners and none of the former tenant farmers have been able to acquire land.

In some respects, the land-reform program has been remarkably successful. An outstanding achievement has been the consolidation of holdings. Farmers no longer have to spend half their working day walking from one field to another, and roads, footpaths, and distribution canals, which previously divided fields even further, now go around rather than through holdings. Less successful has been the attempt to prevent the subdivision of farm holdings. In many instances, more than one family is allowed to work on a holding of minimum size, a situation that obviously amounts to hidden subdivision and quickly reduces the farm holding to an uneconomic size for the occupant families. In so far as this trend affects the per-capita productivity rather than per-acre productivity, which will continue to rise as a result of more intensive irrigation and cultivation, the situation may appear to lack urgency; yet ultimately the pressure to subdivide must threaten the stability of the project. Again, the Canal Law, by permitting all landowners to reacquire land, regardless of whether they were resident or absentee owners, prevented a wider redistribution of land. A major criticism of the reform program, therefore, is that it has provided no opportunity for farmers who previously worked as tenants or casual laborers to settle on land of their own. In this respect, it cannot be claimed that the reforms have benefited the majority of the farm population. Many appear to be worse off than before, because elimination of large estates and consolidation of holdings have led to a considerable reduction in agricultural labor requirements in the project area. To a certain extent this was inevitable; no reform of the land system, however radical, could have provided land for the entire population. This simply demonstrates the limitations of any land-reform program in an area of intense population pressure and limited land resources.

The area currenly irrigated from the East Ghor Canal represents virtually the maximum that can be provided with an adequate water supply from the unregulated flow of the Yarmuk and the side wadis. Extension of the irrigated area to the southern and western parts of the Ghor will therefore require the construction of additional storage dams to conserve the surplus winter streamflow from the lower Jordan Basin, much of which now runs to waste in the Dead Sea.

Suggested Readings

DEARDEN, ANN. *Jordan*. London: Robert Hale, 1958. A survey for the nonspecialist, with a good chapter on the struggle for water.

DOHERTY, KATHRYN B. *Jordan Waters Conflict*. New York: Carnegie Endowment for International Peace, International Conciliation Series No. 553, May, 1965. A review of the various plans to harness the waters of the Jordan.

International Bank for Reconstruction and Development. *The Economic Development of Jordan*. Baltimore: Johns Hopkins Press, 1957. A comprehensive study of Jordan's economy. The formidable social and economic problems facing Jordan immediately after its creation in 1950 considered in detail.

PATAI, R. *The Kingdom of Jordan*. Princeton, N.J.: Princeton University Press, 1958. An excellent comprehensive study of the Kingdom of Jordan emphasizing people and their problems.

SPARROW, G. *Modern Jordan*. London: Allen and Unwin, 1961. A good treatment of modern Jordan.

8 SAUDI ARABIA

John S. Haupert

*Deserts: Heat and Drought • Agriculture, People, and Settlement •
Oil and Industrial Development • Transportation and
Communications • Foreign Trade and Economic Development •
Education • Town Planning*

The Kingdom of Saudi Arabia is large in area—roughly three times the size of Texas—but a third or more of it is dry, barren desert, and almost all of the rest suffers from chronic and severe shortages of water.

For centuries, Bedouins roamed over this vast area seeking water and forage for their herds. Only in the mountains, around intermittent streams, or where there are springs or wells did farmers settle to plant and cultivate crops, but even in these relatively hospitable places they could not hope to eke out more than a meager living.

Today the estimated 6.8 million inhabitants of this harsh land have high hopes for a better life, thanks to a mineral greatly in demand in every industrialized society—petroleum.

Deserts: Heat and Drought

Saudi Arabia occupies about four-fifths of the Arabian Peninsula. For administrative purposes, the nation is divided into a few large regions that may be called provinces. The most important of these are Najd, covering a large part of the interior and containing the capital, Riyadh (Ar Riyad); Hejaz (Al Hijaz), stretching along the Red Sea and containing the

99

holy cities of Mecca (Makkah) and Medina (Al Madinah) and the chief port of Jidda (Juddah); Asir, in the southwest; and finally, the Eastern Province, along the Persian Gulf, where the great oil fields are located.

Topographically, the country is divided into four main zones: the western coastal plain and mountains; the central plateau containing the deserts of An Nafud and Ad Dahna; the eastern Persian Gulf coastal plain; and the extensive southern desert of Ar Rab al Khali.

In the west, on the shore of the Red Sea, the narrow coastal plain extends for 900 miles along the Rift Valley. Adjacent mountains, 2,000 feet high near the Gulf of Aqaba and more than 9,000 feet high in the south, rise boldly and slope gently to the east. Within an arc formed by the An Nafud, a huge desert of reddish sand, and the Jabal Tuwayq (Tuwayq Mountains) is the broad central plateau, about 300 miles wide and varying in elevation from 3,500 to 4,500 feet. A number of oases support irrigated agriculture between Wadi ar Rummah and Hail at the southern edge of the Nafud. To the east, one of the most distinctive geographical features of Saudi Arabia is the long narrow belt of sand known as the Ad Dahna. It extends approximately 800 miles from the Nafud to the Ar Rab al Khali. The area between the sands of the Dahna and the Jabal Tuwayq is the heart of the Najd. North of the Nafud is a barren land of gravel and rocky plains, part of the great Syrian Desert.

The eastern coastline, extending 200 miles from Kuwait (Kuwayt) on the north to the Trucial States on the south, is distinguished by low relief, with salt and mud flats and a somewhat more plentiful water supply.

The southern desert, Ar Rab al Khali, or Empty Quarter, is said to be the largest continuous body of sand in the world. It occupies a great basin bordered by the mountains of Oman (Uman) on the east, a plateau behind the coastal escarpments on the south, and the foohills of the mountains of Yemen and Asir on the west. In this area of 250,000 square miles, sand mountains of complex arrangement attain heights of 500 to 1,000 feet. The sands are not all of one type. Some areas are covered by relatively stable sand sheets; elsewhere mobile dunes are formed by the prevailing winds into star or crescent shapes or into linear veins (*uruq*) many miles long.

The intense heat of the summer months (120° F is not uncommon in the interior) and the low rainfall and humidity are the best-known features of the Arabian climate. However, in the high mountains, winter temperatures may drop to 30° F, and some uplands, such as Asir, often get as much as ten to twenty inches of rain a year. Elsewhere rainfall is extremely scanty and capricious. The average rainfall in Bahrain and Riyadh is about three

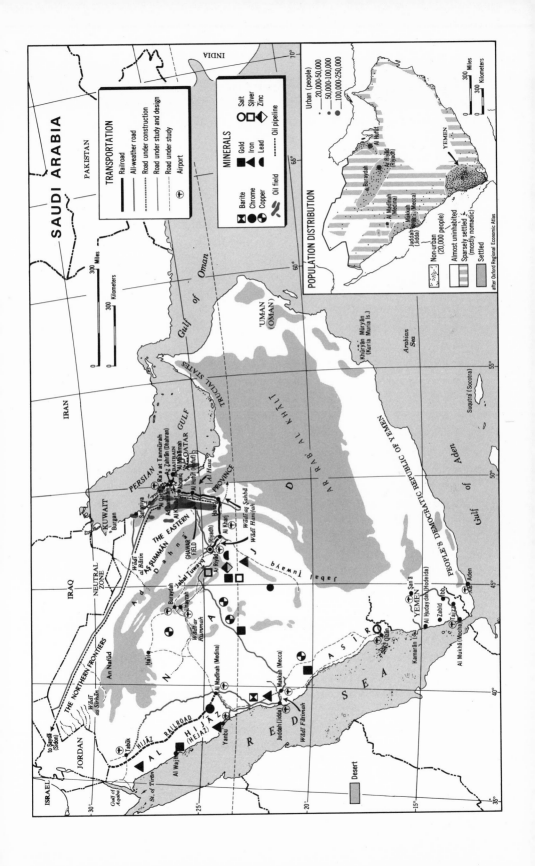

inches a year, but some years have as much as seven inches and others less than one. The over-all average annual rainfall, recorded at six weather stations in 1959–63, was 2.6 inches. When rain does fall, it is usually in the form of torrential cloudbursts, and much of it is lost through evaporation and rapid runoff.

There are no true lakes or rivers on the surface of the land, but artesian reservoirs are found under the central plateau, and there are extensive springs issuing from subsurface water-bearing gravels in the eastern waste-lands. Wadis (intermittent streams) accumulate running water only during periods of runoff from the infrequent rainstorms. Historically, the wadi network determined the distribution of the sedentary population, the course of caravan routes, and the location of commercial centers.

Agriculture, People, and Settlement

Natural vegetation is sparse except in the scattered oases and on the mountainside terraces. The date palm is the most characteristic feature of the oases. Coconut palms are found in the south. There are no true forests, but there are some large trees, such as the acacia, mimosa, carob, and the tamarisk, which is used for windbreaks and sand control. Migrating dunes as well as low rainfall discourage pasturage and shrubs. Annuals, such as grasses, wild flowers, and herbs, spring up briefly after winter rains and supply forage for camels and sheep. Perennial shrubs are also available to animals, including a salt bush called *hamdh*.

It is estimated that only 15 per cent of Saudi Arabia's land is arable, and only 1 per cent is actually under cultivation. Almost all of the arable land is in oases, and 80 per cent of it is irrigated. About 60 per cent of the total land area is used for grazing by wandering Bedouins. It is impossible to determine the precise number of desert nomads; the best estimates indicate that there are about one million of them, in spite of the marked increase in urbanization in the past decade. The Bedouin plays an important part in the nation's economy; livestock products, in fact, surpass date palms as a source of revenue.

The Arabs are not a homogeneous people. Strains of Semitic, Hamitic, and Negroid groups appear among Bedouins and among the coastal peoples. But, as far as customs are concerned, the Saudi Arabians are homogeneous. Almost every action of daily living is determined by tradition, from the wearing of veils by the women to the methods of irrigating and farming of the men. And almost all Saudi Arabs, regardless of their differences in occupation, racial origin, and other features, speak Arabic and are Muslims. Dialects differ, however, and so do sects. The Shia group of the east comprises a minority within the predominantly Sunni population.

Another feature shared by a large proportion of the Saudi Arabians is poverty. The average per-capita income is about $125 a year, but most people have a great deal less, since most of the wealth is in the hands of a few members of the ruling class.

Cultivated land falls into two categories. One type depends upon rainfall at high elevations and diverted runoff adjacent to highlands. On the high terraces of Asir, for instance, coffee is grown, as well as the more profitable *qat,* a leaf chewed for its mildly narcotic effect. Oases constitute the second type. Cultivation here depends upon wells or springs rather than on rainfall and transitory streams. Modern pumping has enlarged the size of existing oases, and new ones have been established, but overpumping, salinization, and excessive evapotranspiration hinder crop production.

The principal agricultural product is dates. They have long been a staple food throughout Arabia, and the wood and fronds of the date palm are used in building huts. Dates are also a major agricultural export; Saudi Arabia is the world's fourth largest producer of dates, from about 8.5 millions palms. Few other crops have been grown in quantity. The typical farmer's methods of irrigation and cultivation are primitive and yields are low. Saudi Arabia therefore depends heavily on food imports. The government is encouraging more diversified farming and the growing of more cereals, vegetables, and fruits. Through agricultural research stations, usually financed by oil revenues, farmers are being taught how to increase yields and hence income through the use of fertilizers, insecticides, and machinery. The government is also establishing cooperatives, which provide the mass-purchasing and marketing advantages of a large organization.

Although cars, jeeps, trucks, and buses are becoming more common, the one-humped dromedary, or camel, is still characteristic of Saudi Arabia. Camels provide meat, milk, clothing, hides for tents, and transportation for the Bedouins and their goods, and they draw water from wells. They are the nomads' chief pride and source of wealth. However, sheep are the principal source of meat and clothing, goats supply much of the country's milk, and cattle are grazed in Asir and near Jidda.

To deal with Saudi Arabia's age-old problem of lack of water, the government is promoting projects to conserve available water and develop new underground sources. Existing sources are being strictly controlled to avoid wastage, and hundreds of new wells have been drilled. One of the new projects is near Wadi Hanifah, where 3,000 acres are now under cultivation.

Another new project is the largest existing oasis of Al Hasa, with its town of Hofuf (Al Hufuf) in the east, where more than seventy artesian springs now provide tens of thousands of gallons of water a minute for more than 30,000 acres; ultimately 68,000 acres will be watered. Seawater is increasingly being put to use. The country's first (1968) desalinization plant, at Al Wajh on the Red Sea coast, currently produces 65,000 gallons of potable water per day. At Jidda, an $18 million desalting and power plant, built with U.S. aid, is virtually completed, and its testing is about to begin. The facility will provide 5 million gallons of potable water and 50,000 kilowatts of electricity daily to the Red Sea port city and its environs. Still another plant is being built in Al Khubar, a port on the Arabian Gulf near Dhahran (Az Zahran), which will furnish 7.5 million gallons of sweet water each day to five towns in the Eastern Province.

With the help of U.N. specialists and money from petroleum, the Ministry of Agriculture and Water has embarked upon an ambitious conservation and dam-construction program. In Asir, for example, in Wadi Jizan, a just-completed dam will store some 12 billion gallons of water and make possible the cultivation of 70,000 acres of dry land. Another aspect of the water program is the construction of irrigation canals. At Wadi as Sahba near Harad, south of Hofuf, the Faisal Model Settlement Project is reclaiming 10,000 acres of desert land for 10,000 Bedouins; 7,000 feet of concrete-lined irrigation canals have already been laid adjacent to fifty newly drilled wells. Sudan grass and tamarisk trees have been planted to anchor the soil and protect villages, and additional fields have been plotted and are being prepared for cultivation. Another project is the planting of 600,000 trees in the northern frontiers to stop dune encroachment.

Oil and Industrial Development

The most important industry in Saudi Arabia is the production of crude oil and petroleum products, and it has been a key factor in the remarkable economic progress of the country during the last few years. It has made possible the construction of highways and ports, new housing, new wells for drinking and irrigation, greater distribution of goods and services, the building of new hospitals, and an ambitious educational program designed to eliminate illiteracy by providing more schools, more teachers, and more teacher-training facilities.

Saudi Arabia in 1970 was the world's fifth largest producer of petroleum, following the United States, the Soviet Union, Venezuela, and Iran, and is estimated to have the largest reserves in the world. In 1970, 176 million tons of oil were produced—slightly more than Libya's total. The nation's income from oil royalties and income taxes levied against the three major oil companies now operating is estimated at over $1 billion, or 85 per cent of the government's revenue for the 1968–69 fiscal year. In 1968, oil income was estimated to have risen 17 per cent over the previous year, when deliveries to the United States and Britain were curtailed because of the Arab-Israeli war and the closure of the Suez Canal. The Trans-Arabian Pipeline (Tapline) gave Saudi Arabia an advantage, because, while competitors had to ship petroleum around the Cape of Good Hope, Saudi Arabia could export from the eastern Mediterranean.

The tremendous oil deposits are found in domed structures in the Dhahran and Ad Damman areas near the Persian Gulf. The world's largest field is the Ghawar area, and the world's largest offshore field is at Safaniya. Terminals for tankers are located at Ras at Tannurah and Ad Damman on the Persian Gulf. The Trans-Arabian Pipeline Company operates a thirty-inch crude-oil pipeline from the producing areas over a distance of 1,069 miles to a marine terminal at Sidon (Sayda), Lebanon. Yearly capacity averages about 24 million tons; the average tanker traveling between Ras at Tannurah and the Mediterranean Sea via the Suez Canal can carry only about 47,000 tons, and the trip takes nine days. Crude oil is refined locally at Ras at Tannurah or piped through Dhahran to the island of Bahrain for refining. Natural gas is liquefied and refrigerated for domestic use. The Arabian-American Oil Company (ARAMCO) holds long-term rights to extensive producing concessions, with Standard Oil of California holding a 30-per-cent interest in this affiliate. Texaco and Standard Oil of New Jersey are other major owners of this concession. Saudi Arabia is one of the six Persian Gulf nations that recently signed an agreement with twenty-three international oil companies (see p. 12). As a result of this pact, its income from oil will increase substantially.

Saudi Arabia's wealth in natural resources is not confined to "black gold." Traditionally, real gold, together with silver, was a main source of income. High-grade iron ores have been discovered recently near Mecca and Yanbu. Nonferrous metals exist in substantial quantities, and gypsum and rock salt are exported. However, the lack, or inaccessibility, of most of the basic raw materials other than petroleum has limited industries and development projects. Currently, the main industrial enterprises (except for petroleum) consist of four large cement plants, a fish-freezing plant, a plastics plant, a detergent factory, a chemical fertilizer factory, and several bottling works. In addition, there are the traditional industries such as weaving, embroidery, smithery, and pearling. But more than three quarters of the hired labor force is employed in the petroleum industry. Labor unions do not as yet exist.

Transportation and Communications

The great distances between population centers have posed a serious transportation problem, which the government is trying to solve through a huge program to develop increased rail, road, and air links and expand air routes and port facilities. A source of national pride is the Saudi Arabian Airlines, the largest air carrier in the Middle East. It began operation in 1947 with three DC-3's, and by 1969 had twenty-six modern jet planes flying on regular schedules into eighteen countries in Asia, Africa, and Europe. The line has more than 2,000 trained employees, mostly Saudis. Dhahran International Airport was completed in 1962, and Jidda also has a large air facility to handle the influx of pilgrims en route to Mecca. In addition, service is available to twenty-two other airports in Saudi Arabia.

Modern surface transport has been greatly increased in the last ten years, and more than 4,200 miles of blacktop highways now connect the main cities, such as Mecca (population, 200,000), Riyadh (225,000), Medina (75,000), Jidda (194,000), Dhahran (12,500), and Ad Damman (40,000). A modern transpeninsular highway links Jidda and Ad Damman – a distance of 950 miles. Plans are underway to build some 3,000 additional miles of highways and roads over the next decade to link all parts of the country and to extend existing routes into Asir and northward to Al Aqabah in Jordan.

The only railway in operation at present, completed in 1951, runs 357 miles from the oil port of Ad Damman on the Persian Gulf through Dhahran to Riyadh. Modern diesels pull freight and passenger cars, including air-conditioned coaches. The line is eventually to be extended to Jidda via Medina. The latter is important in the projected rail pattern because it will be the southern terminus of the rejuvenated Hejaz Railroad, which the Ottoman Turks completed in 1908 but were forced to abandon in World War I. This line, currently being rebuilt, will ultimately connect with the existing one in Jordan and Syria. Reconstruction was delayed by the 1967 Arab-Israeli war.

Shipping remains the chief commercial link with the rest of the world. Along the lengthy coastlines in the west and east are several ports,

Two decades ago there were few roads in Saudi Arabia suitable for motorized transportation. Now, gradual industrialization in the wake of the petroleum boom has made cars and buses almost as common a sight as camels. The Saudi Arabian Government is rapidly expanding its network of asphalt-paved roads to increase contacts among formerly isolated centers in the vast interior desert.

including Jidda, a commercial seaport and trading center, port of entry for pilgrims to nearby Mecca, Holy City of Islam. Until petroleum production and sales became substantial, the annual pilgrimage, or *Haj*, was the main source of foreign exchange; it is still the second largest foreign-revenue–earner. On the Persian Gulf, Ad Damman and Ras at Tannurah handle the bulk of the oil traffic. To meet the demands of increasing oil production and export, programs are underway to expand the facilities at Jidda and Ad Damman. At the former, ten new piers are being added to the existing pier, and new warehouses and buildings, including grain elevators, are also being built. In the Ad Damman project, six new piers will be constructed at the end of a causeway reaching four miles into the Gulf to deep water.

Telecommunications have been improved, and an automatic telephone network for the principal cities is under construction at an estimated cost of $43.5 million.

Foreign Trade and Economic Development

Saudi Arabia's imports have almost doubled over the past five years. In 1967, for instance, the value of imports amounted to $491 million; it rose to $587 million in 1968, an increase of almost 20 per cent. The United States is a major supplier of imported goods—over one fifth of the total. The Arab countries furnish about one fourth of all imports, and Western Europe about the same. Cereals and other foodstuffs account for some 30 per cent at the present time and durable goods for another 30 per cent. These include iron and steel products and building materials; engines, trucks, and tractors; mechanical and electrical equipment; automobiles and earth-moving machinery; and chemicals, air-conditioners, and refrigerators. A feature of the import trade is the continuing shift in favor of capital goods.

The value of exports in 1967–68 was $1.76 billion, with crude and refined oil accounting for more than 90 per cent of the total. About 40 per cent of Saudi Arabian petroleum reaches Western Europe and about the same goes to Asia, mainly to Japan and Australia. The remaining export value consists of skins, hides, wool, and dates.

After years of fiscal irresponsibility, economic development has become the principal concern of the Saudi Arabian government, and a balanced budget of $690.9 million was first achieved in 1965. Under a development plan launched that same year, the lion's share of the budget will be spent to build a solid foundation for further economic development, with special emphasis on irrigation and sewage works, hospitals and schools, and housing and roads. More than $100 million a year has been contributed by the government to the Arab Fund to provide assistance to the United Arab Republic and Jordan after the 1967 war with Israel.

Government expenditures during 1968–69 rose to a new high of $1.23 billion, reflecting an increase of 12 per cent over the preceding fiscal year. The development budget was raised from $369 million in 1965–66 to $596 million for 1970. While this money is playing a leading role in accelerating economic development, investment in the private sector is also rising significantly. Private enterprise is increasingly active in cement manufacturing, the construction industry, electric-power generation, and agricultural schemes. In the public sector, there has been investment in roadbuilding, water and mineral surveys, and selected industrial ventures based on domestic resources. In 1969, a Five-Year Development Plan was approved for 1970–75, which envisages a rise in the Gross National Product from $3.72 billion for 1969–70 to over $5 billion at the close of the period. This would represent an annual GNP growth rate of 9.3 per cent, compared with the growth rate of 8.5 per cent in recent years. This is more than twice the growth rate of the United States and far greater than that of most developing nations.

Since 1962, a development agency called Petromin has had broad authority to initiate and implement projects relating to mineral industries, including oil. In time, it hopes to base 30 per cent of the economy on mineral resources other than oil. One of Petromin's major functions is the establishment of a Saudi-owned and operated petrochemical industry in Jidda and a refinery for Riyadh. Another important project is the first Saudi Arabian steel rolling mill, located near the petrochemical plant in Jidda. The $6-million mill has an annual capacity of 45,000 tons of steel. Petromin has also set up a drilling company to probe for minerals and deep-water wells, and it is organizing plastics and fertilizer industries utilizing the plentiful natural gas. The kingdom's first chemical fertilizer plant, with an annual capacity of 350,000 tons, has recently been completed at Ad Damman.

Education

The Arabian-American Oil Company was largely responsible for launching an education program in Saudi Arabia by offering training for its Arab employees in company-built or financed schools. As late as 1953, when the Ministry of Education was established, there was only one secondary school in the kingdom.

Since 1954, when the government established free public education for boys, a substantial portion of its revenues has been spent on education. In the past ten years, the number of elementary schools and students has more than doubled. Budgetary allocations increased more than 70 per cent in the five years from 1964 to 1969, rising from $78.7 million to $133.8 million. Schools for girls were started in 1963, and, although they enroll only about a third as many students as the boys' schools, reflecting the traditional exclusion of females from the main stream of Arab life, their numbers are growing rapidly. In 1959, enrollment was about 100,000; by 1968, it had reached 271,000.

Before World War II, formal education in Saudi Arabia was confined to the Islamic tradition of religious learning. Today the curriculum continues to stress religion through daily rituals of Koranic recitation, but it is also designed to prepare Saudis for roles in a rapidly modernizing and developing society. Secondary-school enrollment has increased ninefold in the last decade, preparing students for one of the nation's three universities—the University of Riyadh, the Islamic University at Medina, and King Abdul Aziz University at Jidda—all established since 1957. In 1959, there were only 200 university students. Now there are almost 3,000. Many Saudis still go abroad for higher education, but universities at home now offer degrees in nearly every field. Regional vocational centers in five cities, ten technical institutes, and the new Royal Vocational Institute in Riyadh are helping to meet the increasing demand in the kingdom for skilled and semiskilled workers.

Town Planning

Along with its benefits, Saudi Arabia's petroleum wealth has brought some unsettling changes and problems, not the least of which has been unprecedented urban growth. People have moved to urban centers from the hinterland, from other Arab countries, and from Asia, Africa, and Europe.

The traditional towns were simple and suitable to pre-oil-age requirements and means. Social unity, comfort, and privacy were part of Saudi culture. The bazaar, or *suq* (*souk*), in the old city was the main gathering place: It was the center of commerce, news, and gossip and convenient to the mosque. Generally, the *suq* consisted of one main thoroughfare running through the center of the city, crossed by numerous, partly covered side streets. Now, the walls around towns are being pulled down to make room for new houses. With modern transportation available, the cities have expanded along the asphalted roads and become vast expanses of concrete and stone.

Without maintenance or renovation, the old quarters have deteriorated; alarmed by this phenomenon, the Saudi government asked the United Nations for technical assistance to control the development of the cities and towns. The United Nations sent a team of town-planning experts in 1959, and, within five years, technicians were engaged in the development and preparation of master plans for forty-two towns and cities. One of the many problems encountered by the planners was the lack of adequate maps, so the Saudi government asked a British firm to undertake the mapping of thirty-two cities and towns by aerial photography. For the first time in history, Mecca and Medina were photographed from the air.

The government's policy is to allocate a share of its development budget to each municipality, small or large, in order to effect a balanced development over the entire country. Funds are allocated for a wide variety of municipal projects, including telecommunications and water.

As long as petroleum continues to be in demand, Saudi Arabia is likely to have a sizable income and will therefore be in a position to carry out extensive social and economic programs. Standards of living will rise, and eventually an increasing number of citizens should enjoy a greater measure of prosperity. What effect this wealth and the influence of Western technology and ideas will have on orthodox Islamic traditions no one can say, but in Saudi Arabia, as in many other nations in Africa and Asia, a revolution is undoubtedly under way—peaceful here at the moment, and peaceful, it is to be hoped, in the future.

Suggested Readings

Asfour, Edmond Y. *Saudi Arabia: Long-Term Projections of Supply of and Demand for Agricultural Products.* Beirut: Economic Research Institute, American University of Beirut, 1965. A specialized study that assesses the supply of and demand for agricultural products between 1965 and 1975. A joint effort of the U.S. Department of Agriculture and the Saudi Arabia Ministry of Agriculture. Useful for the student of agricultural development.

Hinnawi, David, ed. "Saudi Arabia." *The Arab World,* XI, no. 3 (1965), pp. 84–90. Concise survey of all phases of life in Saudi Arabia. A good brief reference.

9 YEMEN AND THE PEOPLE'S DEMOCRATIC REPUBLIC OF YEMEN

Alexander Melamid

Yemen • People's Democratic Republic of Yemen—
Political Vicissitudes • *Coastal and Inland Regions: A Contrast* •
The People and Economic Development • *The Republic of
Yemen Today*

Yemen

The small country of Yemen lies in the southwestern corner of the Saudi Arabian Peninsula, bordered by Saudi Arabia on the north, the Gulf of Aden on the south, the Red Sea on the west, and the People's Democratic Republic of Yemen on the east. Because the eastern border is undelineated, the area of Yemen can only be approximated at 75,000 square miles. There are some 5 million Yemenites, including the 100,000 inhabitants of the capital, Sana.

Within this country are the best farm lands in Arabia; the Romans called Yemen (and the Republic of Yemen) *Arabia Felix,* or Happy Arabia, in part because of these agricultural areas.

The nation can be divided into three regions. The first is a narrow, arid coastal plain running along the Red Sea; here the temperatures are high throughout the year (frequently exceeding 130° F), and high humidity makes the climate even more uncomfortable. Since it receives less than ten inches of rain per year, this plain is a desert except where springs or seasonal streams permit irrigation; dates, oats, millet, and cotton are the principal crops. In the southern part of the coastal region, a number of small dams irrigate the farmland.

The second region consists of a plateau that rises from the coastal plain in a series of steps to an elevation of 12,000 feet, which makes access rather difficult. Here, average temperatures are substantially cooler and night frost can occur. Large numbers of animals are grazed by mainly sedentary farmers. In summer, up to thirty-five inches of rain falls in the higher parts of the plateau, permitting cultivation without irrigation. These highlands have been skillfully terraced and produce an abundance of vegetables, fruits, cereals, and coffee. Yemen's high plateau, in fact, is believed to be the original home of the coffee tree. In the fifteenth century, pilgrims bringing coffee from Yemen to Mecca (Makkah) spread the use of the beverage in the Islamic world. Turkish invaders in the seventeenth century tasted the brew and exported the art of coffee-making to other countries. Soon, Dutch traders obtained the beans at the Red Sea port of Mocha (Al Mukha), which gave its name to the small, bitter Yemenite beans.

Until recently, coffee was the country's major export. Today, *qat* is the leading export. In the past, the nation was largely self-sufficient in foodstuffs and in good years exported surpluses. However, the disruptions of Yemen's recent civil war and a prolonged drought caused a serious decline in production and made the country partly dependent on food imports.

The third region, east of the plateau, is rugged and dry and consists of deserts, except for a few oases, which obtain their water from springs or seasonal streams.

Little is known about the geology of Yemen. Some iron, coal, uranium, copper, aluminum, and salt have been found, but they are largely unexploited. Several oil concessions have been granted at various times, but no drilling has taken place.

Almost all industries are related to agriculture; there are several cotton textile mills and a cottonseed-oil plant; matches and ammunition are also manufactured. Until recently, Yemen was famous for the excellence of its handicrafts, particularly clothing, jewelry, shoes, and implements, but Jewish artisans dominated these trades, and most of them emigrated after the establishment of Israel.

Little is known of the ancient history of Yemen, although until the revolution of 1962 it was acknowledged to be one of the world's oldest existing monarchies, with a continuous cultural pattern that had lasted for more than 3,000 years. The land once contained the fabled Kingdom of Sheba, and frankincense and myrrh were its principal products. During the sixth century A.D., first Ethiopians and then Persians conquered the kingdom. The inhabitants, formerly Christians or Jews, were converted to the Muslim religion, and Yemen has remained under Muslim law ever since.

After a series of invasions, the Ottoman Turks gained control of the area in 1872. In 1918, they withdrew as a result of the armistice terms of World War I. Yemen then attained complete independence and in 1947 became one of the earliest members of the United Nations. In 1958, it joined the Federation of Arab States, together with the United Arab Republic and Syria, but the U.A.R. became dissatisfied with the arrangement and in 1961 the ties were severed.

King (Imam) Ahmad died in September, 1962, and revolution broke out before his son, Imam Muhammad al-Badr, could begin to rule. In 1964 the insurgents established a republican form of government, complete with National Assembly and a program of planned reforms. However, a civil war between royalist and republican factions ensued, and only very recently has a measure of calm been restored.

The years of political instability have been attributed to two factors: The Yemenites had no background or experience in self-government, and other countries stepped in to aid one side or the other, thus prolonging the conflict. The republicans received help from the United Arab Republic; Saudi Arabia and Jordan supplied the royalist factions. All three countries, however, withdrew their forces from Yemen by mutual agreement in 1967. The Soviet Union announced that it would continue to supply the republicans, and desultory fighting continued, but Soviet personnel who had come with the U.A.R. troops fell into disfavor, and most left by the end of the year. The withdrawal of the U.A.R. troops in particular, since they had not been well regarded by the Yemenites, resulted in gradual acceptance of the purely Yemenite republican forces by many royalist tribes. For a time, their absence made royalist troops bolder, but, in March, 1969, Saudi Arabia halted its arms and financial aid to the royalists; Imam al-Badr and his relatives then abandoned Yemen and the struggle.

In spite of its highly unstable political situation, since 1962 Yemen has taken steps to reduce its age-old isolation. Although there are still only a few roads, a motorable track now connects Aden in the Republic of Yemen to Taizz, Sana, and other towns on the plateau. Parts of this road were paved with the assistance of the United States, and the Soviet Union in 1967 aided the building of a road from Hodeida (Al Hudaydah) to Taizz. Regular aviation services connect the major towns, and there are international flights to the Republic of Yemen and Ethiopia. In addition, the Kuwait Fund for Arab Economic Development is providing money for agricultural development, and Yemen hopes to build flour mills and vegetable and fruit canneries to enlarge its food industry. Electricity has been introduced into many cities and towns. There is reason to believe that oil may be discovered in the coastal plain and offshore areas in the Red Sea, since so much has been found in nearby Arab states. The finally established republican government has taken a decisive step to end isolation by adopting an "open door" foreign policy, which aims at good relations and economic aid from East and West alike and offers incentives to foreign investors. Foreign firms and banks have already begun to open branches in the country, primarily in the main port and business center, Hodeida.

The People's Democratic Republic of Yemen

The territory now known as the People's Democratic Republic of Yemen was one of the last regions in the world to join the ranks of modern states. It acquired sovereignty, territorial boundaries, and membership in the United Nations during 1967.

The nation comprises the lands of the Arabian Peninsula south of Yemen and Saudi Arabia and west of Oman (Uman). It includes a number of offshore islands stretching from the Kamaran Islands, in the Red Sea off Yemen, to Socotra (Suqutra), off the Somali Republic, and Perim, at the entrance to the Red Sea.

Because of inadequately defined boundaries, the area of this region can only be estimated as exceeding 100,000 square miles, somewhat larger than the state of Oregon. Its population is approximately 1.5 million (no census has ever been taken). Today almost all the inhabitants are Arabs, speak Arabic, and are of the Muslim faith.

Political Vicissitudes

During the 1830's, an Indian ship flying the British flag was wrecked at Aden, and its passengers and crew were robbed and mistreated by the local population. Because negotiations for compensation proved fruitless, the East India Company, which then administered India on behalf of Great Britain, sent a warship to the region. In 1839, the Company compelled the local sultan to cede the peninsula of Aden in return for annual payments. In this way, the East India Company, and thus Great Britain, acquired a foothold on the peninsula.

With the end of Company rule in India, Aden became a possession of India; only with the gradual evolution toward Indian independence was the area turned over to direct British administration as a crown colony (1937). To the Aden colony were added by purchase small adjoining lands around the Bay of Aden—a total area of about seventy-five square miles.

The Aden colony was the only part of the mainland of the country actually under foreign administration; to ensure the security of Aden, however, various agreements were made with the chiefs of neighboring areas. These guaranteed the independence of the chiefs and their territories against foreign aggression. In return, the chiefs agreed not to attack Aden or admit any foreigners to their lands without permission from the administrator of Aden. The agreements implied, in fact, that the foreign relations of these chiefs and their areas were to be conducted through foreign agencies: first through the East India Company and subsequently through the government of India and the British Government. The first treaties were made in 1839; more were concluded later in the nineteenth century and early in the twentieth until, ultimately, they covered the whole of the area now called the People's Democratic Republic of Yemen. For the purpose of international relations, they gave the region the status of a protectorate, except for Aden, which remained a colony.

In 1839, several chiefs requested British support in thwarting Egyptian attempts to add their areas to Yemen, which Egypt had occupied in 1818. Again, in 1871, after Turkey (then called the Ottoman Empire) had captured Yemen, these chiefs asked for British aid in repelling Turkish advances. Egyptian and Turkish, as well as subsequent Yemenite, claims were based on Yemenite control of the western part of the region, including Aden, during parts of the seventeenth and eighteenth centuries.

Desultory fighting between British-supported chiefs and Turkish soldiers, backed by Yemenite tribesmen, continued until a series of treaties between Great Britain and Turkey in 1914 established a boundary between the Turkish province of Yemen and the chiefs' areas. This boundary was demarcated from the coast to Wadi Bana; beyond Wadi Bana, a boundary (called the "Violet Line" because of the color of the pencil used to define it on the treaty map) was defined but not demarcated. During World War I, Great Britain and Turkey fought on opposite sides, and Turkey succeeded in occupying large tracts west and north of Aden, until a peace treaty restored the 1914 boundary.

The state of Yemen, however, which evolved in former Turkish territory, was no party to this treaty and refused to recognize the 1914 boundary. In 1920, Yemenite troops and tribesmen invaded and succeeded in occupying parts of the western territory. These forces were withdrawn during 1931–34, when a treaty re-established the 1914 boundary for a period of

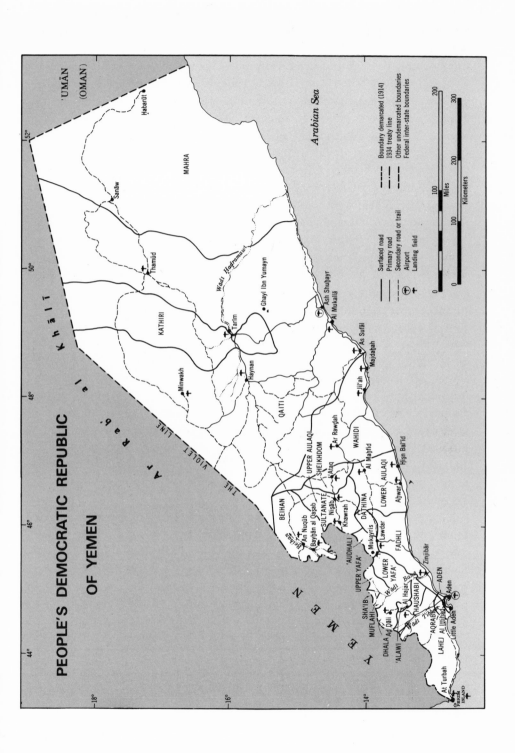

PEOPLE'S DEMOCRATIC REPUBLIC
OF YEMEN

'UMĀN
(OMAN)

Arabian Sea

MAHRA

KATHIRI

QAITI

Al Rab' al Khālī

THE VIOLET LINE

Y E M E N

BEIHAN

'AUDHALI

UPPER YAFA'

SHA'IB

MUFLAHI

DHALA

'ALAWI

LAHEJ

AQRABI

THAUSHABI

ADEN

Little Aden
Aden

At Turbah

PERIM
ISLAND

LOWER
YAFA'

Ad Dāli'

Al Hajar

Wadi Bana

Wadi Tiban

Al Ittihad

FADHLI

Zinjibār

Lawdar

Mukayris

DATHINA

LOWER
AULAQI

Abyan

Hisn Bal'id

WAHIDI

Al Mayfid

Ar Rawdah

Ataq

SULTANATE

SHEIKHDOM

UPPER AULAQI

Nisāb

Khawrah

An Nuqūb

Bayhān al Qasab

Beihan

Ghayl Ibn Yumayn

Tarīm

Haynan

Minwakh

Ash Shuhayr

Al Mukallā

As Suflī

Majdahah

Ji'lah

Wadi Hadramawt

Thamūd

Sanāw

Habarūt

Jil'ah

		Surfaced road
		Primary road
---	---	Secondary road or trail
		Airport
		Landing field

Boundary demarcated (1914)
1934 treaty line
Other undemarcated boundaries
Federal inter-state boundaries

				Miles	
0		100		200	
0	100	200	300		
		Kilometers			

forty years. Conflicting interpretations of this treaty and the lack of a demarcated boundary east of Wadi Bana soon led to a renewal of fighting. Another agreement (1951) to accept the *status quo* along the boundary did not stop the fighting, which continues sporadically to this day.

The boundary with Saudi Arabia had also been disputed since about 1930, but apparently the one unilaterally proclaimed by Great Britain in 1955 has now been generally accepted. No commercial traffic crosses this border. The only undisputed boundary was with Oman, although only one point of it, on the shore of the Indian Ocean, was defined. Today, the Republic of Yemen claims all of Oman as part of its territory.

The Kamaran Islands were taken over by Great Britain from Turkey during World War I but were not mentioned in the peace treaties concluding that war. Great Britain regarded them as part of her Aden colony, but Yemen claimed them as part of the former Turkish province of that name. Their population of about 3,000 is of mixed Arab, Somali, and Ethiopian origin. Perim, with an Arab population of about 400, was also part of Aden colony and was also claimed by Yemen. The island, with its surrounding territorial sea, may be used to close off the entrance to the Red Sea, just as the Straits of Tiran at the entrance to the Gulf of Aqaba were closed off by the United Arab Republic during 1967, prior to the outbreak of war with Israel. For this reason, the island may become a source of dispute between Arab countries and Israel, and it has been suggested that it be turned over to the United Nations. Both the Kamaran Islands and Perim were transferred to South Yemen (now the People's Democratic Republic of Yemen) after an informal poll of the inhabitants' political desires. The Kuria Muria Islands (Khuryan Muryan) in the Indian Ocean near Oman were ceded to Oman in response to the wishes of the population of about 100. These islands are now claimed by the Republic of Yemen.

To promote more efficient local government and to reduce marauding by tribes, British authorities gradually organized the area of the chiefs into a loose association, first known as the Aden Protectorate and renamed the Protectorate of South Arabia in 1962, when the chiefs' areas became states. Tribal guards in each state gradually evolved into police forces, paid out of British funds. At the same time, a military force, called Protectorate Levies, was recruited and used to defend external boundaries. This force, containing both local Arab and British officers, was also paid out of British funds.

Administratively, the protectorate was divided into two parts: the larger Eastern Protectorate—comprising the states of Mahra (which included

Socotra), Qaiti, and Kathiri—and the smaller Western Protectorate, containing thirteen states. Aden colony remained outside the protectorate, since it was under direct British administration.

Later, in the 1960's, the British Government induced some of the states to reorganize themselves into the Federation of South Arabia, including Aden colony (but not Perim), the Kuria Muria Islands, the Eastern Protectorate, and part of the Western Protectorate. According to plan, the federation was to become independent in 1968. In view of the economic contrast between the coast and the interior, however, opposition to the federation developed in Aden. Many, if not most, of the inhabitants of Aden feared that the federation would be dominated by the tribes and states of the interior, to the detriment of the people and institutions of the coast. Aden residents of Yemeni origin contributed significantly to this opposition. Violence erupted in Aden, and British troops had to intervene. It was because of this violence that most of the non-Arab residents of Aden emigrated.

Finally, Aden, the federation, and the states joined together to form the People's Republic of South Yemen, which achieved independence on November 29, 1967. This state is now called the People's Democratic Republic of Yemen.

Coastal and Inland Regions: A Contrast

From time immemorial, the Republic of Yemen has been the world's best-known supplier of incense. This product, the dried sap of bushes that grow in the interior highlands, was used in temple ceremonies by the ancient Egyptians. Jews, Greeks, Romans, Iranians, and Ethiopians also came to the shores of the country to acquire incense. The exportation of incense continues on a smaller scale today.

Collecting, packaging, and transporting incense has always been a simple operation; no foreign experts were required in the interior of the country. Foreign buyers sailed to the coast to buy incense from local traders but hardly ever ventured inland. As a result, the interior remained almost completely unknown to the outside world until about forty years ago. Although cities and states appeared and disappeared and art and especially architecture flourished there, no foreign historians recorded the process.

In the past decades, several thousand inhabitants of the interior temporarily migrated overseas, especially to Indonesia. They brought back, not new ideas, but material goods, such as motor vehicles. When the first modern explorers reached Wadi Hadramawt, thirty or forty years ago, they were amazed to discover that automobiles were already in use there. Unassembled cars had been brought by camel caravans from the coast and over rugged mountains to the flat lands of Wadi Hadramawt. The availability of modern technical equipment, including machine guns, did not disrupt the ancient societies and states of the interior, but it did increase the toll in fighting and help to delay the evolution of modern statehood.

In contrast, the coast has always been open to foreign influences. In the seventeenth century, foreign traders and pirates used its harbors as bases for their operations. These foreign influences increased considerably after the opening of the Suez Canal in 1869, when Aden became a major port on the route from Europe and America to India, Australia, and the Far East. As a result of the divergent development of the two regions, their ways of life and political attitudes differ markedly.

The contrasts between coast and interior are also evident in the landscape and climate. The coast consists mainly of a low plain, up to fifty miles wide, which is frequently interrupted by old lava streams that have eroded into rugged terrain. Temperatures here are high throughout the year, although occasionally they fall below 68° F during the cooler season, from November to March. From May to October temperatures frequently exceed 100° F. Average temperatures are above 80° F throughout the year, and high humidity often makes life unpleasant. Very little rain falls (usually less than two inches per year), desert conditions prevail, and no rivers flow into the sea. Until the introduction of modern well-drilling and reservoir construction, agriculture was virtually unknown, and the population never exceeded a few thousand, who derived their livelihood from fishing, trading, and piracy.

Inland from the coastal plain is a series of parallel ridges, which gradually increase in elevation and merge into a rugged highland plateau. In the west, this plateau varies from 3,000 to 8,000 feet; in the east, elevations do not exceed 5,000 feet. To the north, the plateau falls away in a series of steps to the vast low plains of the Ar Rab al Khali Desert. Both ridges and plateau are broken up by a series of deep, dry river valleys, or wadis. After rains, these valleys carry water, usually in torrential floods. Some of this water seeps into the ground and is recovered from wells at the edge of the wadis, from which it is diverted into irrigation canals leading to plots of cereals and groves of date palms. The total extent of cultivated land, however, is limited. The most important of these agricultural areas lie in Wadi Hadramawt, a gigantic valley running from west to east, which probably owes its origin to geological formations rather than to the action of water. Other important wadis are Bana and Tibban, north of Aden, which are now used for cotton cultivation.

Rain falls almost solely in the summer, and its quantity increases with elevation and decreases from west to east and in the north. About thirty inches per year may fall on the highest mountains near the Yemen border, whereas the average is ten inches near Oman and virtually zero in the Ar Rab al Khali. Here, in contrast to the coast, temperatures vary substantially with the altitude and the season, as, for example, at Mukayris (elevation 6,700 feet), from a minimum of 28° F in January to a maximum of 85° F in August. Vegetation varies with rainfall: Below 3,000 feet, only a few thorn bushes are found; higher up, there are dense thorn thickets. Incense production is limited to a few areas between 3,000 and 5,000 feet, and most accessible groves have been destroyed by excessive cutting. Rugged terrain prevents cultivation in high places despite sufficient precipitation.

The islands close to the Arabian Peninsula are as hot and dry as the coastlands. On Perim, seawater has to be distilled to provide drinking water. Socotra's rainfall resembles that of the higher portions of the interior. Incense production was formerly important here, as was agriculture on the man-made terraces of its wadis.

The People and Economic Development

As in other parts of the Arabian Peninsula, the basic social organization of the population is tribal. Although almost all tribes call themselves Bedouin, not all are nomadic as in northern Arabia. Most tribes live in houses rather than tents and devote part of the year to agriculture. Some live almost exclusively in the cities of Wadi Hadramawt; wandering herds of sheep, goats, and camels, however, still contribute a significant proportion of the food supplies. The few tribes north of Wadi Hadramawt are entirely nomadic and in some years migrate far into Saudi Arabia.

Throughout the region, tribes have always engaged in raiding each other, and caravan traffic suffered from these depredations. In the west, however, traffic with Yemen was always important, and local dialects and habits resemble those of that country. Traffic with Saudi Arabia and Oman was and is less important.

Despite the area's isolation and the interruptions of trade, several cities with more than 10,000 inhabitants developed in Wadi Hadramawt. These cities have some beautiful high-rise residential buildings that reach heights of over eighty feet. Why and when this distinctive urban architecture evolved is not yet known.

On the coast, trade and immigration reduced the social significance of the tribal structure. With the opening of the Suez Canal, Aden became, almost overnight, a coal-refueling stop for vessels passing to and from the Red Sea. Although coal was replaced by oil as a fuel during this century, this did not hinder the growth of the city. Other service industries, such as ship repair, also developed, and Aden, helped by the absence of import tariffs, became famous as a port for shopping and the entertainment of ships' crews and passengers. Merchants and manufacturers from India, Pakistan, and Europe settled there, and labor was attracted, mainly from Yemen, but also from the Somali Republic and the interior. In the 1950's, an oil refinery was built to supply fuel to ships as well as to meet local requirements and provide for exports to neighboring countries that lack refineries. Light industries such as cigarette and textile manufacturing were also established.

Aden's population was about 500 when the British arrived in 1839. By 1963, it had increased to 220,000. Of these, more than 90,000 were immigrants from Yemen or their descendants, 20,000 were from India or Pakistan, 20,000 were from the Somali Republic, and about 3,000 were from Europe. Almost all non-Arab residents departed during the political riots before independence and the closing of the Suez Canal in 1967. The city's population has continued to increase, however, and is now about 250,000.

Other ports, such as Al Mukalla, developed to a lesser degree. For a few decades, Perim was also an important coaling station, but the switch from coal to oil brought an end to this function in 1936. During the era of propeller-driven airplanes, Kamaran Island served for a while as a refueling base.

Agricultural activities in the interior did not benefit much from this economic growth. The increasing population on the coast imported its food from overseas. With British assistance, however, cotton cultivation for export was started in Wadi Bana near Aden in 1949. More than 50,000 acres are now under cultivation and produce a high-grade long-staple cotton similar to that of the Sudan. Production is organized in a partnership of landowners, tenants, and a government agency that operates the irrigation system and handles the processing and marketing. Smaller but similarly organized cotton-cultivation schemes were also established west of

Wadi Bana. Vegetable, fruit, and chicken farming, relying on well or wadi irrigation water, were also developed near Aden.

The Republic of Yemen Today

During the turmoil that preceded the establishment of the republic, some of the local rulers were removed from power, and the process continued after independence. Today, the country is divided into governates. One of these consists of the former British colony of Aden together with the island of Socotra, but little is known of the government and governates of the remainder of the republic. Some of the former political leaders succeeded in escaping to Saudi Arabia, but others rallied support from local tribes and possibly from Saudi Arabia and have clashed with local troops. The latter have been weakened by the dismissal of British advisers, who were well acquainted with the interior, and by the disbanding, for reasons of cost, of the army's celebrated camel corps, established by the British more than forty years ago. As a result, dissident tribesmen and their rulers control portions of the territory.

Although the Republic of Yemen continues to receive financial assistance from Britain, the new rulers are trying to obtain additional aid from the United States and the Soviet Union. So far, the United States has not granted any assistance, and the extent of Soviet aid is unknown. Politically, the Republic of Yemen appears to be closer to Cuba than to any other communist or socialist nation. Because of continuing turmoil in the country and the general lack of such government services as police protection, the search for oil has been curtailed; at present, therefore, there is no hope of obtaining revenues from this resource, which is so significant in other parts of Arabia.

Suggested Readings

BETHMAN, E. W. *Yemen on the Threshold*. Washington, D.C.: Middle East Institute, 1960. The most up-to-date report available.

BRINTON, J. Y. *Aden and the Federation of South Arabia*. Washington, D.C.: American Society of International Law, 1964. A study of political evolution.

HELFRITZ, H. *The Yemen: A Secret Journey*. London: Allen, 1958. A fascinating report.

King, Gillian. *Imperial Outpost—Aden: Its Place in British Strategic Policy.* New York: Oxford University Press, 1964. A British strategic study, which includes much geographical information.

Moseley, Major F. "Exploration for Water in the Aden Protectorate." *Royal Engineers Journal,* LXXX, no. 2 (1966), pp. 124–42. How to find water for economic development.

Newby, J. C. "South of the Empty Quarter." *Geographical Magazine,* XXXIX, no. 2 (1966), pp. 92–101. A general article.

Phillips, Wendell. *Qataban and Sheba.* New York: Harcourt, Brace and World, 1955. Exploring for antiquities in unknown eastern Yemen.

Scott, Hugh. *In the High Yemen.* London: Murray, 1947. Travel and life in interior Yemen.

10 EASTERN ARABIA, KUWAIT, BAHRAIN

Alexander Melamid

Eastern Arabia—*Political Boundaries and Great Britain* •
Deserts and Oases • *The Pre-Petroleum Economy* • *The Petroleum Economy* • *Prospects for the Future* • Kuwait—*Outlook for the Future* • Bahrain—*The People and the Future*

Eastern Arabia

Most of the Eastern Arabian countries have been independent since time immemorial, but few people in the outside world have been aware of the fact, for their diplomatic relations have generally been handled by Great Britain, and until now they have participated little in foreign trade. But today, even though they are not members of the United Nations, these countries are included in world-trade statistics—as present or potential sources of petroleum. The sheikhdoms of Qatar and the Trucial States, located on the southern coast of the Persian Gulf, have been producing oil since 1949 and 1962, respectively; the Sultanate of Oman (Uman), bordering the Arabian Sea and the Gulf of Oman, began to produce oil in 1967.

Political Boundaries and Great Britain

Although these states are independent in that most of their internal affairs have been handled by local Arab rulers (according to the laws of Islam, the only religion in the area), their external boundaries have been a source of much controversy and conflict. The development of the Trucial States in many ways is characteristic of that of Qatar and the Sultanate as well.

At one time, piracy was a major occupation of the inhabitants of the region now known as the Trucial States, so much so that the region acquired the name "Pirate Coast." Because the violence and robbery occurred mainly on the seas, Great Britain in 1820 and 1935 made treaties with the Arab leaders that were followed by a succession of truces outlawing sea battles. Thus, naval piracy gradually came to an end, the old name of the region was forgotten, and the "Pirate Coast" became "Trucial Coast" or the "Trucial States."

The British truces did not, however, outlaw fighting on land, and, as recently as eighteen years ago, prolonged inland conflicts took place among the Bedouin tribes attached to various sheikhdoms. In the course of this fighting, the vague boundaries changed frequently and some sheikhdoms disappeared while others emerged. There were six sheikhdoms in 1835, five in 1914, six again by 1919, and seven by 1937. During 1952, one sheikhdom was eliminated and another appeared. Today the Trucial States include seven divisions, but only a few points of the boundaries between these sheikhdoms have been demarcated, and changes continue to result from minor skirmishes. There are now several disputed territories and at least one area in which rights are shared between two sheikhdoms.

Traveling from west to east along the Trucial Coast, we find Abu Zaby (Abu Dhabi), largest oil-producing state and a signatory to the 1971 pact between Persian Gulf countries and various international oil companies (see p. 12); Dubayy, center of commerce and banking, whose jet airport is serviced by international carriers; Ash Shariqah, where deposits of red oxide are being worked; Ujman; Umm al Qaywayn; Ras al Khaymah; and Al Fujayrah. Six of the states have shorelines on the Persian Gulf, and some have separate land areas, called exclaves, on the Gulf of Oman, where Al Fujayrah is located. Each sheikhdom is centered around its capital city, which bears the same name as the sheikhdom.

Disputes and fighting have decreased considerably in recent years, and peace is being enforced by a regional army staffed by local Arabs and British personnel. The latter are to be withdrawn by the end of 1971. The sheikhs meet occasionally to discuss matters of common interest. There is a development budget that includes financial grants for agricultural and other improvements, which is supported by Great Britain. Trade between the sheikhdoms is proceeding without hindrance, and the main connecting trails are being improved by grading or paving. Thus, the volume of trade is increasing rapidly, and trucks and buses are replacing camel caravans.

According to the treaties with Great Britain, all permits and concessions

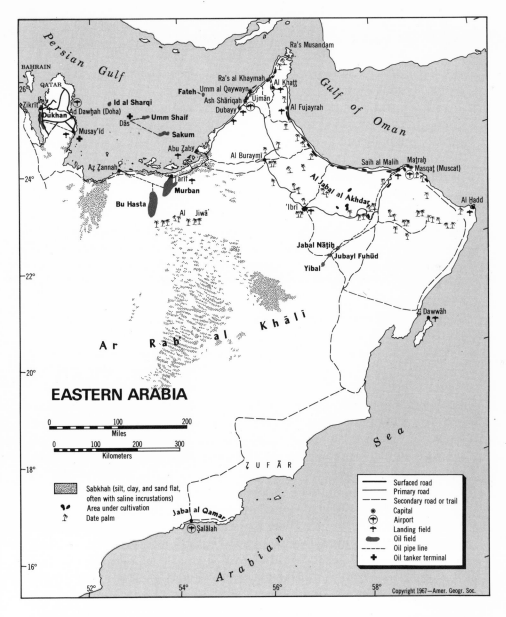

Map legend:

- **Surfaced road**
- **Primary road**
- **Secondary road or trail**
- ⊙ **Capital**
- ⊕ **Airport**
- ✝ **Landing field**
- **Oil field**
- **Oil pipe line**
- ✚ **Oil tanker terminal**

Sabkhah (silt, clay, and sand flat, often with saline incrustations)

♥ Area under cultivation

⚑ Date palm

EASTERN ARABIA

Miles: 0 — 100 — 200

Kilometers: 0 — 100 — 200 — 300

Copyright 1967—Amer. Geogr. Soc.

given to foreign nationals or corporations by the sheikhs require British approval. Under these conditions, oil concessions have been granted to international and American companies, and permits for the establishment of banks have been issued to British, Indian, Pakistani, Iranian, and Lebanese nationals.

The external boundaries of the Trucial States, especially those with Saudi Arabia, are another concern of Great Britain and are as disputed as the internal boundaries of the seven sheikhdoms. However, Britain currently maintains that the borders proclaimed in 1955 delimit the territories of the Trucial States.

The political evolution of Qatar has been similar to that of the Trucial States, but, as sea and then land fighting between various tribes and sheikhs gradually decreased, only one sheikhdom emerged. Here also Great Britain proclaimed the state's external boundaries, and it now approves concessions and permits. The capital is Doha (Ad Dawhah), where the British representative, banks, oil company offices, and the like are located.

In 1798, the Sultanate of Oman signed a separate treaty with Great Britain, but the provisions of this and subsequent treaties resembled those made with the Trucial States and Qatar. An important exception was that the state could establish its own consular treaties. Such treaties were made with the United States, France, the Netherlands, India, and other countries.

Some fighting occurred as recently as 1959, mainly because of an abortive movement to set up a separate state in the mountainous interior of Oman. The purpose of this movement, supported by the United Arab Republic and Saudi Arabia, was to replace the sultan with an elected religious leader. During United Nations discussions of this dispute, the British Government, speaking for the sultan of Oman, described the hearings as a foreign intervention into the affairs of a sovereign state. On the other hand, in 1965 the United Nations passed a resolution stating that the presence of the British prevented the local people from exercising their rights of self-determination and calling for the elimination of British domination. No further action has been taken.

After fighting ceased, economic conditions in Oman began to improve, as elsewhere in the region. Here, too, camel caravans are being replaced by more modern means of transportation. Foreign concessionaires, including American companies, operate with British approval. An American Medical Mission is located in Muscat (Masqat), the country's capital.

Deserts and Oases

Much of Eastern Arabia consists of deserts and semidesert areas suitable only for nomadic grazing. The vast Ar Rab al Khali, one of the world's most barren deserts, which is partially included within the 1955 boundaries of Oman and Abu Zaby, lacks sufficient vegetation even for grazing, and the tribes in adjacent areas cross it only infrequently. As a result, the few explorers who have traveled through it, including Thesiger in 1946 and 1947, have had a hard time finding companions for their journeys.

Most of the deserts are flat and low-lying, and the semideserts are usually covered by gravel or a mixture of gravel and sand. The desert in the western Trucial States is threaded by salt swamps, called *sabkhah*, which make travel difficult, especially after a rainy spell.

In contrast to this barren region, the Sultanate has some relatively fertile areas. Most of the population of 750,000, in fact, is engaged in some form of agriculture, and, until oil production began, dried limes and dates were among the chief exports. Where suitable soil and water exist, a variety of vegetables, cereals, and forage is grown. The rugged peaks of the Al Jabal al Akhdar range, located just south of the Gulf of Oman, and the gentler slopes of the Jabal al Qamar hills, in the province of Zufar, receive more rain than the deserts, and agriculture there is feasible. Also, percolation of water from the Al Jabal al Akhdar range presumably feeds the few wells in the Trucial States and thus provides some irrigation near the towns along the coast as well as in inland oases. The largest of these oases, Al Buraymi, is divided between Abu Zaby and Oman. Al Jiwa, another oasis, is now part of Abu Zaby. Some large sand dunes are found near here and also south of Al Buraymi. There are more extensive oases on the Gulf of Oman and on the Arabian Sea near the foot of the Jabal al Qamar. A few minor oases are located west of the Al Jabal al Akhdar range.

Rain comes in irregular showers during the winter months, and nowhere does the average amount exceed three inches per year except in the Al Jabal al Akhdar range, where the summer and winter accumulation is probably more than ten inches. Not much is known about rain in the Jabal al Qamar, but summer showers are probably caused by winds similar to the monsoons of India. The Qamars are covered by thorn vegetation whose resins were formerly exported as incense.

The weather in Eastern Arabia can be fairly pleasant in winter during a dry spell but is often distinctly unpleasant in summer. In the winter the average temperature near the Persian Gulf is between 60° and 70° F, and near the Gulf of Oman and the Arabian Sea it is about 80°, although night frost is sometimes encountered in the interior. But, from May to October, temperatures along the coast usually exceed 90°, and inland they are even higher. In addition, high humidities along the coasts can make life uncomfortable at any time during the year and in summer prevent cooling off even at night. Farther inland the hot winds that blow down from the Al Jabal al Akhdar range sometimes keep night temperatures as high as 110°, while daytime temperatures often exceed 120° or 130°.

Between April and November, even light outdoor work becomes too strenuous, and oil-company surveys are suspended. However, air-conditioned camps and improved facilities now make it possible to continue drilling and some other activities all year round.

The Pre-Petroleum Economy

Before the discovery of petroleum, nomadic herding was the major agricultural occupation in this dry land, and tribes migrated over large areas to search for fodder. Some boundary claims, especially those of Saudi Arabia, are based on these migrations. Goats, sheep, and camels provided sustenance and transportation (cattle and horses cannot survive on such limited vegetation and water). In the few oases, palm trees supplied dates as well as fronds and wood for building and shade, and barley and vegetables were grown, along with some tobacco.

In the Trucial States, besides practicing piracy, the inhabitants fished and collected pearls from banks in the Persian Gulf. Pearling has declined today because of the competition from cultured pearls, but fishing remains a major source of food and income for many of the states' 180,000 people. Qatar had only a few date gardens, along with a limited supply of pearls, and thus was poorer than its neighbors to the east. In Oman, the richest of the Eastern Arabian states, the major revenue came from trade with India and East Africa, especially the buying and selling of slaves.

The Petroleum Economy

From the beginning, the search for petroleum brought changes in the local economy of Eastern Arabia. Machines and men to operate them were imported, increasing both the means of transportation and the pool of technical skills available. After the discovery of oil, modern ports were built to bring in the steel and other materials required for the development of the oil fields and the storage and export of crude oil. In addition, towns and hospitals were established to serve oil company employees and others. Water supplies were improved by the distillation of seawater, and thus the number of trees and gardens also increased.

When substantial revenues from the petroleum industry became available, the governments were able to undertake development plans, including the construction of schools, hospitals, and agricultural experiment stations. Palaces for the ruling sheikhs and their relatives were also erected. Traders and craftsmen began to supply goods and services, towns grew up with stores, skyscrapers, and hotels, and the tempo of life changed to some degree from nomadism to modern industry and commerce.

An influx of immigrants, attracted by new job opportunities, further changed the picture. They came mainly from other parts of Arabia, but also from Iran, India, Pakistan, and Somalia, probably more than doubling the total population. In addition, a few hundred Europeans and Americans have come to work, usually on short-term contracts. Slowly the standard of living has risen. During 1965, the states of the region, excluding Oman, decided to create their own currency out of their gold and foreign-exchange reserves.

To guard against possible future exhaustion of oil supplies, some of the current income is invested outside of the region; only funds from the balance are used for local development. As a result of these policies, further long-term improvements in the standard of living can be expected.

Despite all these changes, probably about half the people continue to live at present as in the past, making a meager living from the land or the sea, residing in tents or reed huts, wearing traditional gowns, and eating mainly local produce. Indeed, there is a marked contrast between these tribesmen and their brethren who have adjusted to modern industrial and commercial ways of living and who, like the immigrants, live in row houses, wear Western-style garments, and eat imported food. To induce them to live in the area, foreign technicians and executives are given three weeks' paid home leave for every three months of work, are provided with living quarters in clubs or houses near their place of work, and can even play golf on oiled patches of sand.

These changes can be seen most clearly in Qatar, where oil production at Dukhan commenced in 1949. The population was then only about 6,000; today, it is about 80,000 people, most of whom live in the substantially enlarged capital, Doha, whose newly completed deepwater port now handles more of the consumer imports than Zikrit, a port built on the west coast to develop oil production. Oil is currently exported from Musayid on the east coast. Regular ship and airline services connect Doha with Europe and India.

So far, Dukhan is the only oil field discovered on land, but since 1964 an offshore field, Id al Sharqi, has been producing, and additional offshore fields may further increase Qatar's production, which totaled 18 million tons during 1970, or more than the output of Colombia in that year. A small refinery supplies local requirements of petroleum products. Qatar also will receive higher payments for its oil, as a result of the agreement signed in February, 1971.

In the sheikhdom of Abu Zaby, oil was discovered in commercial quantities at Murban during 1960, and production began in 1963 after the necessary harbor facilities and pipelines had been constructed. Az Zannah is the export center for oil from Murban and the nearby field of Bu Hasta. Abu Zaby's offshore field, Umm Shaif, commenced production in 1962, and the oil from this field flows in a submerged pipeline to Das Island, where tankers are loaded and supplies are discharged. This formerly waterless island is at present inhabited by several hundred oil workers and their families. Sakum, another offshore field, which began producing late in 1967, along with other deposits on land and beneath the sea, may eventually increase Abu Zaby's production to well above the 1970 total of 33 million tons. The city of Abu Zaby is located on an island connected to the mainland by a causeway. It now has a good water-supply system, and many Bedouins from Al Jiwa have left the oasis to work in the oil industry.

Elsewhere in the Trucial States, the search for oil has also been successful, and production is expected to begin soon. For example, in 1966 oil was discovered at Fateh in the Persian Gulf. All the oil-producing states have benefited from the new employment opportunities in this industry. In addition, agricultural output has gone up; since the establishment of an agricultural trials station and an agricultural school at Ras al Khaymah, the number of gardens under cultivation has doubled, and the variety of crops has greatly increased.

Petroleum production in the Sultanate of Oman was delayed because of fighting and unsuccessful early drilling ventures. However, in 1967, Oman joined the oil-producing states, and by 1970 output had reached nearly 17 million tons. The oil comes from Jabal Natih, Jubayl Fuhud, and Yibal, located southwest of the Al Jabal al Akhdar range. These fields are connected to the new port on the Gulf of Oman, Saih al Malih, by a pipeline some 170 miles long. Besides the export of petroleum, this port will also handle many imported products, including rice, wheat flour, sugar, cement, vehicles and accessories, cigarettes, coffee, and cotton piece-goods. Muscat and the nearby trading town of Matrah benefit considerably from these developments. In the province of Zufar, oil has been discovered in noncommercial quantities, but the search for more promising prospects is being continued in offshore areas.

Prospects for the Future

The political structure of Eastern Arabia continues to be unstable, illiteracy is widespread, and there is a shortage of arable land, water for irrigation, and transportation facilities. On the other hand, the area now has large revenues from oil that are being used for such projects as better public water-supply systems; more schools, training institutions, and hospitals; new port facilities and better roads; and more efficient agricultural methods. And even larger sums should be forthcoming for further economic and social development as new petroleum fields become productive.

Kuwait

This Arab sheikhdom at the head of the Persian Gulf became fully independent in 1961 and a member of the United Nations in 1963. Its area was about 6,200 square miles until December, 1969, when the Saudi Arabia–Kuwait Neutral Zone was formally divided between the two countries, adding roughly 500 square miles to Kuwait (Kuwayt).

The landscape consists almost entirely of low, flat desert with a few small hills. Summers are uncomfortably humid and hot, with temperatures frequently exceeding 120° F. Winters are more pleasant, with temperatures averaging 70° F. Rain falls rarely and usually in winter. Until recently, a population of less than 50,000 people clustered around the few ponds and wells, all of which were brackish, and made a meager living mainly out of nomadic grazing, the cultivation of date gardens, and a little fishing and pearling along the coasts. Sailors from Kuwait journeyed to East Africa and brought back timber, which they used in the construction of sailing vessels, called dhows; these ships were famous throughout the Indian Ocean, and shipbuilding was Kuwait's only industry.

And yet today Kuwait, whose population has grown to 540,000, is a wealthy nation: It has the highest per-capita income in the world—$3,257 per year compared to $3,153 in the United States. It has free telephone, health, and educational systems, and there is no income tax. This incredibly high standard of living is a direct result of the discovery of petroleum, and of a government policy of profit-sharing.

With the first production of oil in 1946, the oil industry immediately became the major employer, and, through equal profit-sharing, the outstanding revenue-producer for the state and its residents. Other important businesses began to prosper, and there are now banks and other enterprises owned by Kuwait citizens. Fresh water is being distilled from seawater, and additional fresh water is imported from neighboring Iraq. Thus parts of the desert country can be irrigated to produce some vegetables, fruits, and fodder (although the great bulk of food requirements still have to be imported). Kuwait City, once a town of mud huts, has been completely transformed into a modern city of multistoried cement and steel structures, complete with wide boulevards, traffic circles, suburbs, hospitals, dental clinics, theaters, schools, libraries, and a university. And its population is now 150,000.

Oil terminals, refineries, and chemical and other industries are multiplying rapidly; Kuwait is the world's seventh largest producer of oil, with an output of 137.5 million tons in 1970. Oil is produced both onshore (Burgan is the major field) and offshore. In addition, Kuwait has rights to 11.6 millions tons of oil produced per year in the former Kuwait–Saudi Arabian Neutral Zone.

Outlook for the Future

Until Kuwait signed an agreement with Great Britain in 1899, it was a feudal territory, vaguely associated with the Turkish Empire, which frequently suffered invasions from what is now Saudi Arabia. The agreement, precipitated by fear of a particularly deadly raid, placed the country's defense and foreign relations in British hands. Internally, Kuwait remained independent, and Muslim law continued to prevail. The 1899 agreement was canceled in 1961, when Kuwait became fully independent. When Iraq threatened to annex Kuwait later in the same year, British troops were called to the rescue but were subsequently replaced by an international force provided by the Arab League, of which Kuwait is a member.

Except for the 1961 crisis with Iraq, Kuwait has dwelt peacefully with its neighbors for many years. Its boundaries are not fully determined, but there have been no recent disputes. Moreover, Kuwait contributes financially to the upkeep and development of other Arab states.

The present sheikh (or amir) of Kuwait is a constitutional monarch with considerable powers; he appoints the Prime Minister and the Cabinet. However, a parliament (the National Assembly), elected every four years by male citizens, can propose legislation and in some cases can overrule the sheikh's veto.

Financially, the sheikhdom appears to be prospering, and its wealth is apparently being well spent: for increased educational and health facilities, better transportation and communications, and aid to other, less fortunate Arab states. Also, as a result of the 1971 agreement with oil companies (see p. 12) its revenue should continue to rise. However, Kuwait is well aware of the danger of depending so largely on a single product; it is possible that oil will cease to be a prime source of fuel, or that the country's oil resources will eventually be exhausted. Kuwait is therefore attempting to diversify its economy by investing part of its huge revenues in more irrigation to increase agricultural production, in the expansion of chemical-fertilizer and asbestos plants, and in the creation of new petrochemical industries, such as plastics, rubber, and nylon.

Bahrain

Bahrain consists of a group of coral islands that were once famous for their output of pearls, scooped from oysters in the warm, shallow Persian Gulf waters, and are now known for the production of oil. For all practical purposes, Bahrain means Bahrain Island and Al Muharraq Island (a causeway connects the two). It is a virtually independent Arab sheikhdom, associated with the British Commonwealth of Nations, located between Saudi Arabia and Qatar. Its total area is only 231 square miles, and its mainly Arab population is just over 200,000. Al Manamah (population about 80,000) is the capital.

The Bahrain Islands are flat and sandy with only a few low hills. It hardly ever rains, and, were it not for a number of good springs, the islands would be a desert. As far as is known, the sweet water of these springs percolates from aquifers in Saudi Arabia, which pass underneath the salty Persian Gulf. Summers are uncomfortably hot and humid; day temperatures usually exceed 90° F. Winters, with temperatures averaging 68° F, are more pleasant. Spring waters and the hot climate permit intensive cultivation of dates and lucerne (alfalfa). Cereals, fruits (primarily tropical varieties and citrus), and vegetables are also grown, and there are poultry and dairy industries, but the bulk of the food must be imported.

These and other imports are paid for out of oil revenues, which commenced in 1934. Oil production was 4 million tons in 1970. A refinery processes Bahrain oil, as well as oil imported from Saudi Arabia by a pipeline on the bottom of the Persian Gulf. Unless new oil fields are discovered, oil revenues, which are shared equally between the government and the

Courtesy Caltex Petroleum Corporation

Large revenues from petroleum are rapidly bringing modernization and economic development to Bahrain. Buildings of all kinds are going up, especially new housing in response to rising per-capita incomes. This is one of the block-making industries.

producing company, can be expected to decline. Bahrain agreed to share revenues from oil production in an offshore area disputed with Saudi Arabia; thus far, little oil has been discovered there.

For these reasons, the government has invested substantial portions of its revenues in agricultural improvements, profitable ventures overseas, a planned causeway to Saudi Arabia, a first-class international airport, which is the main aviation center for the Persian Gulf region, schools, hospitals, roads, power stations, and, in general, the development of Bahrain as an important trade center for Eastern Arabia. Bahrain also encourages foreign investment that will help to diversify its economy. In 1968, an international consortium was formed to construct a $72-million aluminum smelter, which will provide much-needed jobs and, it is hoped, will also attract subsidiary industries to further strengthen the economy.

The People and the Future

Many burial mounds attest to the large populations on these islands in distant eras. From the beginning, Bahrain had much contact with Iran, and, next to the Arabs, Iranians still make up most of the population. Almost all Arabs and Iranians are Muslims and Muslim law prevails in the islands. Now there are also a few thousand Americans, Europeans, and Indians, primarily employed in the oil industry or in trade. The Portuguese held the islands during most of the sixteenth century, but in 1782 mainland Arab tribes conquered them and established the present dynasty of sheikhs, who have ruled with the help of an advisory council consisting mainly of members of their family. These rulers made the first treaty with Great Britain in 1820, and since 1861 Britain has been responible for Bahrain's defense and foreign relations. Although Bahrain has always been self-governing, a British political agent resides in its capital.

Britain plans to withdraw its military support by the end of 1971, and at that time Bahrain may choose to associate with neighboring states. However, its exact status remains confused: Iran refuses to recognize its independence and claims its territory. Recently, though, Great Britain and Iran have asked the United Nations to consider Iran's claim, and Iran is expected to relinquish it as a result. Bahrain itself claims part of the territory of Qatar, but these two countries, together with the Trucial States, are now in the process of forming a Federation of Arab Amirates for purposes of regional defense and economic cooperation following the withdrawl of British troops. If successful, the federation may also be able to negotiate the settlement of boundary disputes.

Suggested Readings

BELGRAVE, SIR CHARLES. *The Pirate Coast.* London: Bell, 1966. A good local history.

DICKSON, H. R. P. *Kuwait and Her Neighbors.* London: Allen and Unwin, 1956. A primarily historical account.

HAY, RUPERT. *The Persian Gulf States.* Washington, D.C.: The Middle

East Institute, 1959. A good account by a former British resident of the area.

International Bank for Reconstruction and Development. *The Economic Development of Kuwait.* Baltimore: Johns Hopkins Press, 1965. Discusses the country's economic achievements and prospects.

KELLY, J. B. *Eastern Arabian Frontiers.* New York: Praeger, 1964. A thorough study of the evolution of local political boundaries.

LANDEN, R. G. *Oman Since 1856: Disruptive Modernization in a Traditional Arab Society.* Princeton, N.J.: Princeton University Press, 1967. A very interesting study of modernization.

MELAMID, ALEXANDER. "Political Geography of Trucial Oman and Qatar." *Geographical Review,* XLIII (April, 1953), pp. 194–206. The evolution of the state system under the impact of economic development.

OWEN, RODERIC. *The Golden Bubble.* London: Collins, 1957. A lively account of living in Bahrain.

PHILLIPS, W. *Unknown Oman.* New York: McKay, 1966. History and travel in Oman.

SHIBER, SABA GEORGE. *The Kuwait Urbanization.* Kuwait: Government Printing Press, 1966. A documentation, analysis, and critique of Kuwait's rapid urban development.

WILSON, SIR ARNOLD T. *The Persian Gulf.* London: Allen and Unwin, 1928, revised in 1959. A Persian Gulf history written by a famous British administrator of the area.

11 LEBANON*

*Landscape and Climate • The People • Developing Agriculture •
Industrial Growth • Tourism, Trade, and Services • The Future*

Although Lebanon is one of the smallest of the newly independent nations, having an area of only 4,015 square miles, about four-fifths the size of Connecticut, it is currently enjoying a higher standard of living than most—not primarily because of its striking physical endowments, but, rather, because its inhabitants have a remarkable ability for business. Long ago, these people, then known as Phoenicians, engaged in highly successful commercial ventures, notably selling cedar wood to Pharaoh Snefru (*ca.* 2650 B.C.) for his pyramid at Danshur and to Solomon for his temple.

At the height of their power (1200–800 B.C.), they established a string of trading posts and colonies (Carthage, for instance) all along the Mediterranean coast, and were the undisputed rulers of the sea. Later, they sold grain to Rome and for centuries supplied Europe with spices from the Far East. Now they are selling their own fruits, vegetables, and textiles, and American and Western European cars, radios, air conditioners, and the like to their Arab neighbors—always at substantial profits.

Furthermore, economic and social advances have been achieved mainly through private enterprise rather than governmental edicts, and, in spite of several political upheavals, the form of government has remained democratic in fact as well as in name, almost alone among the Middle Eastern nations.

---

* This chapter is based partly on material supplied by Paul P. Vouras.

139

Landscape and Climate

Physically, Lebanon can be divided into four regions. The first is a coastal plain ranging from two to fourteen miles in width, except where it widens out in the south around Sur (Tyre) and Sayda (Sidon), and in the north around Tripoli (Tarabulus), and Halba. This is good farmland and highly productive wherever irrigation is practiced.

Bordering it are the Lebanon Mountains (Jabal Lubnan), which dominate the country throughout its entire length from north to south. They consist of deeply dissected sandstone and limestone formations; one of the deepest gorges is that of the Litani River, some 900 feet deep. Centuries of over-grazing and indiscriminate cutting of trees on these slopes are responsible for their present denudation. The existing forests are chiefly Aleppo pine and oak. The few remaining cedars and firs are in the northern part of the country, about 100 miles from Beirut (Bayrut). The Lebanon Mountains are the source of numerous underground springs, which provide water for irrigation. Their western middle slopes, below 5,000 feet, where soils are relatively fertile and rainfall is adequate, are densely settled. The close proximity of these mountains to the urban centers of Beirut and Tripoli, the availability of good hotel accommodations, the coolness in summer, and the snow-covered slopes in winter (ideal for skiing), all have made the Lebanon Mountains a major tourist attraction, for both Lebanese and foreigners.

East of these mountains lies the Bekaa (Al Biqa), seventy-five miles long and five to eight miles wide, part of the Rift Valley that continues on down through the Red Sea and eastern Africa. This lowland, drained by the Litani River in the south and the Orontes (Asi) in the north, is agriculturally quite productive, especially in the vicinity of Zahlah and Baalbak (Balabakk); farther south, the farmers are hindered by marshes and rocky outcrops.

The Anti-Lebanon Range (Al Jabalash Sharqi), whose slopes rise abruptly from the eastern floor of the Bekaa, forms the boundary between Lebanon and Syria. Because of the steep slopes, thin soils, and scarcity of water in summer, these mountains are sparsely populated; the main economic activities are nomadic grazing and shifting grain cultivation where springs provide water during the dry season.

The prevailing winds coming across the Mediterranean give the coastal plain a semitropical climate with mild, wet winters, and hot, humid, but

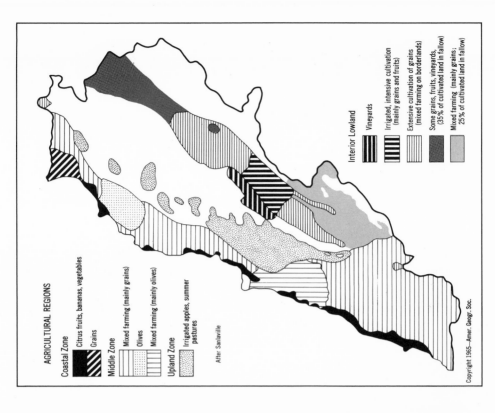

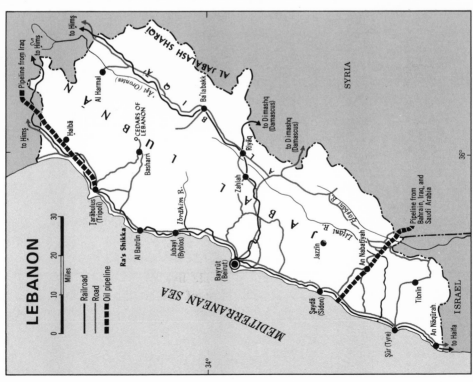

rainless summers (June to September). The average monthly temperatures vary from 57° F in January to 82° F in August. Frosts are rare. The western, windward slopes of the Lebanon Mountains have a temperate and humid climate, with rainfall ranging from forty inches at lower elevations to more than fifty at the crest. Bekaa and the Anti-Lebanon Range, shut off from the tempering effect of the Mediterranean Sea, have cool winters, hot summers, and a long rainless period, lasting from May to October. At Riyaq, the temperature may drop to 18° F, and late frosts (even into May) often cause heavy damage to crops; in the Bekaa, the July and August maximum temperatures frequently exceed 100° F.

The People

The majority of the 2.7 million Lebanese regard themselves as Arabs, and the official language is Arabic. According to recent estimates, Christians predominate (53 per cent) and Muslims constitute a large minority (45 per cent). With an average population density of 670 inhabitants per square mile, or 2,450 per square mile of arable land, Lebanon is one of the most densely peopled countries of Southwest Asia. Its high rate of population growth (*ca.* 2.5 per cent per annum) is aggravating the problem.

Possible solutions that have been suggested include increasing agricultural and industrial production, encouraging birth control, undertaking a better distribution of the land, and promoting supervised emigration. Unrestricted emigration is discouraged because it might upset the delicate politico-religious balance between the Christian and Muslim segments of the population.

Under the Electoral Reform Bill of 1960, the ratio of Christians to Muslims was established at six to five, on the basis of the thesis that the Christians actually constituted the majority. However, the emigration of more Christians than Muslims, together with the high birth rate of Muslims, may have affected this ratio, although no recent census has been taken to substantiate this possibility. The Christians' traditional control of the parliament and the Presidency and the Muslims' control of the Premiership have given the two communities a sense of national identity, thereby contributing to Lebanon's economic and social development.

Approximately 40 per cent of the people live in the urban centers of Beirut, Zahlah, Sayda, and Tripoli. Most of the rest live in more than 2,000 villages, raising crops and livestock. The typical village is an

Courtesy National Council of Tourism in Lebanon

This narrow street in the *suq* of Al Batrun, thirty-five miles north of Beirut, is lined with white houses and craftsmen's workshops. The house fronts, built in "ramleh" stone, the traditional building material, and the corbels and over-hanging balconies typify the architecture of this coastal region. Privacy at street level is much prized in the old sections of Middle Eastern towns.

agglomeration of dwellings concentrated in a small area. Its center is the church, or mosque, and an adjoining square, or *saha,* where the people gather to worship, to exchange news, to trade, or to celebrate national or religious festivals. Since independence, the villagers have become a potent political force ready to exert pressure on the government for a larger share of the national wealth.

In Lebanon, as elsewhere in the world, population is growing faster in the cities than in the countryside. The influx of villagers to the cities has been attributed to such factors as limited arable land, restricted rural employment opportunities, extensive unemployment and underemployment, and the unattractiveness of parts of the rural landscape. If the rural-to-urban migration is not slowed, it may eventually lead to the devitalization of the countryside and to the congestion and sprawl of the cities.

Developing Agriculture

Lebanon's topography, soils, and climate make it possible to raise a variety of crops, in four fairly distinct zones: (1) the coastal plain (citrus fruits, bananas, sugar cane, and grains); (2) a middle zone (olives, grains, tobacco, vineyards, and mixed farming); (3) an upland zone (irrigated apples and summer pastures); and (4) the interior lowland (grains, vineyards, fruits, and some mixed farming).

The most valuable crops are olives, citrus fruits, apples, grapes, vegetables, and tobacco (in that order), and together they bring in more than four-fifths of the agricultural revenue. One of the most dramatic expansions in agriculture has been in the apple crop, which, as a result of new planting and more irrigation, rose from 15,000 tons in 1952 to 154,000 tons in 1968, and many trees planted have not yet matured. The output of many other crops has also been steadily increasing; for example, 88,000 tons of citrus fruits were raised in 1952, compared with 218,000 in 1969.

The remarkable upsurge in agricultural production has been the result mainly of a shift to high-value products, improvement of old terraces on the mountain slopes, expansion of the irrigated area, greater use of fertilizers, pesticides, improved seeds, and better systems of crop rotation.

Most of the agricultural production comes from Lebanon's parcelized holdings. The size of land holdings ranges from less than 5 acres to more than 250. Most of the fragmented holdings are in the mountainous regions and are cultivated by the farmers who own them. The few tenant farmers pay for the use of the land either in kind or in cash. The large farms, which are operated by absentee landowners, are on the coast or in the interior plains. Agricultural credit and other services to the farmers are provided by the Agricultural, Industrial and Real Estate Credit Bank.

The main problem confronting the arboriculture industry of Lebanon is a shrinking market, now that other Mediterranean countries (Greece, Italy, Israel, and Turkey) also have increased their production of fruits. But lower prices, together with improvements in sorting, grading, packing, storing, and transporting, may well bring further increases in exports in the coming years.

At present, agricultural crops come from about 38 per cent of the total area of Lebanon, and, because of the increasing pressure of population upon the land, most of the easily accessible and well-watered mountain slopes have been terraced. One of the chief aims of the government's current Development Plan is to encourage more effective use of the several hundred thousand acres of land classified as cultivable on these slopes. A special agency was created in 1964 to carry out a program of terracing, deep plowing, and constructing irrigation canals and roads to market centers in these areas. The farmers repay the agency for the costs in annual installments over a ten-year period. The agency also promotes reforestation, not only for much needed wood, but because the roots of the trees help to prevent soil erosion.

Another aim of the Development Plan is to raise the quality and quantity of poultry and livestock produce so as to increase the share of produce in the daily diet and reduce imports. Outstanding progress has already been made, especially in the poultry industry; between 1959 and 1968, the number of birds rose from 2 million to 15 million.

A national plan for the rational use of water has been launched, which includes a detailed survey of existing facilities and of the surface and underground water supply, the provision of more mechanical pumps, the digging of irrigation and drainage channels, the building of dams and storage reservoirs, and, above all, greater use of the Litani and Hasbani rivers. A dam now being built on the Litani will provide water to irrigate some 50,000 acres. It will also generate ultimately about 626 million killowatt-hours of electricity per year, or twice as much as is now available. If carried out as planned—and the government has created new departments and agencies and is training technical advisers to do so—these schemes will undoubtedly raise crop production appreciably and may even make it possible to allocate some land to forage crops that could support large herds of cattle and sheep. The planned new highways and asphalted secondary roads will facilitate the transport of agricultural products to local markets and ports.

Industrial Growth

Industry also has grown in the last few years despite such unfavorable factors as the lack of raw materials and cheap power and the scarcity of trained personnel and local capital. The number of industrial workers, the amount of capital invested, and the value of industrial output have more than doubled since 1950. The industries that experienced rapid growth were those of clothing, footwear, textiles, printing and publishing, wool products, furniture, petroleum, mineral and metal products, and foodstuffs and beverages. For example, the number of food-manufacturing plants increased from 616 in 1950 to 2,424 in 1965. Although industrial development has been due mainly to private enterprise, the government has aided it by extending credit, initiating such plans as the Litani River Project to increase the production of electricity, exempting certain raw materials from import duties, exempting new companies from income taxes for several years, promoting free competition, and establishing the Industrial Research Institute.

Apart from oil refining at Tripoli and Sayda, and cement making at Ras Shikka, industries are small, individually or family owned, and concentrate mostly on light consumer goods, such as foods, beverages, textiles, shoes, furniture, and tobacco. Approximately half of the industries in Lebanon are located in Beirut. In order to avoid further concentration of industry in Beirut, the government is thinking of establishing industrial zones or parks in Tripoli and Sayda. The government operates only the key utilities, such as the Beirut Electricity Service.

In spite of the progress made, industry's contribution to the national income is still less than 15 per cent, and any great expansion seems unlikely because of the shortage of basic raw materials and the Lebanese businessman's traditional preference for trade.

Tourism, Trade, and Services

If properly developed, tourism could become the most important industry of Lebanon. The country has much to offer the tourist—old Crusader and Arab forts; ancient Greco-Roman monuments (Baalbak); Byblos (now Jubayl), one of the oldest continuously inhabited cities in the world; Sidon (now Sayda), the greatest of the Phoenician trading cities until 1200 B.C. It also has peaceful beaches and a pleasant summer climate, snow-covered mountains in the winter, picturesque mountain villages, the Cedars of Lebanon, the Baalbak Music Festival, and the first known example of alphabetical writing (in the Beirut Museum). The number of tourists rose from 37,000 in 1948 to more than 1.5 million in 1968, and the government, well aware of the potential income to be derived from tourism, is encouraging the improvement and expansion of accommodations.

At present, tourism, trade, and services provide 75 per cent of the nation's income. Thanks to its foreign-exchange reserves and worldwide contacts and its policy of abolishing exchange controls, the enlarging of the free zone in the port of Beirut, and the building of an international airport, Beirut has become one of the main trading and financial centers of the Middle East, in spite of the fall of the Intra Bank in 1966. It has no less than sixty-eight local banks and seventeen branches of foreign banks and is headquarters for dozens of Western business firms.

Among the principal exports are vegetables and fruits (24 per cent), gold and gems (15 per cent), and textiles (7 per cent); the chief buyers are Saudi Arabia, Iraq, Jordan, and Syria. Although the United Kingdom, France, West Germany, and the United States are Lebanon's main sources of industrial products, their imports from Lebanon are meager. Lebanon's imports consist mostly of food, textiles, clothing, household appliances, machinery, chemicals, petroleum products, transport vehicles, gold and gems, and luxury items, the demand for which is rising with the rising standard of living.

Services in financial and trade transactions go a long way toward paying for the imports. Donations from Lebanese emigrants abroad also contribute sizable sums to the national income. Nevertheless, there is a growing trade imbalance. Exports currently cover only about one-fifth of imports. Were it not for the large inflow of foreign capital and the very large income from transit trade, the situation would be critical. The current emphasis on increasing agricultural production, agricultural exports, and tourism should help to alleviate the imbalance.

The Future

Although heavy reliance on trade and services may be a somewhat precarious economic base, Lebanon's Gross National Product is rising. Agricultural and industrial production and exports are increasing. Almost 90 per cent of the Lebanese are literate. Beirut's universities and technical schools are turning out an increasing number of trained individuals, notably engineers, doctors, and dentists. The average per-capita income of about $350 a year is far higher than in most newly independent states. However, the age-old problem of unequal distribution of wealth remains a serious handicap to development in Lebanon as in many other countries in the Middle East.

The 14 per cent of the population deriving income from commerce, finance, and rents absorb as much as 46 per cent of the Gross National Product, whereas the 50 per cent engaged in agriculture get only 15 per cent. And, unfortunetely, the Lebanese rich have a taste for luxuries. Social legislation put through to distribute taxes more equitably has had little effect because of widespread tax evasion among members of the upper brackets. In any case, most tax revenue comes from sales taxes, which hit the poor relatively far more than the rich. Nevertheless, although the rich are getting very much richer and the poor only a little less poor, there is less real poverty in Lebanon than there was in pre-independence days and than there is in many of the neighboring countries. The development plans now under way should bring further expansion of the economy and tangible benefits to the nation as a whole.

Suggested Readings

FEDDEN, H. R. *Syria and Lebanon*. London: John Murray, 1965. Traveler's description of Syria and Lebanon, with emphasis on history and historic ruins.

GLUBB, JOHN BAGOT. *Syria, Lebanon, Jordan*. London: Thames and Hudson, 1967. A concise history of the area, with several chapters on evolving social customs.

GULICK, JOHN. *Tripoli: A Modern Arab City*. Cambridge: Harvard University Press, 1967. A study by a social anthropologist of urbanization and evolving social attitudes.

HITTI, PHILIP KHURI. *Lebanon in History: From the Earliest Time to the Present*. New York: Macmillan, 1957. A comprehensive and well-documented history.

KHURI, FUAD I. "The Changing Class Structure in Lebanon." *Middle East Journal*, XXIII (Winter, 1969), pp. 29-44. Discusses the evolution of the class structure, the meaning of class, class mobility, and the lack of antagonism between classes.

United States Department of Commerce. *Basic Data on the Economy of Lebanon*, no. 69-28, Washington, D.C., June, 1969. An up-to-date summary of developments in all sectors of Lebanon's economy, with statistical tables.

12 SYRIA*

*The People · Landscape and Climate · Crops and Land Reform ·
Water for Irrigation · Industry, Trade, and Transport · Political
Preoccupations · The Future ·* focus *on the Role of Irrigation
in an Evolving Society*

In Syria as in many other states that have recently achieved independence,
new forms of government, new techniques, and new attitudes and aspirations
are transforming both the social structure and the economy. This evolution
is most apparent in the cities, where the Europeanized middle class is
strongest and where industrialization, commerce, and services are increasing
the opportunities for profitable enterprises and jobs. Although the villages
are strongholds of Arab and Muslim traditions, much is changing there, too.
In the larger villages, modern schools, along with transistor radios, are
transmitting to the young a desire for innovations. New paved roads are
multiplying links with the cities. And, in many villages, the introduction of
new crops and methods has begun to alter the traditional ways of the
farmer and appreciably raise agricultural output and income.

The People

Approximately one third of Syria's 5.7 million people live in cities, mainly
in the modern metropolises of Damascus (Dimashq) and Aleppo (Halab),
which together have over a million inhabitants, and in Homs (Hims),
Hamath (Hamah), Latakia (Al Ladhiqiyah), and Dayr az Zawr. These urban

---

* This chapter is based partly on material contributed by James Hudson.

residents, and especially those who make up the new commercial and professional middle class, are gradually bridging the age-old gap between the very rich and the very poor. They move with equal ease in the old sections of the cities, with their bazaars and craftsmen's shops, and in the modern commercial core, with its high-rise office buildings and rows of stores, restaurants, hotels, cinemas, factories, and warehouses. Many are graduates of Syrian or foreign universities; many enjoy a comfortable standard of living. It is these sophisticated urban dwellers, with their emphasis on youth, knowledge, progress, and the welfare of the country

Courtesy Socony Mobil Oil Company

These modern apartments with their well-watered gardens are in the new part of Damascus, near the border between the fertile oasis, gift of the Barada River, and the surrounding barren, desolate hills. Deep, pillared terraces help to temper the heat of the summer sun.

as a whole, who have sparked a variety of projects that have contributed to Syria's rising prosperity during the last few years.

The majority of the Syrian people, however, live in villages scattered through the country and are dependent upon the produce of their farms. Some of these rural people enjoy a standard of living comparable to that of urban dwellers. Mechanized methods of farming, cooperative operations, and the extension of irrigation through the installation of pumps and the building of huge dams have given many farmers the opportunity to raise their output and improve their health and education. In the Five-Year Plans inaugurated since 1960, the Syrian Government has made a determined effort to expand schooling in rural areas (secondary-school enrollment nearly tripled between 1963 and 1967), and in many places a rural youth now has a chance to step from one way of life to another.

In other villages, life goes on much as it has for untold centuries. Farmers follow ox-drawn wooden plows across fields that they have laboriously irrigated by primitive and time-consuming methods; families crowd in dirt-floored huts, accepting the ills that plague them with little knowledge of their causes or cures.

The vast dry lands bordering the desert are the home of the tribal nomads. These nomads wander in kin groups with their herds of sheep or goats. Their loyalty is primarily to members of the kin group, and they are largely unconcerned with the broader life of the nation. Their numbers have been decreasing as many have shifted to settled farming, and they now make up only about 5 per cent of the population.

Landscape and Climate

Syria is usually divided into five regions: the Mediterranean coast and mountains in the northwest; the central plains, which extend from Homs north to Aleppo and then east to the Euphrates (Al Furat) River; the southwestern area around Damascus; the northeastern plains along and beyond the Euphrates; and the desert.

The Mediterranean region in the northwest consists of a narrow coastal strip backed by rugged limestone mountains and hills. It has about 10 per cent of the people of Syria. Although this area receives considerable rainfall and is thickly populated, it has remained relatively undeveloped, largely because of the social isolation of the main element of the population, the Alouites. Neither irrigation nor terracing has been widely practiced here, in contrast to the physically similar Lebanon Mountains (Jabal

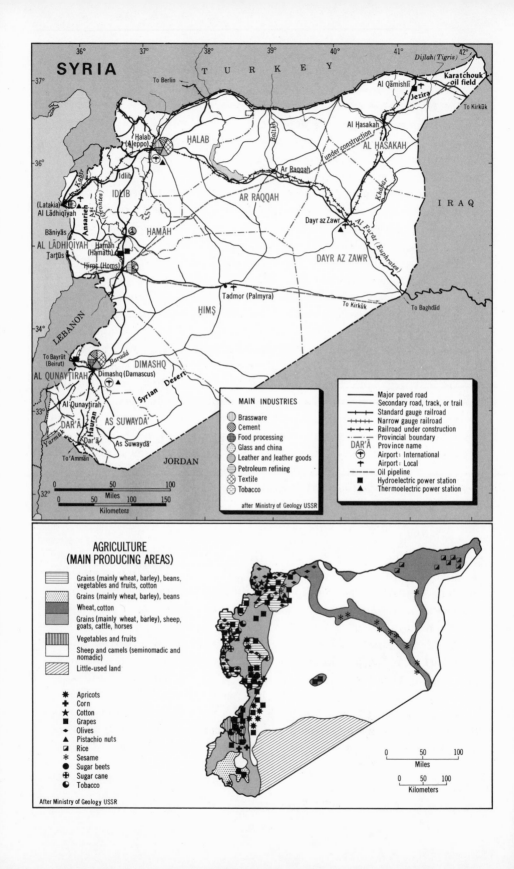

SYRIA

MAIN INDUSTRIES

after Ministry of Geology USSR

- Brassware
- Cement
- Food processing
- Glass and china
- Leather and leather goods
- Petroleum refining
- Textile
- Tobacco

| Major paved road
| Secondary road, track, or trail
| Standard gauge railroad
| Narrow gauge railroad
| Railroad under construction
| Provincial boundary

DAR'Ā Province name
⊕ Airport: International
✛ Airport: Local
Oil pipeline
■ Hydroelectric power station
▲ Thermoelectric power station

AGRICULTURE
(MAIN PRODUCING AREAS)

- Grains (mainly wheat, barley), beans, vegetables and fruits, cotton
- Grains (mainly wheat, barley), beans
- Wheat, cotton
- Grains (mainly wheat, barley), sheep, goats, cattle, horses
- Vegetables and fruits
- Sheep and camels (seminomadic and nomadic)
- Little-used land

- ✳ Apricots
- ✚ Corn
- ★ Cotton
- ■ Grapes
- ◆ Olives
- ▲ Pistachio nuts
- ▨ Rice
- ✳ Sesame
- ● Sugar beets
- ⊕ Sugar cane
- ● Tobacco

After Ministry of Geology USSR

Lubnan) to the south. Wheat, olives, and tobacco have been the traditional crops. Now, however, better communications are bringing increasing contact with other parts of the country, and extensive areas have been planted in cotton and citrus. Also, the coastal cities are being developed as ports. A new general port has been built at Latakia; Baniyas has become a terminal for an oil pipeline from Iraq; and the new port of Tartus has been created.

The Homs-Aleppo-Euphrates region may be termed the core of the nation. Even though it does not contain the capital, it has nearly half (45 per cent) of the total population. Most of this vast, undulating plain is planted with wheat, with patches of olive groves here and there. Along the Orontes (Asi) River are the Ghab marshes, currently being drained and developed for irrigated crops. In the north, Aleppo, Syria's second largest city, with a population of 580,000, is the regional capital. In the south, the rival cities of Homs and Hamath (each having about 200,000 people) serve as local centers.

The Damascus-southwest region, separated from the core by the northern fringes of the Anti-Lebanon Mountains (Al Jabalash Sharqi), has a more varied landscape and about 27 per cent of the total population. Damascus, the national capital, with 620,000 inhabitants, is surrounded by the Ghouta, which consists mainly of small irrigated plots thickly dotted with olive and fruit trees. The Hauran, to the south of Damascus, is mostly wheat fields. Dark basaltic rocks are strewn over the surface, and these are used in construction, giving the villages a somber appearance.

The northeast, along and east of the Euphrates, is known as the Jezira. It consists of plains in the far northeast and along the Euphrates and a flat desert belt in between. Sparsely populated until after World War II, the Jezira has since been developed for large-scale mechanized dry farming and pump-irrigation agriculture. It now has 16 per cent of the population, produces a large share of Syria's wheat and cotton, and has been the site of recent petroleum discoveries, making it one of the nation's richest regions, with fast-growing towns and cities imbued somewhat with a raw frontier atmosphere.

The dry Syrian Desert occupies more than a quarter of the country's 71,228 square miles of land and is of little economic value except to the few herdsmen who trek across its vast empty spaces in pursuit of water and food for their flocks.

Traditionally, the Syrians have tended to cluster in areas where there is a fairly reliable source of water from rivers or wells, or where there is some rainfall, however scanty and seasonal. There are two seasons: a comparatively mild, moist winter and a dry, hot summer. Rainfall occurs almost solely in winter.

The rainfall pattern is influenced by proximity to the Mediterranean Sea and by the mountains, most of which are parallel to the coast. The most humid region, the coast and mountains in the northwest, gets from twenty-four to forty inches of rain per year, enough for the cultivation of rain-fed crops.

East of the mountains, a belt stretching from the Turkish border through Aleppo, Hamath, Homs, and Damascus to the Jordanian border is drier; much of it gets less than fifteen inches a year.

The Jezira, in the far northeastern corner of Syria, however, intersects another belt of rainfall, associated with the Kurdish Mountains of northern Iraq and southeastern Turkey. The annual rainfall here ranges from twelve to twenty-four inches. In the eastern desert, the average is only about six inches or less.

Everywhere rainfall is extremely variable, so that rain-fed agriculture is risky, and widespread disasters caused by long droughts are a recurring threat.

Crops and Land Reform

Wheat and cotton dominate agriculture. Wheat, the traditional crop, is grown throughout inhabited Syria, the most productive districts being the villages of the Aleppo-Homs-Euphrates area and the newly developed farm lands of the Jezira. Since wheat is an unirrigated crop, total production can vary by as much as three times from a humid to a dry year.

Very little cotton was grown until after World War II, when a spectacular increase in production took place. Today, cotton brings in 53 per cent of the total export revenue. More than 60 per cent of the cotton is grown on irrigated lands along the Euphrates and the Jezira; much of the rest comes from irrigated fields around Aleppo. Syria's present dependence upon cotton for a large share of its foreign exchange is a source of some apprehension in view of the fluctuations in the world cotton market; but the Syrians say they could easily shift to a more profitable crop in the event of a big drop in prices.

Other crops include barley, grown in association with wheat in many places, and millet, sorghum, and vetch (a fodder crop). Sugar beets are grown mainly around Damascus and Homs, both of which have sugar refineries. The main olive groves are west of Aleppo and on the Mediterranean coast and nearby mountains; the main grape-growing areas are scattered through the semiarid belt from Aleppo south to the Jordanian border.

The raising of sheep, goats, asses, and cattle is another principal source of income. Sheep, able to find food on the drier lands, are the most numerous (5.4 million), and they are multiple-purpose animals, providing wool, leather, meat, and milk.

In the past, in Syria, as in most Arab countries, a few rich landholders owned a large proportion of the cultivable land, and many of the farmers were poor tenants or laborers. But, since 1958, the Syrian government has made efforts to break up large holdings and redistribute the land to landless peasants on easy terms. Although it has not been entirely successful, this land reform has acted as a powerful incentive to increase farm production. Perhaps equally significant has been the support given to agriculture by private enterprise. The postwar boom in farm output is in large part attributable to a new figure: the urban merchant. Whereas traditionally Syrian merchants have confined their investments to commercial ventures, many are now renting or purchasing unfarmed land and bringing it under cultivation, using machinery, hired workers, and modern irrigation methods.

Water for Irrigation

In view of the scantiness of the rainfall and the seasonal and yearly variations, irrigation is a prime requisite for increasing both yields per acre and the area under cultivation. Irrigation has long been practiced in Syria. Under Roman rule and later under seventh- and eighth-century Arab rulers, extensive irrigation systems were built, which distributed water over large areas. These, however, fell into disrepair over the centuries that followed, and it is only in the last few decades that major efforts have been made to increase irrigation. Now, modern pumps installed by individual farmers are increasingly taking the place of *norias* (great wooden wheels turned by a river's current), bringing water to many thousands of previously dry fields. Much of the newly irrigated land is along the Euphrates and its tributaries, but modern pump systems have also been built in the vicinity of Aleppo and Homs. There are also several government projects under construction, including those in the Ghab-Acharheh-Roudj area, which now drain and irrigate more than 170,000 acres of former swamp along the Orontes River northwest of Hamath. Construction has also begun on a Euphrates dam, which is destined to provide water for an estimated 1.7

million acres. Still in the planning stages is the Khabur River scheme, which is to irrigate 250,000 acres in the northern Jezira.

Industry, Trade, and Transport

The ancient crafts of goldsmithing, silverworking, brassworking, leather-working, and the weaving of superlative damask are still practiced, but modern industry has been expanding rapidly, partly as a result of govern-ment initiative, partly as a result of individual enterprise, often in con-junction with the government.

Agricultural commodities provide most of the raw materials for industry. First in importance are the making of textiles and the processing of foods such as wheat, barley, sugar, olive oil, and fruits. Other factories produce cement, furniture, glass and dishes, toothpaste and soap, and cigarettes.

Most of the factories have been dependent upon imported petroleum for power. However, the recently discovered fields at Karatchouk, in the north-east, are supplying increasing quantities of petroleum, and a recently completed pipeline is bringing it to the new refinery at Homs and to the port of Tartus. Almost all electric power is produced by thermal plants using petroleum products as fuel; the new dam being built on the Eu-phrates should provide large amounts of additional electricity. The problem of energy for homes and industries thus appears to be nearing solution.

The Syrians have long been merchants, and the tradition continues in modern times in the many retail and wholesale establishments, the bazaar shops, and the modern stores that handle both domestic and foreign goods. The chief imports are manufactures, mainly from West Germany, the United States, and, more recently, the Soviet Union. Syria's exports consist almost entirely of agricultural products or items made from such products, such as wheat, barley, and textiles, sold primarily to Lebanon, the People's Republic of China, and Cuba.

Motor vehicles are the most common means of transporting people and goods. Cars, taxis, buses, and trucks provide rapid, cheap, and frequent service. In the populated west, paved roads reach to or near almost all villages; in the more sparsely peopled east, they are rarer. The second Five-Year Plan, inaugurated in 1966, called for widespread improvement of arterial highways, the construction of a new international airport at Damascus, the completion of a railroad between Latakia on the Mediter-ranean coast and Al Qamishli in the agriculturally rich northeast, and further improvement of facilities in the ports of Latakia and Tartus.

Political Preoccupations

Since Syria announced its independence in 1945, politics have been dominated by four issues: Palestine, Arab unity, relations with the great powers, and internal policy.

The Syrians, like many other Arabs, did not accept the loss of the major part of Palestine to Israel in 1949, and this has continued to be a burning issue. In fact, Syria has tended to be more irredentist about Palestine than many other Arab states. The outcome of the June, 1967, war, in which the rest of Palestine and a corner of Syria were occupied by Israel, has apparently reinforced this feeling.

Arab unity is another stated goal of Syrian politicians. The Syrians were the main force behind the 1958 merger with Egypt in the United Arab Republic. Although this merger broke up in 1961, Syria has continued to work for Arab unity and is currently a member of the emerging federation consisting of the United Arab Republic (Egypt), Libya, and possibly the Sudan.

In their relations with the great powers, the Syrians have usually followed a policy that may be described as pro-Soviet neutrality. That is, they have drawn away from the Western powers and closer to the Soviet bloc, but have not become part of it. Most technical advisers, for example, have been from the Soviet bloc.

Internal policy disputes have centered around who was to lead the nation in which direction. Usually, no single group has been strong enough to rule alone; a succession of governments has been formed on the basis of ephemeral alliances and terminated by coups. At present, Syria is similar to Iraq, the United Arab Republic, and Algeria in having a socialist-nationalist-military government.

The Future

Although Syria does not have the vast petroleum reserves of some Arab states, its agricultural resources are relatively rich, and there is no serious pressure upon resources. The rate of population growth is high, nearly 3 per cent a year, but the national income has grown on the average nearly 6 per cent per year. Thus there has been a steady increase in real per-capita income. Although the gap between the rich and the poor is still wide, it is gradually narrowing. Although adequate housing, medical care, and education are still a dream for many, between 10,000 and 20,000 new housing units are being erected annually, and both health and educational services are improving.

If agriculture, industry, and commerce continue to expand at present rates, the average Syrian should enjoy a rising standard of living. If the political situation in Syria becomes more stable, tourism should provide additional income. Syria has much to offer to the tourist in its climate, its crafts, its magnificent Muslim monuments, and its ruins, such as Palmyra (Tadmor), once ruled by the beautiful Queen Zenobia. In general, political rather than economic problems appear to be in the foreground of public consciousness. The Syrians are dissatisfied with the current political situation and are divided on the solutions to be sought. This dissatisfaction and division may be the nation's most basic problem for the future.

focus *on the Role of Irrigation in an Evolving Society*

For many hundreds of years, the Syrian farmer has attempted to find more water for his crops, because of the inadequacy of rainfall or its unreliability during the growing season. The most common sources have been springs and rivers. If there was no nearby spring or river, the farmer sought subterranean sources and ways of getting the water to the surface and onto the land.

Of the earliest farmers and their techniques we know little, except that they probably made water-proofed baskets and skin buckets to transport water from a spring or stream. Perhaps the oldest record of an attempt to deal scientifically with the problems of irrigation is the Hammurabi Code, compiled by the Babylonians in Mesopotamia (in present-day Iraq) in the twenty-third century B.C. Many of the irrigation techniques used in Syria came from Mesopotamia, including the *shaduf* (a long, suspended rod with a bucket at one end and a weight at the other), which was to become so much a part of irrigation in Egypt.

The Persians, who followed the Babylonians, probably introduced the *qanat* system, which was primarily of value to farmers living on a dry plain near a hill. First a canal was dug to the edge of the mountain slope. Then a tunnel about two feet wide and four feet high was bored into the mountain. The bed was kept almost level. Stones and dirt were removed from the tunnel in buckets lowered through vertical shafts excavated at intervals. Digging into the hill continued until water-bearing strata were reached and water began to flow by gravity through the tunnel into the

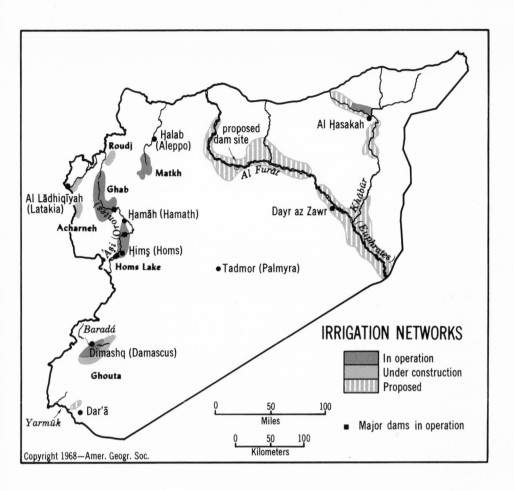

IRRIGATION NETWORKS

In operation
Under construction
Proposed

■ Major dams in operation

Copyright 1968—Amer. Geogr. Soc.

channel and thence to the farmers' fields. Where the vertical shafts used in removing debris filled with water, they became wells. Where other water-bearing strata were found nearby, branch tunnels were dug. Some of these ancient *qanat* networks were five miles long and brought a reliable supply of water to several acres. *Qanats* are still used in Syria today, but few new ones are being built, for, even with modern machinery, it is costly to keep the tunnels free of dirt.

The Persians also brought to Syria two devices for lifting water. One of these was the *challaf* (called the *doulab* in the Aleppo area), used in the Ghouta of Damascus. This consisted of a large vertical wheel set on a horizontal beam across the opening of a well. Attached to the wheel along its circumference were buckets or scoops. The horizontal beam was

SYRIA   159

attached to an upright beam beyond the well. By means of interlocking wooden gears on both beams, turned by a horse or donkey pacing around and around, the horizontal beam and its wheel revolved, and buckets scooped up water and spilled it into a channel. This device gave a continuous supply of water as long as the animal kept circling.

Lifting devices such as the *challaf* could irrigate only relatively small areas, but they can be adapted for modern use. Instead of man- or animal-power, motors can run them, greatly increasing their capacity and effectiveness.

Similar to the *challaf* but more sophisticated is the *noria*, still seen today along the Orontes River. The *noria* is a huge wheel, up to seventy feet in diameter, with buckets attached to it. It is turned by the force of the river's current and lifts water into an aqueduct.

Great cities in Syria generally grew up where such irrigation methods were practiced. Perhaps the most famous of these was Damascus, located near the foot of the Anti-Lebanon ridge. Although the ridge steals from the city most of the moisture coming in from the Mediterranean Sea, it provides a great gift: the Barada River. Without the Barada, Damascus would long since have merged into the neighboring desert. This river coming down from the mountains rushes through a deep gorge where the Damascenes captured it and built an intricate series of channels, creating an oasis of roughly 400 square miles, every square foot of which was cultivated. Wheat or barley was planted among the olive trees, and clover among the apricots, and vegetables were grown wherever there was room for them. Damascus was one of the earliest examples of careful and successful conservation of water resources. It reigned supreme among Syrian cities as a vital link in the trade routes between the great empires of the time.

The glory of Damascus paled when Syria became part of the Roman Empire, not because the Romans challenged its preeminence, but because, through irrigation, they expanded cultivation to many other areas. The Roman road was extended to Syria and so too was the *limes* system, whereby fortified towns formed a protective line of communication along a frontier. With the establishment of fortified towns came the need for water, and the Romans therefore set up elaborate systems of irrigation. Waterworks of all kinds were introduced or expanded: large and small dams, canals, cisterns, aqueducts, and waterwheels. Towns that had never been and would never again be of great importance, such as the desert city of Palmyra, suddenly blossomed under the hands of the Romans. Among the ruins of Palmyra today may be found the remains of a wide Roman road paralleled by the pipes that once carried the precious water to the city.

Syria achieved a peak of agricultural productivity under the Roman Empire such as it was not to achieve again until the seventh and eighth centuries A.D., when for a while its Arab rulers restored and even expanded some of the fine irrigation works built by the Romans. Thereafter, many were allowed to fall into disuse, and large areas that had flourished became barren and deserted.

It was not until the end of World War II that the Syrians once again made massive efforts to realize more fully the potential of their land. Surprisingly, the projects this time were not primarily government-sponsored, as in the past, but, rather, were small projects undertaken by individuals willing to invest in improvements. The scope of their achievements may be indicated by the fact that irrigated lands increased from 586,000 acres in 1947 to 1.6 million acres in 1968, and a large proportion of this increase was due to the efforts of the owners themselves. Most of the irrigation projects they initiated concentrated on getting more water from rivers and wells by improved cement-lined canals to cut down on losses by seepage and improved techniques of pumping. At present, more than 13,000 mechanical pumps are in use, where a few years ago there were none.

However, large projects have also been undertaken by the Syrian Government in recent years: The Five-Year Plan for 1960–65 allocated nearly 40 per cent of all public expenditures to irrigation. One of the most ambitious schemes was the combined irrigation and reclamation of the Ghab-Acharheh-Roudj area, which started in 1954 and is near completion today. Where the Orontes flowed through the Ghab Valley, its course had been blocked for centuries by the building up of a hard basaltic sill, and its waters had backed up in the valley, creating a huge swamp covering well over 800,000 acres. This swamp was drained, dams were built to control the flow of the Orontes and to store water, and thus far more than 170,000 acres have been reclaimed and irrigated, most of which had not previously been used for cultivation. Along with the irrigation works, roads were built and whole new settlements established: Some 50,000 resettled farmers are now growing crops in the area. This was a major undertaking of great value, for it transformed a wasteland into highly valuable farm land producing large summer crops of rice, cotton, sugar beets, and pulses, and large winter crops of wheat, barley, vetch, and clover. More recently, another project was inaugurated nearby that will supply water for a similar area.

Other government projects include a dam southwest of Aleppo, which will eventually irrigate nearly 12,500 acres; another south of Aleppo, to water more than 30,000 acres; and one in the south on the Yarmuk River, to provide controlled winter irrigation and increased summer irrigation for some 16,500 acres. With these projects and others proposed for the Khabur Valley and along the Euphrates, Syria could probably triple its irrigated area.

The extension of irrigation during the last few years has been a prime factor in Syria's rising prosperity and its evolution from a traditional to a modern society. Bringing more water to existing crop lands and to land formerly bare has helped to increase both yields and acreages and hence total farm output.

The growth of Syria's two largest industries, textiles and food-processing, based on its agricultural products, has in turn created new jobs in these and a variety of other industries and also in commerce and services. Furthermore, the rise in cotton exports has supplied larger foreign revenues, which can be used to pay for imported manufactured goods—goods that more people can now afford because they are making more money.

With rising incomes, increasing funds have been available for building roads, schools, and health facilities, which have helped to improve the mobility, education, and welfare of a sizable proportion of the population and to diffuse new attitudes and customs.

Suggested Readings

CANTOR, LEONARD M. *A World Geography of Irrigation.* London: Oliver and Boyd, 1967. A study of irrigation methods (past and present), water supplies, conservation, and the finances involved. Emphasis on regional studies and irrigation projects throughout the world.

FEDDEN, ROBIN. *Syria and Lebanon.* London: John Murray, 1965. Traveler's description of Syria and Lebanon with emphasis on history and historic ruins.

GLUBB, JOHN BAGOT. *Syria, Lebanon, Jordan.* London: Thames and Hudson, 1967. A concise history of the area, with several chapters on evolving social customs.

HOURANI, A. H. *Syria and Lebanon: A Political Essay.* New York: Oxford University Press, 1946. Emphasizes westernization, Arab nationalism, and political history between the two world wars.

U.S. Army Area Handbook for Syria. Washington, D.C.: U.S. Government Printing Office, 1965. Social, political, and economic background.

13 THE REPUBLIC OF TURKEY

John Kolars

Genesis of the Republic and the Kemalist Reforms • Early Efforts Toward Economic Development • Developments Since 1945 • Vexing Problems • The Resource Base • focus *on the Villager's Role in a Half Century of Change*

Turkey occupies a strategic position at a crossroads of land and sea routes between Europe, the Soviet Union, and the other countries of the Middle East and North Africa. This has long made it a center of international controversy and more recently has given it a key role in the North Atlantic Treaty Organization (NATO).

Of even greater interest to many is its continuing program of economic and social development, begun in the mid-1920's. While maintaining the third largest land army in the noncommunist world, Turkey has succeeded in providing its people with the highest per-capita caloric intake among the nations of the Middle East. It produces more steel than Israel and the United Arab Republic combined. Among those Middle Eastern countries that lack significant petroleum reserves, it is third in per-capita consumption of energy, after Israel and Lebanon. It also ranks third in per-capita use of newsprint and, in the last six years, has been surpassed only by Israel in increasing its index of agricultural production.

These and other economic achievements have been accompanied by far-reaching social reforms, despite a turbulent political situation. What, then, is the lesson of Turkey? What are the reasons for its successes, and what are some of the large problems still facing the nation?

Genesis of the Republic and the Kemalist Reforms

Early in the eleventh century A.D., Turkish tribes began moving in large numbers out of their homeland in central Asia. By 1071, one group, the Seljuks, had defeated the Byzantine Empire at the Battle of Manzekirt in eastern Anatolia (Anadolu) and had established a new capital at Konya, from which they ruled for several centuries. Weakened by subsequent Mongol invasions, the Seljuks offered another Turkish tribe, the Osmanlis, the role of guardians of the marches in northwestern Anatolia, on the borders of the shrinking Byzantine Empire. The Osmanlis, known today in the West as Ottomans, gained valuable experience from their contacts with Europeans and rapidly grew in strength. The fairness of their government, especially in contrast with that of the corrupt Byzantines, attracted many Christian followers. Turning their backs on the Seljuks and bypassing the Byzantine capital of Constantinople, the Ottomans moved westward into Europe. Adrianople (modern Edirne) fell to their forces in 1360; the Serbians were defeated in 1389. In the next century, the Ottomans consolidated their position in the Balkans and Anatolia. In 1453, they captured the eastern Roman capital after a long siege; Constantinople of the Byzantines became Istanbul of the Turks. In the sixteenth century, the Ottoman Empire extended as far as the gates of Vienna, and the lands of the declining Arab kingdoms with few exceptions fell under Ottoman control.

Once the empire had reached its height, the indolent court life of Istanbul and the intrigues of the seraglio took their toll. Beginning with Sultan Selim I (1512–20), the character of Ottoman rule gradually changed, and, although there were some great and wise rulers, such as Suleiman I, the Magnificent (1521–66), the evils of farming out the collection of taxes, ruling by proxy, and impressing men into the sultan's army became common. By the end of the nineteenth century, the Ottoman Empire, weakened by corruption, had lost many of its territories and was known as the "sick man of Europe."

But, while the "sick man" continued to decline, forces of reform were at work. Turks who had been educated in the West as well as others who had come to admire Western ways slowly instituted new and liberal policies within the government. By 1909, a group of reformers had ended the absolute rule of the sultan. It is interesting to note that these agents of reform are known to the West as "Young Turks," but they referred to themselves as "Ottoman Liberals."

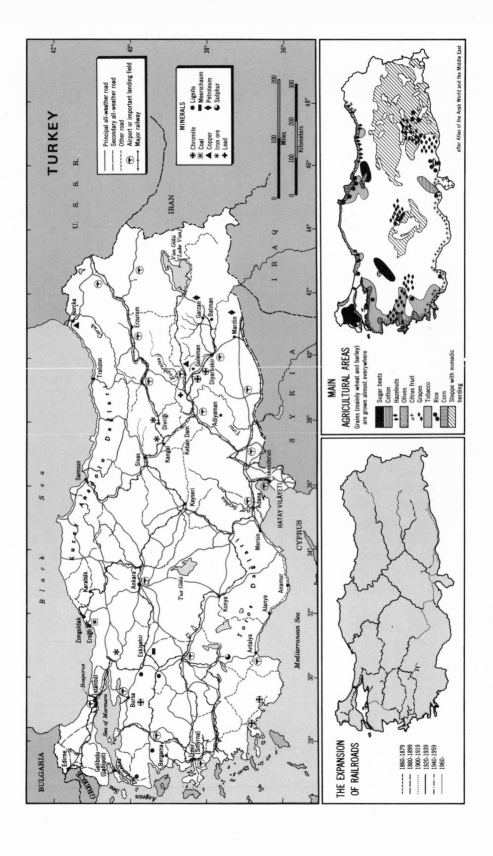

TURKEY

Principal all-weather road
Secondary all-weather road
Other road
Airport or important landing field
Major railway

MINERALS

⊕ Chromite   • Lignite
✠ Coal   ■ Meerschaum
▲ Copper   ◆ Petroleum
✳ Iron ore   ⊕ Sulphur
+ Lead

Miles
0   100   200
Kilometers
0   100   200   300

U. S. S. R.

IRAN

IRAQ

SYRIA

CYPRUS

HATAY VILAYETI

BULGARIA

GREECE

Black Sea

Sea of Marmara

Mediterranean Sea

Aegean Sea

Bosporus

Boncka

Erzurum

Garzan
Batman
Mardin

Guleman
Diyarbakir
Adiyaman

Van Gölü
(Lake Van)

Trabzon

Divriği

Kangal
Keban Dam

Sivas

Kayseri

İskenderun

Seyhan
Adana
Mersin

Anamur

Alanya

Antalya

Konya

Tuz Gölü

Ankara

Karabük

Zonguldak
Ereğli

İstanbul

Edirne

Gelibolu
(Gallipoli)

Bursa

Eskişehir

Bergama

İzmir
(Smyrna)

Samsun

Kuzey Anadolu Dağları

Toros Dağları

Euphrates

Tigris

MAIN AGRICULTURAL AREAS

Grains (mainly wheat and barley) are grown almost everywhere

Sugar beets
Cotton
Hazelnuts
Olives
Citrus fruit
Grapes
Tobacco
Rice
Corn
Steppe with nomadic herding

after Atlas of the Arab World and the Middle East

THE EXPANSION OF RAILROADS

1860-1879
1880-1899
1900-1919
1920-1939
1940-1959
1960-

Although this group helped to change the sultanate for the better, the reformed sultanate, under the leadership of the war minister, Enver Pasher, made the disastrous mistake of committing the Ottoman Empire to the side of the Central Powers in World War I. The defeat of Germany was paralleled by the downfall of the empire. Military disasters on all fronts left the allies in control of Istanbul and opened the way for subsequent occupation of western, southern, and southeastern Anatolia by Greek, Italian, and French forces. When all seemed lost, a leader appeared on the scene who was to initiate a new series of reforms separating the Republic of Turkey from the Ottoman Empire and starting the new nation on the road to economic and social development years in advance of its Muslim neighbors.

The role of Mustafa Kemal (later called Ataturk, Father of the Turks) as the Turkish commander in the Gallipoli (Gelibolu) Campaign and his trials and victories in uniting the people of Anatolia and expelling a Greek expeditionary force are well known. Suffice it to say here that, following the signing of the Treaty of Lausanne on July 24, 1923, a new political entity known as the Republic of Turkey emerged, with Kemal Ataturk as its leader.

At this point, an understanding of the evolution of modern Turkey becomes paramount. Turkey is not simply the remains of the Ottoman Empire, nor are the modern Turks Ottomans renamed. At its height, the empire included North Africa, the Balkans, the Levant, Mesopotamia, and the western shores of Arabia. Its population consisted of Balkan Europeans, Arabs, Berbers, Turkish-speaking peoples, and countless minorities, such as Jews and Kurds. Islam was the state religion, but Christians often constituted the majority of local populations, and there were enclaves of Jewish, Druze, and other religious minorities. The ruling class of Ottomans was defined as those Muslims who spoke an Istanbul dialect of Osmanli Turkish, lived in the capital city, and accepted the culture complex associated with the sultan's court. The Turkish-speaking peasants of Anatolia were recognized as Turks, but the term Turk applied to them often became derogatory.

With the founding of the republic under Ataturk in 1923, all this changed. The capital was moved from Istanbul to Ankara, Turkey renounced all non-Turkish territories of the empire lost during the war, and the rights of the minorities were assured. In the five years that followed, the caliphate was abolished, a national secular education system was established, the courts of religious law were closed, and legal codes based on those of Switzerland, Italy, and Germany were adopted. In addition, the wearing of the fez was forbidden, the International Fixed Calendar was introduced, and the Latin alphabet replaced Arabic script. Thus the new Turkey represents a geographically more unified entity in the form of a secular state oriented toward Europe and the West. Subsequent exchanges of population with Greece brought Muslim Turkish-speakers back to Anatolia and shifted Christian Greek-speaking people outside the borders of the country. This resulted in a largely homogeneous population, in which slightly more than 91 per cent of the 33 million people speak Turkish as their mother tongue and 99 per cent are Muslims. With the exceptions of a Kurdish minority in the southeast and small Turkish minorities in northern Greece, Yugoslavia, Bulgaria, and Cyprus, Turkey is—unlike the Ottoman Empire—the land of the Turks.

In much the same way, universal suffrage and the focusing of national attention on Anatolia, located in a major agricultural area, rather than Istanbul, has shifted popular support of the government to a largely rural, farming people. This is in sharp contrast to the predominance of the urban element in former times. Moreover, with the single exception of Turkey's occupation of the Hatay Vilayeti in 1938, the republic has assiduously refrained from extraterritorial expansion. When the Republic of Turkey is contrasted with the Ottoman Empire, it can be seen that, geographically, socially, culturally, and politically, there is little justification for equating the Ottomans and the modern Turks.

Early Efforts Toward Economic Development

Once the new government of Mustafa Kemal had instituted a program of social and political reforms, thus establishing the basis for economic development, the problem became one of industrializing an essentially agrarian economy. Rescinding of the infamous Capitulations, which had given foreign interests almost complete freedom to exploit Turkish resources, left the republic heavily in debt and with poor credit ratings. Moreover, little private capital was available in Turkey for investment. Between World War I and World War II, the government adopted a system of state-supported development of critical industries and business. The essential purpose of this policy of *étatisme* was to subsidize and manage those elements of the economy—especially heavy industry and a national infrastructure of finance, transportation, and communication facilities— that lay beyond the means of the private sector and involved the general and vital interests of the nation.

One of the major means by which the government stimulated economic development was through the establishment of banks owned and operated by the state. The most important of these was the Central Bank, which coordinated the nation's finances and replaced the foreign-owned Imperial Ottoman Bank as the main dispenser of funds. An agricultural bank was founded to provide credit for farmers and to stabilize farm prices. Three other banks—the Is Bank, the Sumer Bank, and the Eti Bank—became responsible in part for the financing and development of business, general industry, and mining and power, respectively.

Along with this, two Five-Year Plans were initiated. The first of these (1934) had as its goals (1) the increased production of consumer goods, (2) the development of local raw materials, (3) the creation of a textile industry, and (4) the dispersal throughout the country of industry, then concentrated in and about Istanbul and Izmir (Smyrna). Little attention was given to agriculture. The major industries concerned were textiles, chemicals, earthenware products, iron, and paper. The second Five-Year Plan (1936) focused on producer and capital goods, especially the production of machinery and equipment and the development of electrical facilities, mines, and ports. In addition, heavy industries such as the complex of coal mines at Zonguldak and a steel mill at Karabuk were encouraged. Again, agriculture and transportation were recognized as critical but were largely overlooked.

As a result of these efforts, industrialization slowly began to move forward. After Mustafa Kemal Ataturk died in 1938, his policies were continued by his successor, Ismet Inonu. Per-capita income increased from 73 Turkish lire in 1927 to 95 (about $76) in 1939. Industry's share of the national income increased from TL 241 million in 1929 to 314 million in 1939. Trade, banking, services, and transport and communications remained nearly stable; agriculture showed a decrease in income of nearly 25 per cent.

Developments Since 1945

The brief summary in this section is not intended to be comprehensive but, rather, to indicate a few salient events that helped set the mood of the late 1960's.

While industry was achieving a hesitant start, efforts were made to improve the over-all conditions necessary for farm production and to reduce illiteracy. These included the creation in 1940 of Village Institutes, which, although they were in part political organs of Ataturk's People's

Republican Party, provided public education for village youths who agreed to serve subsequently as rural schoolteachers. At the same time, more schools were built. Agrarian reform was instituted in 1945 with a program of land redistribution. In the period 1945–59, some 4.3 million acres of land were distributed to 345,000 recipients chosen from among refugees from Bulgaria and the landless and near landless indigenous population.

In the first years of World War II, Turkey remained neutral, but it finally declared war on the Axis and later became a member of the newly formed United Nations. In 1948, it became eligible for Marshall Plan aid and also joined the Organization for European Economic Cooperation. American technical assistance and financing further stimulated development. Among the important projects undertaken by the Turks and Americans was a major improvement in the road network. In 1950, another significant event occurred: Free national elections were held, and Ataturk's People's Republican Party stepped aside to let the new Democratic Party peacefully assume power. This transition after years of one-party rule attested to the commitment of the new Turks to westernization.

In the decade that followed, Turkey's international commitments increased (in part through NATO and SHAPE) as did its internal efforts in development. Certain tax reductions were granted to encourage foreign investment. Loans were obtained from the International Bank for Reconstruction and Development. Large-scale importing of farm equipment significantly increased the number of tractors and plows in use. By 1965, the agricultural census recorded 54,668 tractors—compared with 2,749 in 1948. Although the average farm is still too small to allow purchase of such equipment, the over-all changes in the amount of cultivated land, production, and productivity are important. In 1948, only 27 million acres were under cultivation; today the figure is 65 million. Harvests of wheat, the nation's principal food crop, increased from 4.8 million tons to 10 million; cotton lint from 58,000 to 382,000; and citrus fruit from 63,000 to 545,000. Productivity has fluctuated somewhat in wheat, but yields of cotton lint have increased threefold since 1948.

Highway mileage increased rapidly, from 5,600 miles of all-weather roads in 1939 to 21,300 miles in 1965. New dams, such as the one on the Seyhan River, with a capacity of 36,000 kilowatts, increased both irrigated farming and electrical production.

All these developments materially improved life in Turkey, but the newly elected government became more and more deeply committed to a program of large-scale deficit spending. The election had been won by promises made to the rural electorate, and the new government had little choice but to continue to build roads and water-supply systems as well as mosques, schools, and factories as rapidly as possible. Indebtedness depleted the treasury, and foreign creditors became more insistent, until only massive infusions of direct foreign credit could stave off disaster. At the same time, the government became more and more sensitive to criticism and imposed harsh restrictions upon the press as well as harassing its political opposition.

Delays in promised elections, combined with student protests, finally precipitated a coup by the Turkish Army on May 27, 1960. Thereafter, a military junta ruled for a year, until constitutional reform and an election returned a coalition government to power, with Ismet Inonu again at its head. In 1965, the Inonu Government was replaced by that of the Justice Party, with Suleyman Demirel as Prime Minister. Six years later, he, in turn, was forced to resign. His successor, Prime Minister Nihat Erim, has announced that his government intends to nationalize some sectors of the economy, to establish stricter controls on foreign trade and foreign investments, and to carry out further land distribution and tax and other reforms.

Vexing Problems

After the 1960 change of government, the role of planning became more specific in the economy. A State Planning Organization was created, which brought forth two new Five-Year Plans and a longer-term, Fifteen-Year Program of development. Achievement of the 7-per-cent annual growth rate, which these plans consider necessary in order to meet increases in population while raising the standard of living, may be an overambitious goal. On the other hand, the economy seems to have stabilized itself once more, and the imminent completion of such projects as the Keban Dam on the Euphrates (Al Furat) River, with an initial capacity of 1.2 million kilowatts, and the new steel plant at Eregli, which went into production in 1965 with a capacity of 500,000 tons, will offer increased opportunities.

Nevertheless, the years ahead pose several serious problems. Fluctuations in agriculture, due largely to the high variability of rainfall in this semiarid land, make it difficult to balance the food and financial budgets. More irrigation is needed. Problems in the inequality of landownership persist, as do those resulting from the migration of hundreds of thousands of rural people to the cities. Population growth continues, although a new program of population planning is under way. The strain put upon educational facilities by new generations is great, and, although the absolute number of literate people is larger than ever, the percentage increase in the literate population is lagging. Finally, in Turkey as in many developing economies, inflation gnaws away at the gains made in the productive sectors.

The Resource Base

These problems may seem insurmountable, but Turkey is well endowed with natural resources on which to build a strong economy. Although it is not one of the oil-rich nations of the Middle East, the production and refining of petroleum has become important. Small fields in the southeast at Garzan now supply oil to refineries at Batman and Mersin. Another refinery at Izmir refines imported crude oil. The costs of transporting petroleum will be cut by the new Batman-Iskenderun pipeline, which has a capacity of 10,000 to 16,000 tons per day. Production of oil rose from 667,000 tons in 1963 to 3.6 million tons in 1970. However, these resources are scarcely enough to meet the internal needs of the country, and it seems unlikely that large reserves will be found. Iron-ore deposits supplying the nation's mills are found near Kangal and Divrigi southeast of Sivas in central Anatolia. Other minerals of considerable value include coal at Zonguldak, copper deposits near Borcka on the Coruh, and chrome mines near Guleman and in the southwest. Except for chrome, of which Turkey is one of the world's largest producers, the supply of most of these minerals is not large by world standards but they help to meet internal needs. Another mineral of slight economic importance but considerable interest is meerschaum, which is produced in limited quantities near Eskisehir and is used primarily in the manufacture of fine pipes.

The patterns of agriculture reflect the nation's great diversity of landscape and climate. There are five main regions, one of which, the rolling plains of Thrace, lies in Europe. The major portion of the country is Anatolia, in Asia, which is shaped like an elongated bowl with high rims and a flat center. Anatolia includes the narrow coastlands; the high and varied central plateau; the surrounding mountains, the Taurus (Toros) in the south and the Kuzey Anadolu in the north; and the eastern highlands and mountains.

The coastlands are a clement area. In the south and west, a typical Mediterranean climate holds sway with hot, dry summers and mild, rainy

Courtesy Turkish Tourism and Information Office

Turkey is making increasing use of its diversified mineral resources, both for rapidly growing local industries and to bring in much needed foreign revenue. One of the specialized banks, Etibank, handles all the extractive (excluding coal and iron) and electrical-power industries, including this copper mine in Ergani, fifty miles northwest of Diyarbakir.

winters. Along the Black Sea in the north, the shores are again mild in winter, but precipitation is greater throughout the year. The interior plateau, cut off by the surrounding mountains from ameliorating maritime influences, is semiarid in character. Enough rain falls everywhere to allow the dry farming of grains, but drought is a recurring problem. The mountain rim and the eastern highlands are better watered because of their elevation but are cold, with winters ranging from mild in the west to severe in the east. In the southeast, along the Syrian border, the influence of the Syrian steppe penetrates and brings near desert conditions.

In Turkey, unlike most countries of the Middle East, rainfall agriculture is the rule. This is particularly true in the interior plateau, where grains such as wheat, barley, rye, and oats predominate, although cereals are produced everywhere as the basis of the rural diet. Only along the Black Sea coast do small grains give way to corn as the subsistence crop, while hazelnuts and tea are raised commercially. In the west near the Aegean Sea, tobacco, figs, and raisins are important crops. The south coast has sizable areas of citrus production, and around the towns of Alanya and Anamur winter temperatures are high enough to permit small quantities of bananas to be grown. Cotton dominates the Adana Plain, some oil seeds are produced in several parts of the country, and sugar beets are increasing on the plateau wherever there is sufficient irrigation water.

Although increasing population creates pressure on the land, and traditional agricultural technology and a history of underdevelopment handicap the economy, Turkey's over-all situation is not without promise. The key to future development lies in the ability of the central government to initiate changes and the ability of the people to accept them.

focus *on the Villager's Role in a Half Century of Change*

It is difficult for a Western urbanite to imagine himself in the village context of modern Turkey, and nearly impossible for him to imagine the narrow world encompassed by the village mind on the eve of World War I. Ignorance, self-sufficiency, and xenophobia were scarcely relieved by the rare visitors and the villagers' infrequent trips to nearby towns. Most visitors were government officials—tax collectors and army recruiters—

and a combination of fear plus the routines of traditional hospitality left little room for establishing educative contacts with such visitors. Deference to authority was extreme, and there was little or no flow of opinion from village to city. Those surviving from that period demonstrate a lack of identification with the issues that led to the end of the Ottoman Empire. Recruits taken from the village were unlikely to return, and only the relatively well-to-do could make the long, difficult, and expensive pilgrimage to Mecca. Thus, knowledge of the outside world remained negligible.

After the founding of the republic in 1923, the development of industry and modernization of agriculture spread outward from urban centers. But change occurred slowly, and officials of the new government at first tended to perform their duties in the manner to which they had been accustomed under the Ottoman regime. Local officials expected and demanded deference from villagers, and villagers in turn anticipated no new attitudes on the part of government representatives. Such stereotyped responses continue to the present time and find expression in the persistence of traditional village attitudes. For example, village patriarchy still survives, and the heads of extended families answer census questions for their grown and married sons; many even supervise the casting of family ballots *en bloc*.

On the other hand, the growth of the multiparty system has helped to bring about new patterns of political behavior. The success of the newer political parties, built as it is upon an appeal to the villagers, has induced a more positive attitude on the part of many officials toward the people they serve.

While traditional patterns of village leadership prevail, the growth of the government hierarchy of offices and the increasing involvement of central agencies in rural affairs mean that someone in each village must more and more represent it before officialdom. Because such contacts, if successful, may result in better roads, an increased water supply, and a variety of other benefits, the role of the village representative is changing. Literacy has become essential as has a certain standard of dress and the ability to conduct oneself with the proper combination of deference and persistence. As urban-rural contacts continue to increase, knowledgeable younger men who have traveled beyond their home territory and who can deal with the bureaucracy effectively are beginning to assume a role much larger than the one assigned to their age group in traditional society. In these situations, the social innovator—that is, a person in and of the village who can act as interpreter between representatives of the urban elite and the rural milieu—becomes increasingly valuable.

The role of such people is expanding as new laws and new development programs create conflicts between the rural populace and the state. Forest conservation laws, for instance, have closed the woods more and more to traditional exploitation by villagers, and in some areas scarcely a grown man can be found who has not paid a fine or served a jail term for violating forest closures. Such situations indicate the discrepancies between the wishes of the state and the realities of the countryside. Only through an exchange of ideas between the governed and the governors can equitable solutions be found, and only the "transformers" in village society can facilitate such *rapprochement*.

Perhaps the greatest source of conflict between villagers and urban administrators is the different geographical scales within which they operate. The administrator, located near the functional center of government, is in a position to perceive and appreciate annual increments of change for the nation as a whole. For example, each year new schools are opened; each year the national ledgers are summed up. Sometimes there are reverses, and sometimes the rate of progress is unacceptably slow, but the over-all effect is one of gradual and steady alteration of past conditions. To the villager, change appears very differently, as a series of quantum jumps often separated by long periods when nothing new happens. For example, the government in a single year may build an all-weather road through a previously isolated village or single out a small community as the site of some agricultural development scheme. Thus, what appears from above as a gradual process of development throughout the nation comes as a series of often precipitous shocks to a given village. However, as more developments take place in a specific area, their effect is cumulative, and with experience the ability of the villagers to interpret, integrate, and accept continuing change improves.

The integration of the villager into the national life of Turkey has become a vital problem for planners and government officials, since nearly 70 per cent of the population lives in farm communities of fewer than 5,000. The integration of the rural population has been directly affected by the creation of government agencies and the services they provide, the growth of urban-centered industries that serve as magnets for excess rural labor, and the improvement in transportation and marketing systems.

Along with the average villager's increasing political awareness has come significant articulation of the service agencies of the government that perform technical rather than political functions. Agencies such as the Directorate of Hydraulic Works, the Farm Irrigation and Conservation Service, and many others have sent their agents and engineers into the hinterland. The hierarchy represented by their branch offices now stretches across the country, and policy determined in Ankara is given tangible expression throughout the nation. The public works thus carried out have an additional aspect, intangible but undeniably important: The presence of educated technicians is no longer regarded as unusual by most villagers, whose exposure to new ideas increases daily.

A case in point is the growing influence of the Ministry of Agriculture upon the rural population. Since this ministry was created in 1937, it has organized departments of agriculture, veterinary services, forestry, agricultural supply, meteorology, soil conservation and farm irrigation, cotton production, plant protection and animal quarantine, as well as state breeding farms and a special showplace, the Ataturk Farm on the outskirts of Ankara. In 1960, the ministry included four regional agricultural schools, four technical agricultural schools, fifteen agricultural experiment stations, five soil-conservation experimental stations, fifteen cattle-breeding stations, nineteen seed stations, and fourteen sugar factories, and it had placed fifty-four home-economics workers in the field. Such a list, incomplete as it is, becomes more impressive when the areal extent of these services is also considered: The Ministry's "4-K" program (similar to the American 4-H Farm Youth Program) has chapters in more than 210 villages in 47 provinces.

The construction of public works and the introduction of improved seeds, livestock, equipment, and farming techniques have had an inevitable effect on rural life. Beyond the difficult-to-evalute question of per-capita change in productivity is the more basic issue of the incorporation of the villager into national life. The expansion of government agencies has undoubtedly accomplished this in addition to other more obvious achievements. A recent study of change in Turkish villages found that 55 per cent of the people interviewed with regard to the causes of change in agricultural practices cited government sources of information and help as most decisive.

The question of urbanization, industrialization, and population growth has directly affected the incorporation of rural peoples into the national milieu. A population growth rate of nearly 3 per cent per year since 1950 has created great pressure on available land resources and an increasing demand for nonagricultural jobs. The inability of rural areas to absorb surplus labor has resulted in cityward migration and a rate of urban growth that exceeds the growth rate of the nation as a whole. For all of

Turkey, cities with more than 50,000 population numbered five in 1927, eleven in 1950, and twenty-seven in 1960. Perhaps the most significant problem associated with this city growth is the presence of migrants living in squatter shantytowns (*gecekondu*) on the outskirts of all the large settlements. In 1965, it was estimated that in Istanbul, Ankara, and Izmir 960,000 people lived in improvised housing units. At the same time, industrial production, though plagued with a variety of troubles, has continued to grow and to provide more jobs for migrant labor. This activity in the urban centers at first might be thought to have little influence upon modes of rural existence, but strong kinship ties link villagers with relatives working in the cities. The feedback of urban-generated capital and ideas to rural areas has a definite effect on village communities. Money and goods find their way to the hinterland, and returning migrants leaven the loaf of village tradition.

Even more dramatic may be the eventual effect on village life of migrant villagers drawn to jobs in Western Europe. For example, in the period 1963–65, more than 122,000 Turkish workers held short-term labor contracts in West Germany. In a sample of 494 Turks employed there, 18.2 per cent had come directly from villages of fewer than 2,000. And of the 200 workers who had lived in Istanbul before departing for Germany, only 86 had been born there. The city thus prepares the villager for further experiences, which in turn will be transmitted by him to rural areas.

The growth of urban markets resulting from city development and increases in both the standard of living and the number of people in non-agricultural activities has been matched by the development of wholesale markets in localities that produce specilized commercial crops, such as citrus. Parallel to these developments has been the expansion of the transportation network. The infrastructure thus provided has enhanced exchanges between the village and the city. The movement of ideas, policies, and material goods from urban to rural areas is increasingly accompanied by the incorporation of rural products into the national market system and rural people into urban activities.

Although a newcomer visiting rural Turkey for the first time might view the scene as uncompromisingly backward, his evaluation would be inaccurate. Many Turks still living can remember the last days of the Ottoman Empire, when geographic isolation left the vast majority of the people out of touch with their government and remote from all but the most rudimentary elements of the developing world economy. Difficult as they have been, the past fifty years have created a new way of life for the Turks and have given them a significant start on the road to better living conditions.

Suggested Readings

HERSHLAG, ZVI Y. *Turkey: The Challenge of Growth*. Leiden: E. J. Brill, 1968. The most comprehensive survey of the Turkish economy available, giving historical as well as current analysis.

KAZAMIAS, ANDREAS M. *Education and the Quest for Modernity in Turkey*. London: Allen and Unwin, 1966. Covers the transition from religious to secular education as well as the role of education following the Ataturk reforms.

KOLARS, JOHN. *Tradition, Season, and Change in a Turkish Village*. Chicago: Department of Geography Research Series no. 82, University of Chicago, 1963. A detailed study of a group of villages undergoing different rates of change in the adaptation to modern agriculture and society.

LEWIS, BERNARD. *The Emergence of Modern Turkey*. New York: Oxford University Press, 1961. Studies the change of the Turkish Government from empire to republic with emphasis on the period immediately before and during the Ataturk years.

ROBINSON, RICHARD. *The First Turkish Republic: A Case Study in National Development*. Cambridge: Harvard University Press, 1963. Full coverage of the period between the founding of the First Republic and the coup of 1960. Pays equal attention to politics, economics, and society.

STIRLING, A. PAUL. *Turkish Village*. London: Weidenfeld and Nicholson, 1965. A comprehensive anthropological work on rural Turkey.

14 IRAQ

Robert A. Fernea and Elizabeth W. Fernea

Landscape and Climate • *Oil and Industries* • *Land and Water Resources* • *The People and Their Future* • focus *on Land Reform and Ecological Problems*

Iraq, which became an independent state in 1932, after centuries of rule by Turks and Mongols and more than a decade under British mandate, is more fortunate than many new nations in having a large source of capital to finance modern technological development and social programs. That source is petroleum, and production has steadily increased since the 1920's. In 1950, state revenues from oil were $15 million, or about 10 per cent of the national income. Currently, oil revenues are approaching $280 million per annum, nearly twice the entire national income of twenty years ago.

A large share of this revenue has gone into long-range projects planned and administered first by a Development Board and now by the Ministry of Planning. Many programs have been undertaken, and important improvements have been made, particularly in flood control and water storage. Between 1950 and 1970, the annual per-capita income more than doubled, from $84 to $200. However, recent history in Iraq demonstrates dramatically that capital alone cannot quickly transform a preindustrial traditional society into an industrial modern state. Today, the Iraqi Government is struggling with a variety of problems, some rooted in the natural environment, some in the local patterns of politics and society, some in the international rivalries between great powers and in the Arab-Israeli conflict.

Landscape and Climate

Only about 6 per cent of Iraq's area of 170,000 square miles is potentially arable land; only 3 per cent is currently farmed.

The nation's total area can be divided into five regions, in which variations in climate and resources have encouraged different social adaptations, and hence differing ways of life.

Iraq's northern and northeastern borders stretch into the foothills of the Zagros Mountains, which skirt Iran and Turkey. A large part of this region is known as Kurdistan, home of over a million Kurds, whose aspirations to independent status have led to bitter civil strife. The summer climate here is cool and pleasant, the winters are snowy and freezing; there is enough rainfall (fifteen to twenty-five inches a year) to support agriculture in the lowlands. During the short summer season, many Kurdish farmers migrate with their families to high mountain meadows, where they pitch their tents, graze their goats and sheep, and plant small crops of grain or tobacco. In the past the mountains were thickly forested, but now they are largely barren owing to overgrazing and erosion for many centuries.

Moving down from the mountains, and following the two great rivers of Iraq, the Tigris (Dijlah) and Euphrates (Al Furat), which have their source in the northern highlands, one passes through a zone of transition from rainfall to irrigation agriculture. Between the two rivers, north and south of Baghdad, lies the Jazirah, where the climate is hot and dry in summer, cold and often damp in winter. Studies have shown that the Jazirah could sustain much more agriculture, but a large portion of the area is now too far from the sources of irrigation water and is used mainly by nomadic tribes who travel in and out of it with their flocks of camels, goats, and sheep along routes where pasture and water can be found.

Central and southern Iraq, from the region around Baghdad and south, is an alluvial plain, composed of silt laid down through the centuries by the flooding Tigris and Euphrates, which flow independently southward into marshes and then join in the Shatt al Arab to empty finally into the Persian Gulf. This is the principal agricultural zone of the country, ancient Mesopotamia, site of one of the earliest known civilizations. Archaeological evidence shows that the area has been cultivated intermittently by settled farmers at least since Sumerian times, 5,000 years ago, and probably much earlier. In addition to dates, wheat, and barley, the

principal crops are vegetables, rice, and cotton, planted and harvested twice a year in many places. Summers are hot and dry, with temperatures in the shade of over 110° F. Winters are cold and rainy, with occasional freezing weather at night.

Traditionally, the settled farmers of this alluvial plain have been members of great confederations of tribes. Although tribal loyalties and ties are weakening, they are still a significant fact of life for many of these cultivators and have been a divisive factor in the efforts of the national government to unify the country.

Farther south lie the marshlands, about 6,000 square miles of lagoons, mud flats, reed beds, and tiny rivulets, where small enclaves of the Madan people are found. The major resource of the Madan are the reeds, which they feed to their water buffalo and with which they build their homes. Reeds are also woven into mats sold throughout Iraq and Kuwait. The climate is hot and humid in summer, cool and damp in winter; life in the marshes is difficult and, until very recently, stood at a bare level of subsistence.

South of the marshes, along the banks of the Shatt al Arab, rich date orchards produce Iraq's most important agricultural export crop. Most of the dates are processed and shipped through Basra (Al Basrah), the southern port city that lies near Iraq's only outlet to the sea—a short stretch of land along the Persian Gulf. Basra also serves as a focal point for the refining and shipping of oil.

Almost all the rest of Iraq—more than half of it—is desert, part of the vast desert that stretches into Syria, Jordan, and Saudi Arabia. Here, water and pasture are so scarce that only nomadic life is possible.

Oil and Industries

Iraq has proved petroleum reserves of some 3.4 billion tons and, with an annual output of 77 million tons, is the eighth largest oil producer in the world, the fourth largest in the Middle East. Since the 1920's, production has been in the hands of internationally owned consortiums, the biggest of which are the Iraq Petroleum Company (IPC) and its associated Basra and Mosul Petroleum Companies. But in recent years, the government has been restricting the expansion of foreign-owned companies. In 1961, the companies' areas of operation were cut back to their producing oil fields, equivalent to about 0.5 per cent of previously held lands, and they lost the remainder of their concessions. In 1967, the state-owned Iraq National Oil Company (INOC) was given exclusive rights over all areas except those left to the IPC in 1961. No further concessions to oil-rich areas are to be given, although INOC may operate in association with foreign corporations. In accordance with a 1952 agreement, Iraq has been receiving half of the oil companies' profits, the companies having guaranteed a minimum annual output of 30 million tons from January 1, 1956 (later raised to 31 million tons). Its revenues from oil will increase as a result of the 1971 pact between producing countries of the Persian Gulf and international oil companies (see p. 12).

Courtesy United Nations

Much of Kurdistan in Iraq is too mountainous and barren to support many people, but it has one of the richest oilfields in the world, and this has been a source of conflict between the Baghdad government, which controls the fields, and the Kurds, who wish to control them. In addition to the political disturbances, the prevalence of malaria posed serious problems for the Kurds until a successful campaign against the disease was launched by the World Health Organization during the 1950's. Better health conditions combined with more irrigation now allow the Kurds to produce larger crops of wheat and other grains each year.

Kirkuk has traditionally been the richest of Iraq's oil fields. Other significant fields are at Ain Zalah, northwest of Mosul (Al Mawsil), and at Al Amarah, Ratawi, and Rumaila, in the southern alluvial plains. The North Rumaila field, thought to be capable of producing some 20 million tons a year, is to be developed by INOC with a Soviet loan of $70 million. Iraq is to repay the loan by crude-oil shipments to the Soviet Union beginning one year after the start of production. The Soviet agreement also provides for the extension of a new pipeline to southern Iraqi oil terminals and the building of a dock at Basra for river traffic and a navigation canal at Al Faw, Iraq's Persian Gulf oil-tanker terminal. At present, about two-thirds of the country's oil is carried by pipeline to the Syrian Mediterranean port of Baniyas and the Lebanese port of Tripoli (Tarabulus); only one-third passes through Basra. The new line from Rumaila to Al Faw should increase Iraq's profits from oil exports.

One of the largest industries associated with oil is the state-owned sulphur-recovery plant at Kirkuk, which began operations in 1968. Scheduled production is 120,000 tons of sulphur annually out of gas from the Kirkuk field; by-product gases will be sent by pipeline to Baghdad, the capital city. Another pipeline from Kirkuk to Baghdad (completed in 1966) carries natural gas and liquid petroleum gas for use in the city's power stations and industries.

Iraq has seven refineries in operation, the most important of which have been at Kirkuk and Baghdad. The latter, completed in 1955, has an annual capacity of 2.2 million tons. A new refinery at Basra, the largest so far, was completed in 1968 with an initial capacity of 2.5 million tons.

Efforts are being made to develop industries based on local resources other than oil to manufacture things needed for the domestic market, but large-scale industrialization has made little headway to date. Nor have attempts to decentralize industrial development as yet stopped the flow of people to the capital city. Of the 1,200 establishments employing ten or more persons, more than half are located in Baghdad. These industries are mainly concerned with food-processing, brewing, cigarette-making, spinning and weaving, chemicals, metal manufacturing, and the making of clothes and furniture. The largest plants produce electricity, bricks, and cement, and regulate water supplies.

Important factories elsewhere include a bitumen plant at Quiyara south of Mosul, which produces 60,000 tons of asphalt a year and employs 250 workers; a million-dollar 644-loom textile mill at Mosul, which provides work for 1,200 workers and produces 25 million square yards of calico annually from locally grown cotton; two cement plants, each with a daily output of 350 tons; and several smaller textile mills and canneries. Mosul also boasts a sugar factory with an annual production of 35,000 tons.

Land and Water Resources

Aside from oil, Iraq's principal natural assets are its land and water resources. It is potentially one of the most fertile and productive parts of the Middle East, but misuse of the land and lack of control of the rivers have made their present development a task of staggering proportions. In the north, erosion of the hillsides has reduced the amount of livestock that can be supported. In the south, the topsoil is largely silt, but, because of the flatness and the impervious subsoils, the alluvial plain is poorly drained and tends to become saline with too much irrigation.

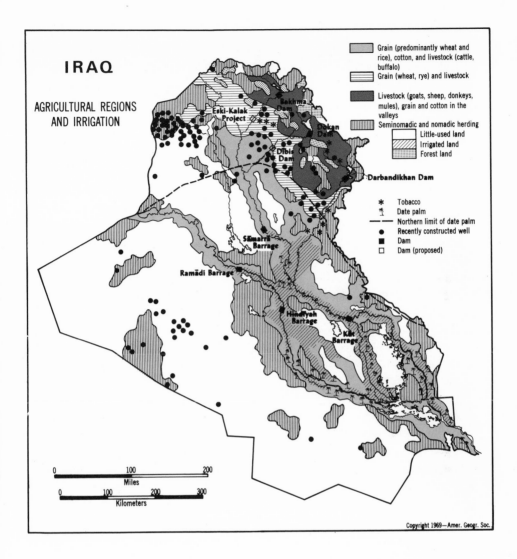

IRAQ

AGRICULTURAL REGIONS
AND IRRIGATION

Grain (predominantly wheat and
rice), cotton, and livestock (cattle,
buffalo)
Grain (wheat, rye) and livestock
Livestock (goats, sheep, donkeys,
mules), grain and cotton in the
valleys
Seminomadic and nomadic herding
Little-used land
Irrigated land
Forest land

Eski-Kalak
Project
Bakhma
Dam
Dokan
Dam
Dibis
Dam
Darbandikhan Dam
Sāmarrā
Barrage
Ramādi Barrage
Hindiyah
Barrage
Kūt
Barrage

* Tobacco
🌱 Date palm
— Northern limit of date palm
● Recently constructed well
■ Dam
□ Dam (proposed)

0   100   200
Miles
0   100   200   300
Kilometers

As the soil salts up, the land becomes less productive and must be artificially washed and drained or permitted to lie fallow to regain its fertility.

Although the Tigris and Euphrates have an abundance of water, it is largely wasted because so much of it spills out into the southern marshes or flows into the Persian Gulf. The river system is also marked by extreme annual variation in flow, resulting in years of flood and years of drought. The Tigris, the larger river, reaches its maximum in April, the Euphrates in May—too late for best results with winter crops and too early for maturing summer crops. Flooding has been a constant and serious problem. Baghdad was almost destroyed by a flood at the end of the nineteenth century and was badly flooded in 1954 and again in 1968, despite measures taken by the government to construct flood-control devices.

A major aim of Iraq's various economic-development plans has been better regulation of its water resources: the storage of more water for increased, year-round irrigation, and the provision of proper drainage systems to enlarge the cultivable land areas; the prevention of floods; and the creation of hydroelectric power. To supplement the existing dams and canals on the Euphrates, Tigris, Diyala, and Little Zab (Zab as Saghir) rivers, four major irrigation works have been built with oil revenues. These are the Samarra Barrage, with regulators and channels leading from the Tigris to the Wadi Tharthar storage reservoir; the Ramadi Barrage, with regulators and channels from the Euphrates to the Hawr al Habbaniyah; the Dokan Dam in the far north on the Little Zab River; and the Darbandikhan Dam on the Diyala River.

In 1961, the government announced other major projects, including the Dibis Dam on the Little Zab, part of a scheme to irrigate large tracts in the Kirkuk area; the Eski-Kalak Project on the left bank of the Great Zab River, halfway between Irbil and Mosul, designed to irrigate more than 30,000 acres; the Shatt al Gharraf Project and associated Ash Shatrah drainage, west of Al Amarah, which should make cultivable some 175,000 acres; and an artesian-well project in the northern and southern deserts. Some 800 such wells had been completed by 1962, according to government sources, and 1,000 more are planned.

Together, the dams and reservoirs completed, under construction, and planned should almost double the area of cultivated land, provide ample protection against floods, and supply the nation with some 635,000 kilowatts of electric power.

The People and Their Future

About 95 per cent of the Iraqis are Muslims, and the rest are mainly Christians (Armenians, Assyrians, Catholics) and Jews. The Muslim majority is itself split between two major sects of Islam, the Sunni and the Shia. Sunni membership is further divided between Kurdish Sunni Muslims and Arab Sunni Muslims. Since the Kurds consider themselves Kurds first, the largest homogeneous religious group in Iraq is the Shia Muslims, numbering from 4 to 5 million. Through pilgrimage, the Shia have close ties with the Shia congregations of Iran and Pakistan, since four of the twelve major Shia shrines lie within Iraq's boundaries, at An Najaf, Karbala, Samarra, and Kadhimain in Baghdad.

Until recently, 90 per cent of the Iraqis were illiterate, and the great majority lived barely above the subsistence level. Sanitation, health, and nutrition were substandard, and child mortality rates were very high. In the countryside, a small percentage of wealthy landowners owned most of the cultivable land and farmed it through the labor of tenant share-croppers. The Ministry of Agrarian Reform estimated that in 1958 half the area under cultivation was held by 3 per cent of the landowners.

A sharp division also existed between town and rural dwellers. There have always been great cities in Iraq—from the time of Ur, Babylon, and

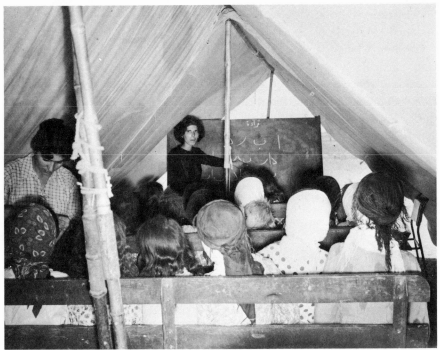

Courtesy United Nations

Educational facilities for the villages are part of a plan designed to improve the standard of living of the Iraqi people. Community-development programs, some of them sponsored by the United Nations, promote literacy, advise people about modern agricultural methods, and provide training in health care and nutrition. These young women are learning reading and writing as well as sewing and other household arts. The class is being held in a tent until a brick schoolhouse can be built.

Nineveh—for it stands in an important position midway on the trade routes from India to the Mediterranean, but the rural and urban populations have generally feared and suspected each other. Yet the differences between rich and poor and between town and country dwellers were scarcely greater than those between nomad and settled tribesman, Sunni and Shia, Kurd and Arab.

Contemplating the diverse groups that the government is now attempting to unite into one nation, one might ask how it was ever possible for such disparate peoples to live as a nation. The answer is that until 1932 Iraq was not a nation in the modern sense of the word. Until the British arrived on the scene in 1914, pacified the countryside, and brought the area under the control of a central administration, Iraq was a group of largely self-governing units. Towns, tribes, and nomads had been organized rather loosely into vilayets or provinces by the Ottoman governors, but these operated primarily for purposes of trade and taxation.

Carleton Coon's famous metaphor of the Middle East as a mosaic fits Iraq particularly well. For many centuries, Iraq was a relatively stable mosaic, a social pattern of differing peoples, religions, and languages, with varying occupations. Until the central government began to reach into the mountain villages of Kurdistan, the clusters of reed huts in the isolated marshes, the tribal guest houses in the alluvial plain, the townhouses of the wealthy Baghdad merchants, the tents of the nomads, these people existed together but separately. Tribal strife and attacks on the cities occurred occasionally, but only in recent decades have the basic differences among the pieces of the mosaic become abrasive and disturbing to the general peace, as each group struggles to find its proper place in the new state.

This is because the mortar that held the mosaic in place is breaking up. The mortar—age-old tradition, shared expectations, and acceptance of one's role and place in life—is disintegrating. The compromises worked out over centuries by previous administrations were shattered by the 1958 revolution and the fall of the monarchy. The government of Abdul Karim Qassem came to power with promises that the great oil revenues were to be used for the benefit of all the people. The present government is striving to make these promises good. It is not easy.

The population of the country has jumped from 6.7 million to nearly 9 million in ten years. Indications are that the annual rate of growth is 2.5 per cent. This high rate is due largely to improved health services and a consequent lowering of the child mortality rate. Iraq at present has no population pressure comparable to that of, say, the United Arab Republic; on the contrary, the population is still rather sparse in relation to natural resources. But, with this high rate of growth, the pressure is bound to mount unless these resources can be utilized to better advantage than at present.

With the growth in population has come a shift in its distribution. Twenty years ago, two-thirds of the people lived in rural areas and were engaged in agriculture. The other third were concentrated in the principal cities— Baghdad; Mosul, in the far north; Kirkuk, on the edge of the oil fields; the two holy cities of Ar Najaf and Karbala; and Basra, port city in the south. Traditionally, city people were engaged in trade, small-scale manufacture, the professions, and education.

Today, all this is changing. By 1957, nearly 50 per cent of the population had become concentrated in urban areas, and, although recent figures are difficult to obtain, evidence suggests that the trend to move to the cities is accelerating. Baghdad, for example, has doubled in size in ten years. With more than 1.8 million people, it presently has one-fifth of the country's total population. Proportionately fewer people are engaged in agriculture than was the case a decade ago. More and more people in the smaller towns as well as in the cities are working in factories and businesses and in government offices, as the bureaucatic organizations managing the central government's affairs have increased year by year.

The continued migration of rural dwellers to the cities has added to the financial burdens of the government. Housing, education, and social services must be provided for the new arrivals. Many constructive steps have been taken by the government in this general direction. Low-cost housing is going up around the cities. Under direct government-sponsored construction programs about 20,000 low-cost houses have been built annually, and the government has assisted private builders in constructing another 20,000—a small step toward the elimination of the nearly 3 million substandard dwellings. More health centers have been opened, and social services have been expanded. Roads to outlying areas have been paved to link farm with market.

One of the country's most impressive accomplishments is in the field of education. Primary-school enrollment leaped from 640,000 in 1960 to 960,000 in 1964; secondary-school enrollment, from 130,000 to 235,000. Public expenditure on education has risen to 25 per cent of the national income. Iraq has announced that it plans to enforce its compulsory-education law for boys by 1975 and for girls by 1980. Illiteracy has dropped from 90 to 75 per cent and is estimated to be declining each year. Iraqi sources claim that at present only one-third of the men in the age group fifteen to forty are illiterate.

These social services, and the land-reform programs discussed below must all be paid for. Further, the government has become increasingly involved in both domestic and regional conflicts, with the result that military spending has climbed steadily. The migration from the countryside, coupled with several bad drought years, has caused agricultural production to drop. Thus, the government has been forced to dip more deeply into oil revenues. Whereas in past decades, surplus agricultural products were exported, now many basic commodities must be imported in response to the decrease in farm output and the needs of an increasing population. In the years 1951–53, the value of non-oil exports was $61 million; by 1959–61, it had dropped to $25 million; for 1962–64, it rose again, but only to $48 million. Even the export of dates fell from 436,000 tons in 1962–63 to 345,000 in 1966–67.

Before 1958, the government invested in infrastructures such as dams and flood-control projects but was unwilling, and perhaps afraid, to spend large amounts on developing its human resources. The revolutionary governments have tried to redress this imbalance by making long-overdue investments in social services—education, health, and housing. This has led to rising expectations on the part of the people.

The government must continue to spend oil revenues to build a solid economic base within the country itself, through expanding industry and improving agriculture. It must also satisfy the newly felt needs of the people for health and educational services. But large-scale improvements in education and medical facilities take time. With the pattern of ethnic, religious, and political dissonance that constantly threatens the stability of any central government in Iraq, deferring present expectations in favor of future rewards of over-all economic growth is a difficult and even dangerous step. Nevertheless, it is surely the central problem confronting the Iraqi nation today.

focus *on Land Reform and Ecological Problems*

Land reform is often advocated as a means of stimulating agricultural production in developing countries. Iraq is no exception. Although the nation lies within the Fertile Crescent, the principal grain-producing region of the Middle East, in the last century agriculture has not provided more than bare subsistence for the average Iraqi farmer and has yielded crops of uneven quality and quantity.

Economists and planners have consistently stated that the country has far greater agricultural potential than is currently being realized and that one of the major obstacles in developing that potential is the land-tenure system. The problem of Iraqi agriculture has been fundamentally social, not technical. The average *fellah* (small farmer) is poor because the land is not very productive and the landowner takes most of the crop.

Even before 1957, experts engaged by the prerevolutionary government to assess and propose remedies for the nation's agricultural woes recognized the need to improve the status and standard of living of the individual farmer if agriculture itself were to be upgraded. As a result, legislation was passed to initiate model land-development and resettlement projects. These model schemes, somewhat like the homestead projects of frontier America, utilized, not the large estates, but *miri sirf*, or state land, which had been largely uncultivated in the past because of lack of water. The first of these schemes was at Dujaila, near Al Kut on the Tigris River. More than a thousand plots of 60 acres (100 *donums*) each were allotted to landless farmers who agreed to settle and farm them under government supervision. Intensive cultivation—that is, farming without traditional fallowing, and planting three rather than two crops a year—was part of the government-supervised program.

Later planners pointed out that such land-development schemes could be enlarged and more potentially arable land brought under cultivation through increasing irrigation, both pump irrigation in the rain-fed north and flow irrigation in the alluvial south. Flood water from the rivers could be stored in natural depressions through the use of barrages, regulators, and large dams, to be released for irrigation at times of greatest benefit to crops. Barrages and dams would assist in controlling the unpredictable and often disastrous floods that have devastated Iraq periodically throughout its history. The increased amount of water available for irrigation would also allow more intensive cultivation of the soil, through fertilizing and using soil-enriching crops rather than fallowing, and through providing enough water for summer crops. The assumption was that such intensive cultivation would increase over-all production and raise the individual *fellah*'s income.

By 1958, when the *miri sirf* land-settlement project at Dujaila had been in operation for over ten years, farming had begun at other projects, including Hawija, Latafiya, and Shahrazoor. Dujaila did indeed suggest that ownership of the land might act as a stimulant. The farmers were producing more, and they were almost twice as prosperous as the tenant farmers on neighboring estates; but the scheme revealed an unforeseen difficulty: The land began to salt up after less than two years of cultivation and became progressively less fertile.

The revolutionary leaders who came to power in 1958 with the fall of the monarchy and the collapse of the Nuri Said regime were not satisfied with measures like the *miri sirf* projects. They believed that privately owned land holdings exceeding 625 acres of irrigated land or 1,250 acres of rain-fed land should be expropriated and redistributed, and they passed a law to this effect in 1959. According to Iraqi Government figures, altogether 4.25 million acres of privately held land were to be taken over. In addition, 2.9 million acres of *miri sirf* land, which had remained uncultivated, were to be distributed, as were 2.3 million acres of land with unsettled title—land that, in law, was state domain, but in fact was in the usufructuary possession of tribal sheikhs.

Confiscation of the large estates was to be only the first step in implementing the law, followed by a period of temporary management of the land by the Ministry of Agrarian Reform and then redistribution. But the postrevolutionary governments have been plagued by administrative and political problems. In addition, officials were faced with the gigantic task of surveying and registering over half the nation's arable land. Consequently, implementation of the law has been slow. According to official Iraqi figures, by 1966 the total area covered by the reform was only 6.1 million acres, slightly less than two-thirds the amount projected earlier. This included the area privately owned and the area in "temporary tenancy." Subsequent reports indicate that much land has yet to be distributed and that large numbers of farmers are still landless or tenants or uncertain of their status and, hence, are unwilling or unable to undertake projects that would increase their yields and total farm output. Cooperative societies have been formed to invest capital, run demonstration plots, introduce new crops and crop rotations, and increase the use of insecticides and fertilizers, but there are not enough of them, and management problems have arisen in many. Where formerly the landowner or his agents directed all operations on large estates, including the supplying of seeds, the repairing of pumps, the maintenance of some canals, the settlement of disputes between cultivators, and the vital distribution of irrigation water, now local conflicts between new small owners, tenants, and government administrators frequently disrupt operations so much that no crops are planted or crops are planted but not properly watered and harvested.

Despite these problems, production might be expected to remain approximately the same, if not to rise, because of the agrarian reformers' attempts to establish scientific cropping and fertilizing patterns, the extra crops produced under the intensive cultivation program, and the improved irrigation and drainage systems. This is not, however, the case. Exports of dates, barley, and wheat have declined, and Iraq is now annually importing grains, vegetables, and other foodstuffs in which it was largely self-sufficient before 1958. Oil revenue, the primary source of capital for national development, thus is being used increasingly to balance the food budget. Therefore, despite millions of dollars of investment and a determined though still unfinished attempt to break up the old land-tenure system and reassign the land to individual farmers, the agricultural situation has not improved.

The agrarian-reform movement and the earlier homestead schemes appear to have failed to take into account the ecology and history of the land and the indigenous solutions evolved over centuries for dealing with that land.

The rain-fed area of northern Iraq offers many possibilities for agricultural development if the current erosion of the mountainous hillsides is halted. It has been suggested that a long-range program of reforestation, combined with supplementary pump irrigation, may in the long run increase production of grain and allow much more crop diversification than at present. The northern hill country can support tobacco fields as well as fruit and nut orchards, all excellent export crops.

But the rain-fed area represents only a small portion of the nation's arable land. In the principal agricultural area, the alluvial plain between the Tigris and Euphrates rivers, the flatness of the land and the impermeable subsoils tend to prevent the runoff of irrigation water. High temperatures cause rapid evaporation of the standing water, and the excess salts remain. This is the salinization process, which gradually renders the ground infertile. The International Bank Mission of 1952 found that 20 per cent to 30 per cent of all cultivated land had been abandoned because of salt accumulation, and yields had declined on the remaining land by 20 per cent to 50 per cent and often more. The increased irrigation provided by the government has in many places increased the salting-up process since that date.

Recent engineering studies have shown that in many parts of southern Iraq, unless tile drains are laid under the fields, a fantastically costly process, the land will continue to salt up under the levels of water use necessary for intensive cultivation. It now seems clear that intensive use of land that must be irrigated and failure to fallow regularly will cause the land to salt up and result in decreased fertility. Current drainage systems are inadequate.

In the past, cultivation followed a pattern of extensive rather than intensive land use, combined with livestock production. Small groups of people settled on the land, dug canals from the river, farmed the land for a time, and, when it became salty, moved on and left the land fallow to recover its strength. Gradually the *niren-niren* system of fallowing developed, whereby half the land under cultivation was farmed and half left fallow each year. The fallow land offered pasture for the livestock, which has always provided an important part of the farmer's income, whether he was a sharecropper or freeholder. Irrigation, required if the land was to be cultivated at all, necessitated social management of water distribution, whether from the small, individually dug canals, the larger tribal canals, or the more complex irrigation works constructed during the great periods of empire in ancient Mesopotamia: Sumeria, Akkadia, Babylonia, and Abbasid. In drought years, the people returned to a pastoral existence; the tribes of both the northern rain-fed area and the southern alluvial plains have alternated between pastoralism and settled agriculture for many centuries.

When the patterns of extensive (rather than intensive) farming have been violated, the land has become infertile, production has dropped, and the people have left the farms. This is exactly what is happening in many places in Iraq today.

Extensive land use sufficed for the rather smaller population that occupied Iraq in the past. Today, the population is nearly 9 million and is increasing at an annual rate of 2.5 per cent. This rising population and its needs may exhaust the agricultural base of the country more quickly than planners and economists have suspected. Yet switching from extensive to intensive cultivation and single-family farms does not seem to be the answer, at least with present techniques.

But perhaps the lessons of the past can be the basis for new attempts, in light of the present government's desire to improve the agrarian economy. More attention must be paid to the managerial functions, the sets of social relationships between farmer and landlord that in the past handled such vital problems as seed distribution, irrigation cycles, cropping, fallowing, and grazing rights. The cooperatives may eventually be successful, if traditional patterns of tribal enmity can be overcome. Other changes might be considered. Assigning individual plots of land to families may ultimately prove less satisfactory than forming larger units of land under private, cooperative, or governmental direction, permitting less intensive patterns of cultivation.

Iraq has oil money to develop its agricultural potential by educating managerial farm personnel, improving livestock strains, diversifying crops, reforesting the northern hillsides, and experimenting with drainage and fallow crops as methods of reducing salinization. These actions are not so dramatic as confiscating estates and distributing land to the landless, yet, in the long run, they may be the factors that will help this ancient land to break the cycle of rural poverty and minimal production, encourage some of the hundreds of thousands of rural migrants to the city to return to the farms, and help establish a sound agricultural base for the future.

Suggested Readings

BAALI, FAUD. "Agrarian Reform in Iraq: Some Socio-economic Aspects." *The American Journal of Economics and Sociology,* XXVIII, no. 1 (Jan., 1969), pp. 61–76. A concise summary of the events leading up to the Agrarian Reform Law of 1959 and an evaluation of its implementation to the present.

AL-BARAZI, NURI K. *The Geography of Agriculture in Irrigated Areas of the Middle Euphrates Valley.* 2 vols. Baghdad: Al-Aani Press, 1961. A detailed analysis of the physical geography, land use, and irrigation policies of Iraq, and a study of its agriculture in relation to population growth and distribution.

FERNEA, ROBERT A. "Land Reform and Ecology in Post-revolutionary Iraq." *Economic Development and Cultural Change,* XVII, no. 3 (April, 1969), pp. 356–81. The role of social, cultural, and ecological factors in the development of agriculture.

LANGLEY, KATHLEEN M. "Iraq: Some Aspects of the Economic Scene." *Middle East Journal,* XVIII, no. 2 (Spring, 1964), pp. 180–88. A study of economic policies in the light of political changes: some of the econmic problems facing the country, agrarian reform needs, and industrial possibilities.

SEVIAN, VAHÉ J. "The Evolution of the Boundary Between Iraq and Iran." In Charles A. Fisher, ed., *Essays in Political Geography.* New York: Barnes and Noble, 1968, pp. 211–23. A factual, up-to-date account of politicogeographical factors in the evolution of the present Iraqi-Iranian boundary.

15 IRAN

John S. Haupert

A Mountainous Terrain • Water and Agriculture • People and Cultural Cleavages • Land Reform • Natural Resources and Industries • focus *on the Education Corps,* by Gad Soffer

Iranians call their land Iran, but their expressive and poetic language is Farsi, or Persian, in which they preserve the memory of the royal province of the Achaemenids (today called Fars) and their capital, Persepolis. Twenty-five hundred years ago, the Persian Empire spread as far as Egypt and Greece in the West and the Hindu Kush in the East. The ancient Greeks alone kept the advancing tide from penetrating into Europe. Later, the country's geographical position amid opposing forces in the Middle East—Arabs and Turks to the west and Mongols and Russians to the north and east—provided some sense of national purpose. The Iranian legend—maintained in the language, religion, literature, and ancient customs—has been a far more cohesive force in a land occupied by countless conquerors through the ages.

A Mountainous Terrain

Iran has an area of about 628,000 square miles (slightly larger than Alaska) and a varied landscape, although most of the country consists of a complex of mountain chains enclosing a series of interior basins 1,000 to 4,000 feet in elevation. The four main physiographic units are the Zagros Mountains and adjacent lowlands of the Khuzestan region (the latter are associated with the Mesopotamian and Persian Gulf lowlands); the Alborz chain and Caspian littoral; the eastern and southeastern upland rim; and the interior basins.

The Zagros Mountains are a series of folded parallel ranges, which were modified by fracturing followed by differential warping. They extend for about 1,400 miles in a long arc from Turkey's Armenian highlands to the borders of Pakistan. The northwestern sector of the Zagros is characterized by a complex of fault scarps and down-throw basins, the largest containing Lake Urmia (Rezaiyeh), a salt lake from which there is no outlet. One of the spectacular topographic features of this area is the superposition of large volcanic cones upon high plateaus, such as Mount Savalan (15,784 feet), west of Ardabil, and Mount Sahand (12,138 feet), south of Tabriz.

The distinguishing characteristics of the central Zagros are the synclinal valleys, which were created by surface folding rather than by faulting and down-throw. A number of perennial streams, such as the Dez and Karkheh, have cut intricate valleys through these ranges to the Mesopotamian lowlands. The south-central Zagros give rise to the Karun River, navigable only in the flat alluvial flood plain of Khuzestan. In the southern Zagros, water courses are short and ephemeral, draining into either the Persian Gulf or the Dasht-e Lut, the interior sandy desert.

In the north, between the Caucasus and the Hindu Kush, are the Alborz and the Kopet mountains. The former rise abruptly in a series of steep, narrow folds that form a crescent-shaped spur extending eastward from the massifs of northwestern Iran. The Alborz are high and include the country's highest peak, Mount Damavand (18,955 feet), a volcanic cone lying about 40 miles northeast of Tehran. The rainy northern slopes drop precipitously to the Caspian shores, which are 88 feet below mean sea level and are covered with a lush, subtropical, deciduous forest. In marked contrast, scrub vegetation characterizes the dry shadow of the southern slopes, which trend more gradually toward the immense salt wastes of the Dasht-e Kavir. The Caspian plain extends for about 400 miles from west to east and inland up to 20 miles.

On the eastern side of the central plateau, the upland rim of barren peaks rises above vast and sterile basins of drifting sands and salt flats. These enclosed basins occupy about half the total area of the country. One of these, the Sistan, contains the complex drainage area of the Hirmand (Helmand) River, the source of which is in Afghanistan. In Pleistocene times, these depressions were inundated by extensive lakes that disappeared when the climate became arid and evaporation rates high.

Water and Agriculture

Extreme variations in rainfall and temperature are common. Relief is a major factor, for the highlands obstruct the prevailing westerlies in winter and northerly winds in summer. The mean annual precipitation for the entire country is 15.7 inches, which decreases generally from north to south and west to east. Most of the rain comes in winter. Heavy rainfall well distributed throughout the year is confined to the Caspian lowlands and varies from 50 or 60 inches in the west to 20 inches in the east. The northern Zagros average about 10 inches. Half the total area of Iran gets less than 4 inches. The driest regions are the central deserts and the southern coast.

Summer temperatures are high throughout the country: Tehran has a mean daily maximum in July of 99° F, and, in Khuzestan and Sistan provinces, temperatures may rise to over 120° F. Average January temperatures fall to well below freezing on the interior plateau and below zero in Azerbaijan.

Annual surpluses of water are rare and are confined to the northwestern mountains enclosing the central plateau. In general, the ten-inch isohyet follows the inner foothills of the Zagros-Alborz-Kopet systems and marks the minimum limit where crops can be cultivated without irrigation. One-third of all cultivated land is irrigated, from rivers, wells, and *qanats*, underground conduits that convey water long distances by gravity to a point where it reaches the surface for distribution to fields and villages. *Qanats* are declining in numbers because of their high maintenance requirements and are being replaced by more efficient diesel pumping from deep wells and simple stream-diversion projects.

Only about 12 per cent of the country is devoted to crops, but this is a fairly high proportion in the Middle East. An additional 18 per cent consists of forests and pasture lands. More than 75 per cent of Iran's 28 million people depend upon agriculture for their livelihood. Wheat is the chief bread grain and the staple food for the vast majority. It is grown mainly as a winter crop in Azerbaijan, in the interior Zagros valleys, and in Kermanshah, Esfahan, and Khorasan provinces. Until recently, wheat was seldom produced in sufficient quantities because of capricious rainfall and primitive cultivation methods. For the past three years, however, wheat output has been 3.6 million tons a year, exceeding requirements. In 1968, about 225,000 tons were exported. Favorable weather conditions rather than improved production techniques made this possible. In the long run, sub-

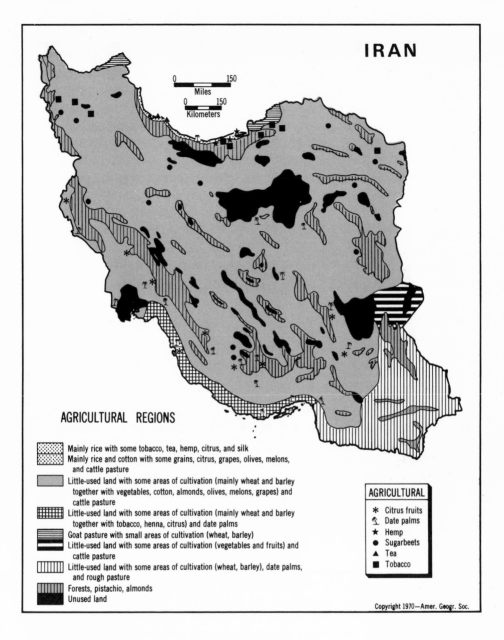

IRAN

AGRICULTURAL REGIONS

- Mainly rice with some tobacco, tea, hemp, citrus, and silk
- Mainly rice and cotton with some grains, citrus, grapes, olives, melons, and cattle pasture
- Little-used land with some areas of cultivation (mainly wheat and barley together with vegetables, cotton, almonds, olives, melons, grapes) and cattle pasture
- Little-used land with some areas of cultivation (mainly wheat and barley together with tobacco, henna, citrus) and date palms
- Goat pasture with small areas of cultivation (wheat, barley)
- Little-used land with some areas of cultivation (vegetables and fruits) and cattle pasture
- Little-used land with some areas of cultivation (wheat, barley), date palms, and rough pasture
- Forests, pistachio, almonds
- Unused land

AGRICULTURAL

* Citrus fruits
🖑 Date palms
★ Hemp
● Sugarbeets
▲ Tea
■ Tobacco

stantial expansion to bread-grain production will be necessary to keep pace with the country's high annual population growth rate of about 3 per cent.

The current Economic Development Plan (1968–73) emphasizes con-

Courtesy United Nations

Agricultural workers weed a rice field with modern machinery at the Sari Agricultural School, one of twenty schools in Iran engaged in training middle-level agricultural personnel. Increased output through improved farming methods and training of agricultural technicians is a basic objective of the nation's development plans.

tinued self-sufficiency in wheat, setting a target of 4.4 million tons. Under this plan, the annual growth rate for all agricultural products is to be 5 per cent. Production goals for wheat and other products are affected, not only by rainfall factors, but also by the construction of new water projects. Significant expansion of wheat acreage is also contingent upon the growing demand for increased plantings of barley, rice, sugar, tobacco, cotton, dates, fruits, and vegetables and for increased output of meat products. The traditional handicaps to agricultural development persist. Cultivation without proper crop rotations and fertilizers continues to deplete soil fertility, and irrigation without adequate drainage creates greater soil salinity. As always, the occurrence of timely and sufficient rainfall is a crucial factor; however, the use of high-yielding wheat varieties that are adaptable to arid lands and the availability of fertilizers, insecticides, machinery, and improved milling and storage facilities all hold promise for continuing improvement in grain and other crop yields.

Rice is the main food crop of the wet Caspian lowlands, with an output of 1.25 million tons in 1969. Barley, maize, and millet have been grown since antiquity, and Iran has long been famous for a wide variety of high-quality nuts, fruits, and vegetables. In Khuzestan Province, after several centuries of dormancy and neglect, irrigated crops of grains, cotton, dates, and sugar cane have increased sharply since the completion of the giant Mohammed Reza Shah Pahlavi Dam on the Dez River in 1963. The reservoir capacity is 3.3 billion cubic yards of water, which will eventually irrigate more than 300,000 acres throughout the year. A huge agro-industrial complex, based on large-scale farming units, is being implemented. Additional dams under construction on the Dez and Karun rivers will irrigate another 2.5 million acres and generate 6 million kilowatts of hydroelectric power yearly.

People and Cultural Cleavages

About 90 per cent of the Iranians are Shia Muslims and speak Farsi, which belongs to the Aryan or Indo-Iranian branch of languages. Farsi is remarkably similar to ancient Persian, but is written as a modified form of Arabic. Ethnically, Iranians are of mixed ancestry, with marked Arabic and Turkish influences. At least two-thirds consider themselves to be "true" Persians. The second largest ethnic-linguistic group is comprised of people of Turkish extraction in Azerbaijan who speak a Turki dialect. The Kurds, a semisedentary tribal society numbering over a million, live in the mountainous districts bordering Turkey and Iraq, but are Sunni Muslims. In Khuzestan and the south coastal regions, there are more than 2 million people of Arabic background. To the west and south of Esfahan, the capital of Persia in the Middle Ages, Bakhtiari tribesmen practice transhumance, moving their flocks vast distances between Khuzestan and the interior plateau; they speak yet another dialect of Persian. A Gilaki dialect is spoken by Turkish elements on the Caspian coast. Still other variations are found among Mazandaranis and Turkomans to the east. The presence of non-Islamic religions contributes to further cultural differences. An example is Zoroastrianism, which dominated Persia until the arrival of Islam in the seventh century and still prevails in a few areas. It considers earth, fire, and water to be sacred elements in a world divided between good and evil.

The greatly diverse ethnic groups and tribal communities were by-products of foreign invasion, internal dynastic struggles, tribal warfare and raiding, and the insecurity of land tenure. Tension has always existed between the sedentary, semisettled, and nomadic populations. The balance has been precarious and marked by a tendency of the cultivators to encroach upon grazing lands.

Population distributions are determined mainly by physical conditions. The dominant type of settlement has been the village, for irrigation works could best be implemented as a communal enterprise. Rural villages were characterized by high densities and close clustering of habitations, often surrounded by protective walls, with gardens, fields, and orchards arranged along the periphery of the settlements. Government policy encouraged high-density settlements to enhance political cooperation and effective tax collection. When the central government was ineffective or ceased to exist, semi-autonomous agricultural and pastoral societies maintained and passed on their traditions. Despite the tendency toward local particularism and fragmentation, there was a unifying factor: the great trunk roads, such as the Khorasan Road, which ran from Baghdad into central Asia and had connecting routes linking important provincial centers. Invaders followed these highways, but so did commerce and the Islamic civilization, which became integrated with provincialism.

Two sorts of cleavage, therefore, have persisted in Iranian society to the present. One is between the government and the rural population, the former extracting taxes and soldiers from the latter; the other is between urban and rural life. In spite of the economic interdependence of farms and cities, landlords became absentees integrated into urban society, thus lessening contacts between these two main sectors. A privileged class of large landed proprietors with arbitrary powers determined the economic and social conditions of the small landowners, peasant sharecroppers, tenants, and farm laborers.

Land Reform

The movement for land reform was a response to the desire for political, social, and economic changes stimulated by powerful national forces and Western influences that have emerged in recent years. In the 1950's, the Shah initiated his own program by selective distribution of crown lands. Landowners, however, showed no tendency to follow his lead, maintaining that decreasing production would result because the peasants did not have the means to maintain irrigation works or the incentives to increase farm output.

With the advent of a stronger and more effective government, a national referendum held in 1963 approved a comprehensive land reform law, which called for (1) limiting landlords to ownership of only one village, (2) compensating landlords on the basis of the taxation rates paid previously, (3) allocating land to the peasants without altering the morphology of the village and associated crop and pasture lands, (4) permitting peasants to purchase land on installment payments over a fifteen-year period, and (5) requiring membership in a cooperative society as a condition of land tenure.

Additional amendments to the basic reform law regulated disputes concerning title and deed to land parcels and fixed the maximum size of holdings on the basis of crop types and the extent of irrigation. For example, in the densely populated Gilan, rice plantations could not exceed fifty acres, but larger acreages were permitted for extensive wheat-farming and grazing lands. In most districts, share-cropping relationships were concluded. The initial mechanics of land reform have essentially been completed, affecting about 53,000 villages with over 2 million families of some 12 million members. But more than a million holdings have not yet been distributed, because of problems associated with uncertain ownership and registration difficulties. Not all peasants have benefited; agricultural laborers, for example, have been affected only indirectly. In addition, small landowners resent the new position of the peasants as well as the compensation paid to the large landowners. The danger persists that existing fields will be subdivided into inefficient and unproductive units.

On the positive side, it is now evident that the land already transferred is better tended, for farmers regard it as their own. The introduction of advanced technologies has resulted in crop diversification, expansion of cultivated land, and increased production of cash crops. Consolidation of scattered plots, however, is not yet accomplished, and this policy has not been forced on a reluctant peasantry in the hope that the demand for it will probably occur anyway. The emphasis in the current phase of land reform is on improving agricultural extension services, cooperatives, and credit facilities of the Agricultural Credit and Rural Development Bank of Iran. The number of cooperatives jumped from 711 in 1960 to about 8,600 in 1968, and membership now exceeds a million. The cooperative movement has made notable progress by providing the members with practice in cooperation and self-help and by giving them a new sense of responsibility.

Natural Resources and Industries

Land reform is only one phase of modernization. Rapid expansion of the nonagricultural sector is desirable as well, if only to absorb surplus farm workers who lack land or are likely to be displaced by improved technology. Industrialization also has captured the imagination of many Iranians who would like to see a reversal of the present ratio of rural to urban population. This is a long-term policy, however, requiring capital, mechanization, and social interaction and integration.

The private, traditional nonagricultural sector consists of the "bazaar" economy, the local system for the exchange of goods and services, which continues to be a strong influence in daily life. The modern nonagricultural sector of the economy is dominated by petroleum production and refining. For the past ten years or so, oil revenues have provided capital funds for multipurpose dam projects, irrigation schemes, roads, railroads, telecommunications, schools, and hospitals. A secondary effect has been the rapid rise of private investment and enterprise. During the past five years, the Gross National Product (GNP) has increased by more than 10 per cent

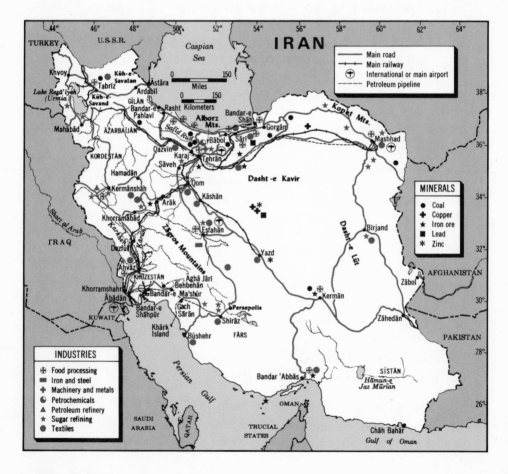

annually. This rate is one of the most accelerated in the world, comparable to that of Japan. The per-capita GNP in 1969 had risen to $328. The petroleum industry at present contributes about 20 per cent of the GNP. The industry began in 1908 with the discovery by the British of commercial quantities of oil in Khuzestan.

The refinery completed in Abadan in 1913 was the first in the Middle East, and, with its new petrochemical complex, it is still the largest. Iran is estimated to have over 10 per cent of the world's known reserves. In 1970, it was the largest producing country in the Middle East and ranked fourth in the world, following the United States, the Soviet Union, and Venezuela. Production in 1970 reached 191 million tons, an all-time high.

Operation and development of the industry proceeded almost independently of the rest of the country for many years, but, in 1951, the Anglo-Iranian Company was nationalized. Production lagged when trained British personnel were withdrawn and, a few years later, a consortium therefore undertook to operate the National Iranian Oil Company (NIOC) temporarily. The nine-member consortium pumps about 90 per cent of the nation's oil at present. The foreign-owned companies include British Petroleum, Royal Dutch Shell, Standard Oil, Gulf, and Compagnie Française des Petroles. The consortium owns no oil but merely acts as a legal agent of the NIOC, which in turn pays the oil companies a fee. The national company retains sufficient oil for domestic needs after disposing of the major portion of the production.

The present 50-50 partnership arrangement with the NIOC is being challenged by a government demand for a 20-per-cent increase in oil output that would yield about $6 billion in additional revenues for the current development plan. The consortium responds, however, that, because production costs are the highest in the Middle East and because it has also made recent investments in new offshore oil fields and terminals, a 10-per-cent rate of increase would be more realistic. But, whether or not production rises, Iran's revenues from oil will increase substantially as a result of the 1971 agreement between six Persian Gulf nations and twenty-three oil companies (see p. 12). The consortium constructed one of the world's largest oil jetties on Khark Island in the Persian Gulf, twenty-five miles from the mainland; it is capable of handling ten ships at once, providing the fastest loading rate yet achieved, up to 10,000 tons per hour. The excessive size of supertankers and the restricted channel of the Shatt Al Arab at Abadan and the main cargo port of Khorramshahr have necessitated the construction of other facilities on the Persian Gulf, such as the new port city of Bandar-e Mashur, fifty miles east of Abadan.

Mineral resources other than oil are fairly plentiful but have not been intensively developed. Bituminous coal is found in the Alborz Mountains and lead and iron near Yazdi; chromite and zinc are also mined. Traditionally, textiles, food processing, woodworking, and some metals industries are significant. More than 40 per cent of the employment in manufacturing is located in or near Tehran, whose population is now 2.7 million.

A 600-mile railroad to Khorramshahr from Tehran and a parallel 10-inch pipeline connect the Persian Gulf with the interior. Other important rail lines extend to Tabriz and Mashhad. Tehran also has an international airport and an extensive internal network served by Iran Air. Of the country's 16,000 miles of roads, 10 per cent are paved and suitable for all-weather use. But some regions are still isolated and inaccessible. National efforts to develop heavy industry have been hampered by insufficient electric power. Two multipurpose dams near Tehran and a refinery now provide additional heat and power. Oil- and gas-fired thermal plants exist in other large cities.

Foreign capital has played a vital role in Iran's spectacular economic growth and will account for about 15 per cent of the current development-plan investment. The United States contributes about half of all private foreign investment, concentrated mostly in the petrochemical, rubber, and pharmaceutical industries. Also, since World War II, U.S. aid in the form of military assistance has been substantial; this has now been considerably reduced. Furthermore, in 1967, the U.S. Agency for International Development (AID) closed its mission after sixteen years of operation in view of the fact that sufficient economic development had taken place to stimulate the flow of private foreign capital from other sources. AID projects were related to agriculture, hydroelectric development, telecommunications, and the construction of airports, railroads, highways, and ports.

Another goal of Iranian industrial diversification is the realization of a national steel industry. The Soviet Union is currently constructing an integrated steel mill at Esfahan, the second largest city, and sufficient iron ore to last for a century is located near Yazd, about 150 miles to the southeast. Coking coal, however, will probably have to be imported. Although the absence of railroad service to Esfahan will limit development, the plant will eventually produce 1.2 million tons of steel per year.

Until recently, Soviet economic aid has been negligible. A number of factors are responsible for a *rapprochement*. Like Turkey, Iran wants to be more independent of the United States in political and economic affairs. In addition, the closure of the Suez Canal in 1967 has begun to stimulate the routing of Iranian trade by way of the Caspian Sea across the lengthy

PROPOSED INDUSTRIAL PROJECTS
(FOURTH NATIONAL DEVELOPMENT
PLAN 1968-72)

1 AŽARBĀĪJĀN-E BAKHTARĪ
2 AŽARBĀĪJĀN-E KHAVARĪ
3 GĪLĀN
4 KORDESTĀN
5 FĀRS
6 HAMADĀN
7 KERMĀNSHĀHĀN
8 MĀZANDARĀN
9 SEMNĀN
10 KHORĀSĀN
11 EŞFAHĀN
12 KERMĀN
13 KHŪZESTĀN
14 ĪLĀM
15 LORESTĀN
16 BAKHTĪĀRĪ VA CHAHĀR MAḤĀLL
17 BANĀDER VA JAZĀYER-E KHALĪJ-E FĀRS
　　VA DARYĀ-YE OMĀN
18 BALŪCHESTĀN VA SĪSTĀN
19 TEHRĀN
20 BOYER AHMADĪ-YE SARDSĪR VA KOHKĪLŪYEH

O	Agricultural implements	⊞	Hides and skins
●	Aluminum smelting	■	Lead smelting
★	Animal fodder	✳	Machinery
✱	Cement	◔	Petrochemicals
◑	Chemicals	⊕	Pumps
■	Cold storage	✳	Sugar refining
□	Copper smelting	◉	Telephone equipment
✚	Electrical equipment and tools	◪	Tractor plant
✛	Electrical motors	▲	Turbines

Turkish and Soviet land boundaries. Of greatest importance to the Soviet
Union are Iran's vast reserves of natural gas. A forty-inch pipeline was laid
in 1970 from the oil fields near Ahvaz in Khuzestan to the Soviet border at
Astara, one of the longest of its type in the world. Western companies con-

structed the gas line from the fields northward to the vicinity of Saveh, a city eighty miles southwest of Tehran. A Russian team completed the northern half of the line as well as a spur to carry gas to Tehran. It will cost $550 million, most of the funds being provided by the current development plan and some by the Soviet Union.

The revenue from initial gas deliveries will cover outstanding debts incurred by the steel mill and the cost of purchasing some military equipment. Additional credits have also been extended by several East European countries to supply industrial machinery and build machine-tool plants in exchange for oil.

The foreign trade balance currently is quite advantageous, with imports valued at about $1.5 billion and exports, including petroleum, slightly in excess of this amount. Rapidly increasing oil revenues in the past few years are largely responsible for the favorable balance of payments. Agricultural products comprise but 7 per cent of all exports and include cotton, wheat, fruits, hides, and skins. Future exploitation of other mineral resources and the development of petrochemical industries represent a further export potential. Iran is now by far the biggest importer in the Middle East, with a steady rise of about 20 per cent yearly, and the United States has been a leading supplier of imports, including vegetable oils, machinery, and vehicles. With the exception of petroleum, almost 30 per cent of all exports now go to the Soviet Union and Eastern Europe.

The government has altered or abolished many of the traditional institutions of Iran, and the country is well launched on a program of modernization. It has abundant resources, both human and natural; harmony is being attained among its diverse societies; and, despite the problems associated with the rapid increase in population, a growing number of Iranians are participating in the nation's social and economic evolution.

focus *on the Education Corps*—Gad Soffer

Aware that a literate and healthy population is a prime requisite for prosperity, the Shah of Iran in 1962 proclaimed an all-out war on illiteracy. He estimated at that time that 80 per cent of the population could neither read nor write; yet the country's developing industries needed hundreds of thousands of engineers and technicians. Farmers, too, were singled out as targets for the literacy program, for modern methods were needed to inincrease production and productivity, and these required mastering and keeping up with current trends.

This copper artisan is one of many at work in the main square of Esfahan. The government is currently promoting work-oriented literacy training for artisans and other workers, geared specifically to their trade or job.

At present, nearly 20 per cent of the national budget is being invested in education, but the illiteracy rate in 1970 was still between 60 and 70 per cent. Also, there is a wide gap between towns and rural centers. Some 75 per cent of the Iranians live in scattered and often isolated villages. Literacy has been extremely low in these areas because of the disproportionately distributed efforts and means of the Iranian Ministry of Education, which put its major emphasis on education in urban areas. Only 24 per cent of the rural children of school age had a chance of going to school before 1962, compared to 84 per cent of the children in urban centers. However, in the nine years since then, the situation has improved in the villages. Between 1964 and 1968, the average rate of increase in the number of pupils attending classes was 8 per cent in urban areas and 19 per cent in the villages, thanks to the creation of the Literacy Corps.

One of the major difficulties in carrying out an education program has been the acute shortage of teachers in the rural areas. To combat this situation, the Literacy Corps was organized in 1962. The name was later changed to Education Corps, since it was decided that the objective was to bring general education to the villager rather than just literacy. The corpsmen are high-school graduates who have been inducted for compulsory military service and given the choice of either helping to bring education to the village population or performing routine military jobs. Between April, 1963, and September, 1969, 52,601 corpsmen were sent to villages. Since October, 1968, a Women's Division of the Literacy Corps, made up entirely of volunteers, has sent out 2,720 corpswomen.

Interest in Iran's Education Corps, especially in the Middle East, has been considerable. The corps is being recognized as a valuable weapon in the battle against illiteracy. UNESCO and the U.S. Government are giving encouragement; the Shah of Iran has personally backed and supported the corps' efforts.

With this growing interest, there would appear to be a need for a study of the Education Corps to evaluate its organization, success, and future direction. The Ministry of Education has published pamphlets explaining the project and taking note of its success, but they contain little objective material.

The following observations were made during a visit to the provinces of central south Iran, Kurdistan, and the Caspian Sea region. A total of ninety-three corpsmen were interviewed, as well as three governors and numerous directors and supervisors. Sixty schools and ten training centers were visited.

The difficulties of visiting Education Corps schools and obtaining meaningful interviews with their soldier-teachers are numerous. In the first place, many of the schools are virtually inaccessible by car; some can be reached only on foot or horseback or by jeep. Furthermore, the schools are often widely scattered, so that only one or two can normally be visited in one day. In addition, no matter what the time of the visit, one runs the risk of interrupting a class or a project. In many cases, classes are dismissed for the remainder of the morning or afternoon because of a visit, or a corpsman may be occupied elsewhere during normal school hours. Some Education Corps schools are operated with a great deal of flexibility.

Large villages often have two corpsmen working as a team, while, in other instances, a single corpsman may serve two or three small villages through a common school. Some divide their classes into grades; others do not. All build their schools according to the same plan, furnished by the Ministry of Education. Schools differ only in minor ways. Some have chairs; others have benches; many have no furniture of any kind. Current plans call for the supply to all schools of chairs with small attached tables. These are being purchased locally by district, and small carpenter shops can produce them for about 200 rials ($2.67) each. Many schools have stoves, but some claim they cannot get oil. In principle, the government provides each corpsman who is charged with building a school with a maximum credit of 5,000 rials ($66) for the purchase of building materials that the villagers are unable to furnish; but the money is not always received.

Unfortunately in many villages, the school is purposely built outside the village. The reason given is the wish to provide a quiet environment for the children. Apparently, there is some fear of letting the "government" into the center of the village, where for the purposes of integration, status, and convenience, the school should have been located.

Supervision over corpsmen is sketchy at best. Each Education Corps guide is charged with supervising up to twenty teachers, and he finds it impossible to do much more than visit each school once or twice monthly. The guide delivers pay to the teachers, sometimes gives them rides to town or from one village to another, brings them necessary supplies, keeps them informed of Ministry of Education affairs, and assists them in various ways. Although most corpsmen seem satisfied with the relationship between themselves and their guide, some welcome the infrequency of the guide's visits.

Villagers on the whole seem to cooperate willingly with corpsmen. They provide labor for building schools, baths, roads, bridges, and mosques. Most villages have a community fund to which all villagers contribute. This fund is cash on hand and permits some otherwise unfinanced projects to be carried out. When records are kept, it is usually the corpsman and the village chief who handle the books. However, some cases of noncooperation still exist. In one case, a corpsman was badly clubbed by a village man who opposed the changes and new ideas introduced.

Landowner pressures on the villagers *not* to cooperate are dwindling but still exist. Cases of pressure and bribes given to corpsmen by landowners in order to discourage the introduction of changes also could be found. In some border villages, the corpsmen had to face the threat of being killed by smugglers, who used the villages as a haven.

Education corpsmen live at least as well and usually better than the average villager. Most of them live in the school building. The more successful corpsmen are able to live within the village in a rented room—a factor that contributes to their acceptance. Most state their average monthly expenditure at around $20. This means that they could conceivably save some money each month: Monthly salaries for corpsmen with the rank of sergeant are from 3,500 to 4,500 rials ($47 to $60).

In many classrooms, boys and girls study in mixed classes, usually with a preponderance of boys. In some villages, only boys are taught by the corpsmen; the common explanation is that "the girls have their own teacher and a separate school; they aren't ready yet to be taught by a man."

Normal school hours are from 8:30 to 11:30 A.M. and 2:00 to 4:00 P.M. for children, and 6:30 to 8:00 P.M. for adults. But, in fact, this schedule does not appear to be closely followed. The dearth of evening classes, the lack of adherence to schedules, the expected allocation of some school hours to religious study—these all add up to considerably reduced productive time. Also, a sharp decline in enrollment occurs during the planting and harvesting seasons, when boys and girls are needed as helping hands in the fields. One possible solution for the seasonal absences is a mandatory attendance during these periods of at least three days a week, with the threat of withdrawing the program from the villages that do not abide by it. The use of films and the early evening radio and television programs that are now getting under way should increase motivation. These programs will deal with farming methods, family matters, and hygiene and will include Persian music and poetry.

In addition to teaching, corpsmen initiate village projects, such as wells, which are essential to sanitary living. Several have been instrumental in making access roads passable and in building underground bath houses, bridges, and even mosques.

So far, the program can be termed a success. Its continued effectiveness, however, will require further efforts on a large scale. A problem that is causing increasing concern is the provision of reading materials, at the village level, to Iran's thousands of newly literate people. According to present plans, some twenty volumes of special reading materials will be produced for new literates and will be distributed by the Educational Corps, other teachers, and rural cultural centers. Textbooks for special groups, such as the Baluchi and the Turkish-speaking Iranians, are to be prepared. Inadequate textbooks will, hopefully, be replaced by better ones and ones more meaningful to the villager.

No one can deny that the corps is doing its job. It is teaching villagers not so much a new way of life but ways of attacking the problems that plagued their old way of life. Village children are learning to read and write; village improvements are being made. The statistics are impressive. As of 1970, the concrete results of the corpsmen's efforts include:

Schools built	11,100
Schools repaired	7,600
Mosques built	1,000
Mosques repaired	8,800
Mortuaries built	700
Mortuaries repaired	1,300
Miles of feeder roads laid	37,000
Bridges built	26,500
Qanats drained	10,400
Trees planted	2,214,400
Public baths built	4,300
Culverts built	24,500
Model farms established	8,700
Village societies organized	7,500

The corps can boast of having given an education to nearly 1.5 million school-age children and 400,000 adults. Even allowing for a 50-per-cent "exaggeration factor," this is still quite good.

But Iran needs many more teachers. It is estimated that in the next twenty years the population will reach 40 million. By 1985, Iran is likely to have over 4 million children in elementary schools. Plans designed to meet the rising demand for teachers include expansion of the corps program; the radio, television, and book programs already mentioned; greater investment in the Work-Oriented Adult Literacy Project; a special program to provide teachers for private schools in return for the free education of a number of needy students; encouraging university students to devote their free time to teaching in secondary schools. Other projects include special courses for outstanding students, the granting of more scholarships to students and professors, and more classes for women in rural areas. The aim is to achieve more than the minimal standards of some less developed nations, where people who can read or write only their names are classified as literate.

Suggested Readings

AVERY, PETER. *Modern Iran*. New York: Praeger, 1965. A perceptive study of the recent history of Iran, with emphasis on political and social change.

Fisher, W. B., ed. *The Land of Iran*. The Cambridge History of Iran, vol. 1. Cambridge, England: The University Press, 1968. One of the most comprehensive geographies of Iran in existence, providing intensive study of the physical environment, flora and fauna, anthropology, and economic life. Gives excellent insight into land-man relationships.

Lambton, A. K. S. *The Persian Land Reform, 1962–1966*. London: Oxford University Press, 1969. A current evaluation of the land-reform law and its implementation and reception in the various provinces against the background of the prevailing physical, social, and tenurial conditions.

INDEX

Abadan, 18, 20, 205
Abu Rudeis, 76
Abu Simbel, 59
Abu Zaby, 126, 129, 132
  petroleum production in, 12, 126
Acre, 66, 75
Ad Dahna, 100
Ad Damman, 105, 106–7, 109
Adana Plain, 173
Adasiya, 94
Aden, 6, 114–16, 118, 119, 120, 122, 123
Aden, Gulf of, 112
Aegean Sea, 173
Afghanistan, 3, 5
Agency for International Development, 206
Agriculture, 28–31, 33
  in Eastern Arabia, 129
  in Iran, 198–201, 203
  in Iraq, 180–82, 189, 190–95
  in Israel, 65, 69, 71, 74
  in Jordan, 29, 86, 87, 89, 94–98
  in Lebanon, 143–45
  in People's Democratic Republic of Yemen, 120–23
  in Saudi Arabia, 102–4
  in Syria, 151, 153, 154–55
  in Turkey, 163, 168–73, 176
  in United Arab Republic, 47–51, 55, 60, 62
  in Yemen, 112–13
Ahvaz, 207
Ain Zalah, 183
Al Amarah, 183
Al Aqabah, 89, 90, 91, 106
Al-Badr, Muhammad, 114
Al Faiyum, 46
Al Faw, 183
Al Fujayrah, 127
Al Hasa, 104
Al Jabal al Akhdar Mountains, 129
Al Jiwa, 129, 132
Al Mafraq, 30
Al Manamah, 135
Al Muharraq Island, 135
Al Mukalla, 122
Al Qamishli, 156
Al Wajh, 104
Alanya, 173
Alborz Mountains, 197, 206
Aleppo, 18, 149, 151–55, 161

Alexandria, 18, 19, 23, 24, 46, 53, 54, 55, 61
Algeria, 6
Alouites, 151
Amiran, David H. K., 36n
Amman, 15, 87, 90, 96
Amoco-U.A.R. Oil Co., 53
An Nafud, 100
Anamur, 173
Anatolia, 166–67, 171
Anglo-Iranian Co., 205
Ankara, 17, 24, 166, 177
Anti-Lebanon Range, 140–42, 153, 160
Aqaba, Gulf of, 44, 68, 70, 100
Ar Najaf, 189
Ar Rab al Khali Desert, 100, 120, 121, 128–29
Ar Rusayfah, 90
Arab-Israeli wars, 66, 106, 108, 118, 157
  Arab unity and, 6, 7
  Jerusalem and, 78–79, 83
  Jordan and, 89, 92, 94
  refugees from, 70–71, 87
  United Arab Republic and, 51, 53, 56, 62–63
Arab League, 6–7, 134
Arab states, 3 (see also specific country)
Arabian-American Oil Co., 105, 109
Arabian Peninsula, 99
  nomadism in, 32
Arabian Sea, 129
Arabs
  in Israel, 70–71, 78, 81
  unity of, 4–8, 157
Arad, 74, 76
Arid regions, 28–33
  potentialities of, 36–37
  (see also Deserts; Irrigation)
As Salt, 90
Ash Shariqah, 126
Ash Shatrah, 186
Ashdod, 66–68, 70, 74
Ashqelon, 68, 76
Asir, 100, 103, 104, 106
Astara, 207
Aswan, 46, 52, 55, 61
Aswan High Dam, 46, 52, 54, 57–62
Asyut, 44, 46
Ataturk (see Kemal, Mustafa)
Az Zahran, 104

Az Zannah, 132
Azerbaijan, 198

Baalbak, 140, **146**
Baghdad, 17, 18, 19, 24, 180, 184, 189
Bahrain, 100, 105, 135–37
  climate of, 135
  economic development in, 135–37
  petroleum production in, 135–37
Bakhtiari, 32, 201
Balance of payments
  in Iran, 208
  in Israel, 76–77
  in United Arab Republic, 56
Balance of trade (see Exports and imports)
Bandar-e Mashur, 205
Baniyas, 153, 183
Barada River, 160
Barth, F., 32
Basra, 18, 182, 183, 184, 189
Batman, 171
Bedouins, 32, 99, 102
  in Eastern Arabia, 126
  in People's Dem. Rep. of Yemen, 121
Beersheba, 69, 74, 75
Beirut, 15, 18, 24, 26, 140, 142, 146
Bekaa, 140, 142
Berbers, 4
Bet Shemesh, 75
Bethlehem, 91
Bidonville, 20, 23
Bilharzia, 47
Bill, James A., 9–16
Black Sea, 172
Borcka, 171
Burgan, 134

Cairo, 15, 17–26 passim, 46, 55, 61
Carmel Range, 66
Caspian region, 197, 198, 200, 210
Caspian Sea, 206
Central Treaty Organization, 8
Challaf, 159–60
Christianity, 4
  in Iraq, 186
  Jerusalem as center of, 77–78
  in Lebanon, 142
  in Turkey, 166–67
Cities, 15, 17–26, 121–22
  morphology of, 20–22
  (see also Town planning; Urbanization)
Climate, 28–31
  of Bahrain, 135
  of Eastern Arabia, 129–30
  of Iran, 197–98
  of Iraq, 180–82
  of Israel, 65

of Jordan, 84, 85–86
of Kuwait, 133
of Lebanon, 140–42
of People's Democratic Republic of Yemen, 120–21
of Saudi Arabia, 100
of Syria, 151–60
of Turkey, 172
of United Arab Republic, 46
of Yemen, 112–13
Commerce
  and growth of cities, 18, 23–25
  in Lebanon, 139, 146–47
  (see also Exports and imports)
Communications
  in Israel, 74
  in Saudi Arabia, 106–7
Coon, Carleton, 188
Cooperatives
  in Iran, 203
  in Iraq, 192, 194
  in Saudi Arabia, 103
  in United Arab Republic, 50
Coruh River, 171
Crops (see Agriculture)
Cyprus, 6

Damascus, 17, 18, 19, 24, 149, 153, 154, 156, 160
Darbandikan Dam, 186
Das Island, 132
Dasht-e Lut, 194
Dayr az Zawr, 149
Dead Sea, 31, 64, 66, 68, 75, 84, 88, 89
Delta, Nile, 46, 47, 52, 61
Demirel, Suleyman, 170
Desalinization plants, 73–74, 104
Deserts
  in Eastern Arabia, 128–30
  in Iran, 198
  in Iraq, 182
  in Jordan, 83, 84–85
  in Saudi Arabia, 100
  in United Arab Republic, 44, 46
  in Yemen, 113
  (see also Arid regions)
Development (see Economic development)
Dez River, 197, 201
Dhahran, 105, 106
Dibis Dam, 186
Dimona, 74, 75
Divrigi, 171
Diyala River, 186
Doha, 128, 131
Dokan Dam, 186
Druze, 71
Dubayy, 126

Dujaila, 191
Dukhan, 131

East Bank (Jordan), 84, 86, 88, 91
East Ghor Irrigation Project, 88, 92–98
Eastern Arabia, 125–33
  agriculture in, 129, 130, 132
  economic development in, 131–33
  landscape and climate of, 128–30
  petroleum production in, 125, 127, 130–33
Eastern Province (Saudi Arabia), 100
Ecological balance, 31, 37
Economic development, 7, 9–10, 12
  in Bahrain, 135–37
  in Eastern Arabia, 131–33
  in Iran, 199, 204–8
  in Iraq, 186, 190
  in Israel, 76
  in Jordan, 86
  in Kuwait, 133–35
  in Lebanon, 139, 147–48
  in People's Democratic Republic of Yemen, 121–23
  planning for, 14–16
  in Saudi Arabia, 108–9
  in Syria, 157–58, 162
  in Turkey, 163, 167–71, 177
  in United Arab Republic, 50–63
  in Yemen, 115
Education, 15–16, 26
  in Iran, 208–13
  in Iraq, 189–90
  in Lebanon, 147
  in Saudi Arabia, 109–10
  in Syria, 151–58
  in Turkey, 168–69, 171
  in United Arab Republic, 55
Education Corps, 208–13
Egypt, 23, 34 (see also United Arab Republic)
Egyptian General Petroleum Corp., 53
El Alamein, 54
El Arish, 52
El Faiyum, 54
El Ghor (see Jordan Rift Valley)
El Mahalla el Kubra, 52
El Maks, 53
El Morgan, 53, 54
El Siwa, 44
El Wahat el Bahariya, 44, 52
El Wahat el Dakhla, 44
El Wahat el Kharga, 44
Elat, 65, 68, 70, 74, 75, 76
Employment
  in Jordan, 87
  in Lebanon, 143
  in Saudi Arabia, 106
  in Turkey, 176–77

in United Arab Republic, 54, 56
urbanization and, 20
ENI, 53
Eregli, 170
Erim, Nihat, 170
Erosion, 31, 65, 180, 184, 193
Esfahan, 17, 24, 198, 201, 206
Eski-Kalak Project, 186
Eskisehir, 171
Euphrates River, 34, 151, 153, 155, 156, 162, 170, 180, 185, 186, 193
Exports and imports
  of Iran, 208
  of Iraq, 190, 193
  of Israel, 72, 73, 76
  of Jordan, 91–92
  of Lebanon, 147
  of People's Democratic Republic of Yemen, 119
  of Saudi Arabia, 108
  of Syria, 154, 156, 162
  of United Arab Republic, 51, 54, 56
  of Yemen, 113

Faisal Model Settlement Project, 104
Farming (see Agriculture)
Farms, size of
  in Israel, 71
  in Jordan, 96–97
  in Lebanon, 144
  in United Arab Republic, 49–50
Farsi language, 196, 201
Fateh, 132
Federation of Arab States, 114
Federation of South Arabia, 119
Fellahin, 47–50
Fernea, Elizabeth W., 179–95
Fernea, Robert A., 179–95
Flood control, in Iraq, 186, 191
Ford Foundation, 60
France, influence of, 5–6

Galilee, 65, 66, 75
Garzan, 171
Gaza Strip, 64, 71, 73
Gebel Katherina, 44
Ghab-Acharheh-Roudj irrigation, 155, 161
Ghab marshes, 153
Ghawar, 105
Ghouta, 153, 159
Gilan, 203
Golan Heights, 71
Grazing
  in Jordan, 89, 92
  in Saudi Arabia, 102
  in Yemen, 113
  (see also Nomadic pastoralism)
Great Bitter Lake, 62

Great Britain
  Bahrain and, 135–37
  Eastern Arabia and, 125–28
  influence of, 5–6
  Iraq and, 188
  Kuwait and, 134
  People's Democratic Republic of Yemen and, 115–19, 122, 123
Great Zab River, 186
Gross National Product, 12
  of Iran, 203–5
  of Israel, 76
  of Lebanon, 147
  of Saudi Arabia, 109
  of United Arab Republic, 109
Groundwater resources, 34–37
Guleman, 171

Haifa, 18, 22, 65, 66, 68, 70, 74, 75, 76
Hail, 100
Haim, S. G., 4n
Halba, 140
Hamath, 149, 153, 154
Hammam, 20
Hara, 21
Harrison, Robert S., 17–26
Hasbani River, 145
Hashemite Kingdom (See Jordan)
Hatay Vilayeti, 167
Haupert, John S., 64–82, 99–111, 196–208
Hauran, 153
Hawija, 191
Health care, 15–16, 26
  in Iraq, 188, 189–90
  in Syria, 158
  in United Arab Republic, 47, 55
Hejaz, 99
Hejaz Railroad, 87, 106
Helez, 75
Helwan, 52
Hindu Kush, 197
Hirmand River, 197
Hodeida, 114
Hofuf, 104
Homs, 149, 151, 153, 154, 155, 156
Housing, urban, 15, 20
  in Iraq, 189
  in Turkey, 177
Hudson, James, 149n
Hula Valley, 65, 74

Id al Sharqi, 131
Immigration
  in Eastern Arabia, 131
  in Israel, 70
Imports (See Exports and imports)
Incense, 119, 121
Income, per-capita

in Iraq, 179
in Israel, 66–70, 73, 76, 77
in Lebanon, 147
in Saudi Arabia, 103
in Syria, 157
in Turkey, 168
in United Arab Republic, 55, 57
Industry
  in Iran, 204–6
  in Iraq, 184
  in Israel, 66–70, 73, 76–77
  in Jordan, 86, 90–91
  in Lebanon, 145–46
  in Saudi Arabia, 105
  in Syria, 156, 162
  in Turkey, 167–70, 177
  in United Arab Republic, 51–57
  in Yemen, 113–15
Inonu, Ismet, 168, 170
Iran, 5, 7–8, 11, 15, 17, 196–214
  agriculture in, 198–201, 203
  Bahrain and, 139
  economic development in, 199, 204–8
  education in, 208–13
  industry in, 204–6
  irrigation in, 34, 198, 201
  land reform in, 102–3
  landscape and climate of, 196–98
  people of, 32, 33, 201–2
  petroleum production in, 11–14, 204–8
Iraq, 5, 6, 7, 8, 11, 15, 179–95
  agriculture in, 180–82, 189, 190–95
  economic development in, 186, 190
  industry in, 184
  irrigation in, 36, 180, 186, 191, 193
  Kuwait and, 134
  land reform in, 190–95
  landscape and climate of, 180–82, 184
  people of, 186–90
  petroleum production in, 12–14, 179, 182–84
  urbanization in, 19, 184, 189
Iraq National Oil Co., 183
Iraq Petroleum Co., 183
Irbid, 84
Irrigation, 27, 28, 33–37
  in Iran, 34, 198, 201
  in Iraq, 36, 180, 186, 191, 193
  in Israel, 36, 66, 69, 72
  in Jordan, 88, 92–98
  in Lebanon, 140, 145
  in Saudi Arabia, 36, 103–4
  in Syria, 151, 153, 155–56, 158–62
  in United Arab Republic, 46, 60–61
  in Yemen, 112–13
Islam
  in Bahrain, 137
  in Iran, 201

in Iraq, 186–87
in Lebanon, 142
in People's Democratic Republic of Yemen, 115
in Saudi Arabia, 103, 110
in Turkey, 166
in United Arab Republic, 47
in Yemen, 113
Islamic world, 3–5
social system in, 10–11
Israel, 3, 4, 6, 8, 64–82, 94
agriculture in, 65, 69, 71–74
industry in, 66–70, 73, 76–77
irrigation in, 36, 66, 69, 72
landscape and climate of, 64–70
refugees and immigrants in, 70–71
United Arab Republic and, 43, 47
urbanization in, 19
(see also Arab-Israeli wars)
Issawi, Charles, 7
Istanbul, 17, 18, 19, 20, 164, 166, 168, 177

Jabal al Qamar hills, 129
Jabal Natih, 132
Jabal Tuwayq Tuwayq, 100
Jaffa (see Tel Aviv-Jaffa)
Jazirah, 180
Jericho, 36
Jerusalem, 18, 31–32, 65, 66, 74, 80–82, 83, 91
Jews
in Iraq, 186
in United Arab Republic, 47
(see also Israel)
Jezira, 153, 154, 156
Jidda, 18, 100, 103, 104, 106, 107, 109, 110
Jordan, 7, 11, 15, 83–98
agriculture in, 29, 86, 87–89, 94–98
industry in, 86, 90–91
Jerusalem and, 78–81
landscape and climate of, 83–86
mineral resources of, 89–90
people of, 86–87
Yemen and, 114
Jordan Rift Valley, 84, 92
Jordan River, 65, 84, 92–95
Jordan Valley, 36, 65, 84, 85–86, 88, 92
Jubayl, 146
Jubayl Fuhud, 132
Judea, 65, 66, 83, 84, 88

Kallia, 89
Kamaran Islands, 115, 118, 122
Kangal, 171
Karabuk, 168
Karatchouk, 156
Karbala, 189
Karkheh River, 197

Karun River, 197, 201
Kathiri, 119
Keban Dam, 170
Kemal, Mustafa, 7, 166–68
Kenya, 3
Kermanshah, 198
Khabur River, 156, 162
Khan, 20
Khark Island, 205
Khorasan, 198
Khorramshahr, 205, 206
Khuzestan, 196, 197, 198, 201, 207
Kibbutz, 71
Kinneret-Negev project, 73
Kirkuk, 183, 184, 186, 189
Kolars, John, 163–78
Kollek, Teddy, 80
Kopet Mountains, 197
Kurdish Mountains, 154
Kurdistan, 32, 180, 210
Kurds, 4, 32, 167, 180, 186, 201
Kuria Muria Islands, 118, 119
Kuwait, 7, 15, 56, 100, 133–35
economic development of, 133–35
landscape and climate of, 133
petroleum production in, 11–12, 133–35
Yemen and, 114
Kuwait City, 15, 134
Kuwait Fund for Arab Economic Development, 7, 114
Kuzey Anadolu Mountains, 171

Lachish region, 73
Lake Kinneret, 65, 73 (see also Lake Tiberias)
Lake Nasser, 46, 57, 60–61
Lake Tiberias, 65, 84, 88, 92 (see also Lake Kinneret)
Lake Urmia, 197
Land reform
in Iran, 202–3
in Iraq, 190–95
in Jordan, 96
in Syria, 155
in Turkey, 169, 170
in United Arab Republic, 47–51
Landscape
of Bahrain, 135
of Eastern Arabia, 128–29
of Iran, 196–98
of Iraq, 180–82, 184
of Israel, 64–70
of Jordan, 83–85
of Kuwait, 133
of Lebanon, 140–42
of People's Democratic Republic of Yemen, 112–13
of Saudi Arabia, 99–102

Landscape (cont.)
  of Syria, 151–54
  of Turkey, 171–73
  of United Arab Republic, 44–46
  of Yemen, 112–13
Latafiya, 191
Latakia, 149, 153, 156
Lebanon, 4, 6, 7, 11, 15, 94, 139–48
  agriculture of, 143–45
  commerce and trade in, 139, 146–47
  economic development of, 139, 147–48
  industry in, 145–46
  landscape and climate of, 140–42
  people of, 142–43
Lebanon Mountains, 65, 140–42, 151
Lewis, Bernard, 4
Libya, 7, 56, 157
Libyan Desert, 44
Litani River, 140, 145–46
Little Zab River, 186
Lur, 32
Luxor, 44

Madaba, 84
Madan, 182
Maghreb, 6
Mahra, 118
Mandelbaum Gate, 78, 80
Manners, Ian R., 3–8, 27–37, 83–98
Manufacturing, 24 (see also Industry)
Mashhad, 206
Matrah, 132
Mazandaranis, 201
Mecca, 18, 100, 105, 106, 107, 111
Medina, 18, 106, 110, 111
Medinas, 20–23
Mediterranean Sea, 65, 151, 154
Melamid, Alexander, 112–23, 125–37
Mersin, 171
Mesopotamia, 180, 194
Middle class
  professional, 11, 14
  in Syria, 149–50
  in United Arab Republic, 43
  urbanization and, 25–26
Middle East
  cities of, 17–26
  composition of, 3–8
  ecology of, 27–37
  petroleum and, 9–16
Mineral resources
  in Iran, 206–8
  in Israel, 75–76
  in Jordan, 89–90
  in Saudi Arabia, 105, 109
  in Turkey, 171
  in United Arab Republic, 52–54
  in Yemen, 113

(see also Petroleum production)
Minority groups in cities, 21 (see also specific groups)
Mizpe Ramon, 68
Mohammed Reza Shah Pahlavi Dam, 201
Morocco, 3, 6
Moshav, 71
Mosque, 20
Mosul, 184, 189
Mount Damavand, 197
Mount Sahand, 197
Mount Savalan, 197
Muhammadanism (see Islam)
Mukayris, 121
Mukheiba Dam, 7, 89
Munkhafad el Qattara, 44
Murban, 132
Musayid, 131
Muscat, 128, 132
Muslims (see Islam)

Nablus, 96
Najd, 99–100
Nasser, Gamal Abdel, 4, 43, 57
National Iranian Oil Co., 205
Near East, 5
Negev Desert, 65, 68–70, 73, 75
Nile Delta, 46, 47, 52, 61
Nile River, 34, 44, 46, 47, 55, 57, 60–61
Nomadic pastoralism, 28, 31, 32–33
  in Eastern Arabia, 130
  in Iran, 32, 33
  in Jordan, 87
  in Lebanon, 140
  in People's Democratic Republic of Yemen, 121
  in Saudi Arabia, 102, 103
  in Syria, 151
  (see also Grazing)
Noria, 160
North Atlantic Treaty Organization, 163, 169

Oases, 102
Oil (see Petroleum production)
Oman, 115, 118, 121
Oman, Gulf of, 126, 129, 132
Oman, Sultanate of, 125, 128–32
Oman Mountains, 100
Organization of Petroleum Exporting Countries, 12
Oron, 74, 75
Orontes River, 34, 140, 153, 155, 161
Ottoman Empire, 4, 5, 113, 116, 164–67, 174
  (see also Turkey)

Palestine, 6, 7, 83, 90, 92
  partition of, 78

Syria and, 157
(see also Israel; Jordan)
Palestinian refugees, 70, 86
Palmyra, 158, 160
Pan-Arabism (see Arabs, unity of)
Pastoralism (see Grazing; Nomadic pastoralism)
People's Democratic Republic of Yemen, 112, 115–23
economic development of, 121–23
history of, 115–20
landscape and climate of, 120–21
Perim, 115, 118, 121, 122
Perrin de Brichambaut, G., 28
Persia (see Iran)
Persian Empire, 196
Persian Gulf, 5, 6, 133, 135, 182
Eastern Arabia and, 125, 126, 129, 130
Iran and, 197, 205, 206
Saudi Arabia and, 100, 105–6
Petroleum production, 11–14, 16
in Bahrain, 135–37
in Eastern Arabia, 125, 127, 130–33
in Iran, 11–14, 204–8
in Iraq, 12–14, 179, 182–84
in Israel, 75–76
in Kuwait, 11–12, 133–35
in Saudi Arabia, 11–12, 104–6, 107, 108, 111
in Syria, 153, 156
in Turkey, 171
in United Arab Republic, 52–54
Petromin, 109
Phillips Petroleum Corp., 53
Political systems, 9–10, 16
in Lebanon, 139
in People's Democratic Republic of Yemen, 119, 123
in Syria, 157
in Turkey, 163, 167, 169–70, 174–76
in Yemen, 114–15
Population
of Iran, 201–2
of Iraq, 186–89
of Israel, 70–71
of Jordan, 86–87
of Lebanon, 142–43
of Saudi Arabia, 102–3
of Syria, 149–51, 157
of United Arab Republic, 47
Population growth, 14, 18–21, 26
in Iran, 199
in Iraq, 188–89, 194
in Israel, 71
in Jordan, 86
in Lebanon, 142–43
in Syria, 157
in Turkey, 170–71, 176

in United Arab Republic, 47, 57
Port Said, 55, 62
Protectorate of South Arabia, 118–19

Qaiti, 119
Qanat, 34, 158–59, 198
Qassem, Abdul Karim, 188
Qatar, 13, 125, 128, 130, 131–32, 137
Qiryat Gat, 73
Quiyara, 184
Quseir, 52

Rainfall, 28–33
in Eastern Arabia, 129
in Iran, 198, 200
in Iraq, 180
in Israel, 65, 66
in Jordan, 84, 85, 92
in Lebanon, 140–142
in People's Democratic Republic of Yemen, 120–21
in Saudi Arabia, 100–102
in Syria, 153–54
in Turkey, 170, 172
in United Arab Republic, 44, 46
in Yemen, 112–13
Ramadi Barrage, 186
Ramla, 75
Ras al Khaymah, 127, 132
Ras at Tannurah, 105, 107
Ras el Sudr, 53
Ras Shikka, 146
Ratawi, 183
Red Sea, 44, 100, 112, 115, 118, 121
Red Sea Highlands, 44
Refugees, 70–71, 86–87
Religion, 18, 25–26 (see also Christianity; Islam)
Revolution, 9, 11
Rift Valley, 44, 68, 75, 84, 100, 140
Riyadh, 99, 100, 106, 109, 110
Riyaq, 142
Roman Empire, 160–61
Rumaila, 183
Rural-urban differences, 24–26
in Iran, 202
in Iraq, 187
in Turkey, 174–77
(see also Urbanization)

Sadat, Anwar, 43–44
Sadd el Ali (see Aswan High Dam)
Safaniya, 105
Safi, 89
Saih al Malih, 132
Sakum, 132
Salinization of land, 184–85, 192, 193–95
Samaria, 65, 66, 83, 84, 88

Samarra Barrage, 186
Sana, 112, 114
Saudi Arabia, 6, 11, 15, 36, 56, 99–111
  agriculture in, 102–4
  Bahrain and, 135–36
  Eastern Arabia and, 128, 130
  economic development in, 108–9
  education in, 109–10
  industry in, 105–6
  Kuwait and, 133, 134
  landscape and climate of, 99–102
  mineral resources in, 105, 109
  petroleum production in, 11–12, 104–6,
    107, 108, 111
  town planning in, 110–11
  transportation and communication in,
    103, 106–8
  Yemen and, 114, 115, 118
Saveh, 208
Sayda, 140, 142, 146
Sea of Galilee, 65 (see also Lake Kinneret)
Sedom, 65, 89
Seyh, 21
Shah, Reza, 7
Shahrazoor, 191
Sharon Plain, 64, 65, 66
Shatt al Arab, 8, 180, 182, 205
Shatt al Gharraf Project, 186
Shefelah, 65, 66
Sheikhdoms in Eastern Arabia, 126, 128,
  131, 132 (see also Bahrain; Kuwait)
Shia sect, 3, 103, 186–87, 201
Sibaiyah, 52
Sidon, 105
Sinai Peninsula, 44, 52, 71
Sistan, 197, 198
Sivas, 171
Social change, 9–16
  cities and, 24, 26 (see also Urbanization)
Social class, 21 (see also Fellahin; Middle
  class; Villages)
Social system in Islamic world, 10–11
Socotra, 115, 119, 121, 123
Soffer, Gad, 208–13
Somali Republic, 122
South Yemen (see People's Democratic Re-
  public of Yemen)
Soviet Union (see Union of Soviet Socialist
  Republics)
Standard Oil of California, 105
Standard Oil of New Jersey, 105
Sudan, 7, 57, 61, 157
Suez, 55, 62
Suez Canal, 55, 62–63, 122
  closure of, 54, 56, 62, 69, 105, 207
  improvement of, 7
Suez Canal Zone, 6, 47
Sunni sect, 3, 103, 186, 201

Suq, 21–23, 110
Sur, 141
Syria, 4, 5, 7, 11, 12, 15, 94, 149–162
  agriculture in, 151, 153, 154–55, 157
  cities in, 17, 149–50
  economic development of, 157–58
  industry in, 156, 162
  irrigation in, 151, 153, 155–56, 158–62
  landscape and climate of, 151–54
  people of, 149–51, 157
Syrian Desert, 100, 153

Tabriz, 206
Taizz, 114
Tartus, 153, 156
Taurus Mountains, 171
Tehran, 15, 17, 19, 198, 206
Tel Aviv-Jaffa, 24, 65, 66, 68, 74
Temperature range (See Climate)
Texaco, 105
Thesiger, W., 129
Thrace, 171
Tigris River, 180, 185, 186, 191, 193
Timna, 70, 74
Toros Daglari Mountains, 4
Tourism
  in Israel, 68, 76
  in Jordan, 91–92
  in Lebanon, 140, 146
  in Syria, 158
  in United Arab Republic, 56
Town planning, 110–11 (see also Cities)
Trabzon, 18
Trade (See Commerce)
Trans-Arabian Pipeline, 90, 105
Transjordan, 6, 83
Transjordan Plateau, 84
Transportation
  in Iran, 202, 206
  in Israel, 74
  in Jordan, 91
  in Saudi Arabia, 103, 106–7
  in Syria, 156
  in Turkey, 169, 177
  in United Arab Republic, 55
  in Yemen, 114
Tribal life
  in Eastern Arabia, 130
  in Iran, 201
  in Iraq, 181, 188
  in People's Democratic Republic of Yem-
    in, 118–19, 121–22, 123
  (see also Nomadic pastoralism)
Tripoli, 21, 25, 26, 140, 142, 146, 183
Trucial States, 100, 125–32, 137
Tunisia, 6
Turkey, Republic of, 7–8, 11, 163–78
  agriculture in, 163, 168–73, 176

economic development in, 163, 167–71, 177
history of, 164–70
industry in, 167–70, 177
landscape and climate of, 171–73
political system of, 163, 167, 169–70, 174–76
urbanization in, 18, 170–71
Yemen and, 116, 118
Turkomans, 201

Ujman, 126
Umm al Qaywayn, 126
Umm Shaif, 132
Unemployment (See Employment)
Union of Soviet Socialist Republics, 8, 43
Iran and, 206–8
Iraq and, 183
People's Democratic Republic of Yemen and, 123
Syria and, 157
United Arab Republic and, 51, 52, 56, 58, 60
Yemen and, 114
United Arab Republic, 3, 4, 6, 7, 11, 15, 43–63
agriculture in, 47–51, 55, 60
Eastern Arabia and, 128
economic development in, 51–63
industry in, 51–57
Israel and (See Arab-Israeli wars)
land reform in, 47–50
landscape and climate of, 44–46
petroleum production in, 12, 52–54
Syria and, 157
urbanization in, 18, 54–55
Yemen and, 114
United Nations
in Eastern Arabia, 128
in Israel, 70
in Jerusalem, 78, 81
in Jordan, 86–87
in Saudi Arabia, 104, 110
in United Arab Republic, 59, 60
United States
Eastern Arabia and, 128
Iran and, 206
People's Democratic Republic of Yemen and, 123
Saudi Arabia and, 104, 108
Turkey and, 169
United Arab Republic and, 51
Yemen and, 114
Urbanization, 14–15, 17–26
in Iran, 15, 17
in Iraq, 19, 184, 189
in Jordan, 86–87
in Lebanon, 143
in Saudi Arabia, 110

in Syria, 149–50
in Turkey, 18, 170–71, 176–77
in United Arab Republic, 54–55
(see also Cities; Rural-urban differences)

Villages
in Iran, 202, 209–13
in Israel, 71
in Lebanon, 142–43
in Syria, 149, 151
in Turkey, 172–78
Vouras, Paul P., 139n

Wadi, 33–34, 102
Wadi ar Rummah, 100
Wadi Araba, 84
Wadi as Sahba, 104
Wadi Bana, 116–17, 122
Wadi Hadramawt, 120, 121
Wadi Hanifah, 103
Wadi Jizan, 104
Wadi Yabis, 95
Wadi Zarqa, 88, 91
Wallen, C. C., 28
Water supply, 27–37
in Iran, 198, 200
in Iraq, 184–86
in Israel, 73–74
in Jordan, 83–85, 88, 94
in Saudi Arabia, 102, 103
in United Arab Republic, 57–62
(see also Irrigation; Rainfall)
Wells, 35–36
West Bank (Jordan), 7, 71, 80, 83, 84, 86, 88, 91, 92
Western Desert, 44
Women, status of, 26

Yanbu, 105
Yarmuk Project, 7
Yarmuk River, 88, 92, 94, 98, 161
Yazd, 206
Yazdi, 206
Yemen, 7, 100, 112–15, 121
history of, 113–15
landscape and climate of, 112–13
Yibal, 132
Yizreel, 65, 66
Yotvata Kibbutz, 69
"Young Turks," 164

Zagros Mountains, 4, 32, 180, 196–97, 198
Zahlah, 140, 142
Zevulun, 65
Zikrit, 131
Zonguldak, 168, 171
Zoroastrianism, 201
Zufar, 129, 132

THE CONTRIBUTORS

JAMES A. BILL is Assistant Professor of Government, University of Texas.

ELIZABETH W. FERNEA is author of *Guests of the Sheik* (1969).

ROBERT A. FERNEA is Professor of Anthropology and Director of the Center for Middle Eastern Studies, University of Texas.

ROBERT S. HARRISON is Associate Professor of Geology-Geography, C. W. Post College, Long Island University.

JOHN S. HAUPERT is Associate Professor of Geography, State University of New York at Bufflalo.

JAMES HUDSON, formerly Assistant Professor of Geography, American University of Beirut, is now at Morgan State College.

JOHN KOLARS is Associate Professor of Geography, University of Michigan.

IAN R. MANNERS is Assistant Professor of Geography, Columbia University.

ALEXANDER MELAMID is Professor of Economics, New York University.

GAD SOFFER is Associate Professor of History, University of Dayton.

PAUL P. VOURAS is Professor of Geography, Paterson State College.